AARDVARKS TO ZEBRAS

AARDVARKS TO ZEBRAS

A Menagerie of Facts, Fiction, and Fantasy About the Wonderful World of Animals

Melissa S. Tulin

A Citadel Press Book

A Citadel Press Book
Published by Carol Publishing Group
Citadel Press is a registered trademark of Carol Communications, Inc.
Editorial Offices: 600 Madison Avenue, New York, N.Y. 10022
Sales and Distribution Offices: 120 Enterprise Avenue, Secaucus, N.J. 07094
In Canada: Canadian Manda Group, P.O. Box 920, Station U, Toronto,
Ontario M8Z 5P9

Queries regarding rights and permissions should be addressed to Carol Publishing
Group, 600 Madison Avenue, New York, N.Y. 10022
Carol Publishing Group books are available at special discounts for bulk purchases,
sales promotions, fund-raising, or educational purposes. Special editions can be creat-
ed to specifications. For details, contact Special Sales Department, Carol Publishing
Group, 120 Enterprise Avenue, Secaucus, N.J. 07094

Manufactured in the United States of America

10   9   8   7   6   5   4   3   2   1

Designed by Andrew B. Gardner

Library of Congress Cataloging-in-Publication Data

Tulin, Melissa S.
    Aardvarks to zebras : a menagerie of facts, fiction, and fantasy about the
    wonderful world of animals / by Melissa S. Tulin.
        p.   cm.
    "A Citadel Press book."
    ISBN 0-8065-1548-1
    1. Animals—Miscellanea. 2. Animals—Folklore. I. Title
QL50.T825 1994
591—dc20   94–17474
                                                            CIP

For Samantha and Isaiah
So that they will learn to respect all God's creatures

And in memory of
Sasha and Rachel, a.k.a. "The Germantown Cats"

Contents

PART II
TALES OF THE DREAMTIME: ANIMALS
IN MYTHS, FOLKLORE, AND SUPERSTITION

PART III
THE PEACEABLE KINGDOM:
ANIMALS IN RELIGION

PART IV
ANIMALS IN POPULAR CULTURE

Acknowledgments

Special thanks go to my agents, Michael Larsen and Elizabeth Pomada, for having such faith in this project; Arthur Melanson, for spiritual support; the staff of the Northeast Regional Library, Philadelphia, Pennsylvania, for their invaluable assistance; and last but not least, my husband, Mark Tulin, for his advice and support, and for putting up with my late night typing sessions.

Author to Reader

Every October 17, on the Feast of St. Francis of Assisi, patron saint of animals, residents of Manhattan's Morningside Heights are treated to an unusual sight at the famous Cathedral of St. John the Divine. Led by the bishop of the Episcopal Diocese of New York, thousands of animals of all types, ranging from the exotic—huge, lumbering elephants, stately giraffes, dark-eyed llamas, and chattering monkeys, all "borrowed" from local zoos—to the more everyday, including dozens of dogs and cats, brilliantly feathered birds, even a New York sewer rat and a one-celled amoeba, make their way up the stone steps of this national landmark accompanied by their human attendants. The occasion is the Blessing of the Animals, which has become an annual event at the cathedral.

Like the ceremony at St. John the Divine, this book is a celebration of the rich diversity of the animal kingdom. From simple sponges that spend most of their lives rooted to one spot to highly advanced mammals such as whales, dolphins, chimpanzees, and gorillas, the world of animals is an amazing one. Perhaps more than any other society, America is a nation of animal lovers. There are currently 100 *million* cats and dogs in this country, not counting the birds, rabbits, fish, snakes, iguanas—you name it, we have it. Many of these animals are pampered shamelessly. Every year, Americans spend billions of dollars on high-tech medical care for their pets, including CAT scans, dialysis, joint replacements, and even liposuction. Millions more are spent on food, toys, and even clothing for these animals, and when Fido or Fifi dies, he or she can be buried in style at one of hundreds of pet cemeteries around the country. Americans spend more on pet food than on baby food.

Why are pets—or, to be politically correct, "companion animals"—so popular? One reason is that as more and more young people delay starting families, or forego having them altogether, an animal such as a dog or a cat can be a child substitute. For others who live alone, a dog or cat makes good company. Animals can be downright therapeutic for their human companions; scientists have discovered that people exhibit marked improvements in blood pressure when they care for pets. Nursing homes, hospitals, and other establishments have started programs in which dogs, cats, and other animals "visit" patients. To many residents at these institutions, the visits from these four-legged therapists are the high point of the day.

And it is not only dogs, cats, and other domestic animals that fascinate us. On a recent trip to South Carolina's beautiful Low Country, I had the opportunity to watch a brown pelican, a species that has just now come back from the brink of extinction, fishing for its dinner. We had seen many interesting animals on this short trip, including dolphins, egrets, blue and great herons, and even a bark-brown alligator sunning itself on a log in a black-water swamp, but this bird held my attention like none of the others had.

Its huge bill and dangling pouch, heavy body, and short, thick legs looked odd flying above the surface of the blue-green water, as if various parts of different birds had been patched together to make this one ungainly creature. As the pelican sailed across the water, it spotted a fish and, without wasting so much as a fraction of a second, dive-bombed into the water, its body a ruler-straight, vertical line.

I watched, amazed, as the bird emerged a few seconds later, shedding bright drops of salt water, holding in her beak a glittering, chrome-colored fish that flapped wildly before it disappeared into the bird's pouch. It was the hundredth, or the thousandth, time the pelican had gone through these motions, but to me, city born and bred, it was as if I had seen something rare and wonderful, and I watched the pelican silently as it fished again, stunned by its awkward beauty.

Part I of this book, "The Animal Kingdom," is not only about pelicans, but ponies, pythons, and scores of other animals. Starting off with an explanation of how animals are classified, it goes on to tell the "where," "what," and "why" of their existence: where they live, what they eat, why they act the way they do. It also tells of humankinds' relationship with the animal kingdom through the centuries, which has not always been a happy one. One section of "The Animal Kingdom," "The Hall of Shame: Extinct, Endangered, and Threatened Animals," takes a sobering look at the dozens of species that have vanished from the face of the earth, including the well-known passenger pigeon and less familiar animals such as the quagga, which once roamed the savannahs of southern Africa in the thousands.

Part II of this book, "Tales of the Dreamtime: Animals in Myths, Folklore, and Superstition," relates how animals have influenced the myths and legends of every society, from the ancient Greeks to African bushmen. Every culture has its own stories of creation, many of them involving animals. The Kooris of Australia, for example, believe that a giant rainbow serpent once crawled along the earth. The winding riverbeds are a legacy of this multicolored serpent, who etched them in the earth with the movements of his great, sinuous body. At the other end other spectrum, the Cherokees tell of the Great White Grandfather Beaver of the North, who they say will someday bring about the end of the world. Unicorns with shining horns, fire-breathing dragons, devil dogs, and demon cats populated the imaginations of our forbearers, leaving us a rich treasury of myths, legends, and folklore about animals.

Part III, "The Peaceable Kingdom: Animals in Religion," illustrates how animals have played a role in the world's great faiths, dating from the days of the ancient Egyptians, whose vast pantheon of gods often took on the characteristics of animals such as the crocodile, cat, and lion. Animals have been sacrificed, have been portrayed as symbols of faith or faithlessness, and have been cronies of sinners and companions of saints. The title of this section was inspired by the book of Isaiah, which describes a utopia where "the wolf will lie down with the lamb, and the leopard shall lie down with the kid, and the calf and the lion and the yearling together, and a little child shall lead them."

From the sacred we go to the secular in Part IV, "Animals in Popular Culture." From Mickey Mouse to the late, great Spuds MacKenzie, animals are an integral part of popular culture. Think about it: In an age of film screens cluttered with R-rated gore, movies starring animals (*Beethoven, The Incredible Journey, Benji*) continue to make money and tug at our heartstrings. As a child I remember going to see the movie *Old Yeller*, in which the canine hero becomes the devoted companion of a troubled little boy in the Old West. Toward the end of the film, during the scene in which the dog is "put to sleep," at least three quarters of the audience, including myself, was weeping. Such is the power of animals, even fictional ones, to move us.

It is hoped that this book will entertain, educate, amuse, enlighten, and leave the reader with the same sense of wonder I felt while watching that pelican in South Carolina several years ago. So sit back, turn the pages, and step inside the wonderful world of animals.

Philadelphia, Pennsylvania
October 1994

Part 1

A
Z
THE ANIMAL KINGDOM

Chapter One

ANIMAL MISCELLANY

Before we embark on our journey through the animal kingdom, from aardvarks to zebras, let us take a look at some preliminary information, including albinism in animals, how animals are classified, and animal intelligence.

ALBINISM

Most animals, including human beings, possess *melanin*, a substance that gives color to the skin, eyes, and hair. Albinos, however, are unable to produce this pigment. Albinism can be complete or partial. True (complete) albinos have white skin and hair and very pale eyes. Often the eyes appear pink because the blood in the tiny vessels of the iris, the colored part of the eyeball, shows through.

Albinism is rare, occurring in about one in every twenty thousand human births and just as infrequently in animals. In the wild, albino animals rarely survive for long, because their distinctive coloring makes them an easy target for predators.

In many cultures, albino animals, because of their rarity, have been considered sacred. In ancient Siam (now called Thailand), albino elephants were considered the exclusive property of the king and could be ridden, owned, or killed by another only with the monarch's consent. Crafty Siamese rulers often used albino elephants as a device for punishing their enemies.

A rare albino alligator. For an animal to be born with this disorder, both parents must carry the gene that causes it. Photo by Steven Dorand, Audubon Zoo. Courtesy of Zoological Society of Philadelphia.

The opposite of albinism is *melanism,* an excess of pigment. The so-called black panther of Asia, for example, is actually a melanotic form of the leopard. The black molly, a popular aquarium fish, is also a melanotic animal. ·

CLASSIFICATION OF ANIMALS

The system used to classify the hundreds of thousands of animals in the world was developed in 1758 by Carl von Linné, a Swedish taxonomist and botanist. Linné's system used Greek and Latin, the languages of the scholars of the day. Today we know Linné by the Latin version of his name, Carolus Linnaeus.

According to the Linnaean system, all known life on earth can be divided into five kingdoms: *Animalia, Plantae, Fungi, Protista,* and *Monera,* with *Animalia* being the largest. The Linnaean system gives every organism two names, a sort of "first name" (species) and "surname" (genus), but in scientific notation, the surname comes first, just as your last name is listed first in the telephone book. This system is known as *binomial nomenclature.*

Besides species and genera, animals are also divided into phylums, subphylums, classes, orders, and families. As we go from larger (phylum) to smaller (species) units, the animals become more and more closely related. Within a species, all the animals have very similar characteristics and can interbreed to produce offspring who are themselves capable of interbreeding. For instance, the common house cat, *Felis domesticus*, is of the genus *Felis* and species *domesticus*, while the tiger is of the genus *Panthera* and the species *tigris*. Both, however, are of the family *Felidae* (in zoology all names of families end in "idae").

Here's how both species are classified according to the Linnaean system:

	Tiger	**Domestic Cat**
Phylum:	Chordata	Chordata
Class:	Mammalia	Mammalia
Order:	Carnivora	Carnivora
Family:	Felidae	Felidae
Genus:	*Panthera*	*Felis*
Species:	*tigris*	*domesticus*

ANIMAL INTELLIGENCE

For many years, the behavior of animals was thought to be driven solely by instinct. Charles Darwin (1809–1882), who revolutionized science with his theory of evolution, however, argued in his 1871 book *The Descent of Man* that animals possess some power of reasoning. He was convinced that "the difference in mind between man and the higher animals, great as it is, certainly is one of degree, not kind."

Scientists now know that animals do possess intelligence, which varies greatly among the different groups. Intelligence in an animal is usually measured by giving it certain problems to solve and observing how quickly and in what manner it solves them. A rat running through a maze is an example of an intelligence test with which many of us may be familiar. Some indications of high intelligence among animals are: (1) they quickly learn to solve complicated problems, (2) they play when they are young, and (3) they try new experiences as adults.

The most intelligent animals are the *primates*—apes, monkeys, and man. Next to man, apes and monkeys, which have brains similar to those of human beings, are the brightest animals. They can follow simple instructions and perform fairly complicated tasks. Bonobos (close relatives of chimpanzees), chimps, and gorillas have been taught to communicate using American Sign Language (ASL) and can understand human speech to a limited extent. A bonobo named Kanzi, who lives on the campus of the Georgia State University Language Research Center outside of Atlanta, has been found to have the grammatical abilities of a two-and-a-half-year-old. Kanzi makes his desires known by pointing to symbols printed on a board or by punching the symbols on a specially designed keyboard that then generates the words in English. In the wild, other apes have been observed using tools, an indication of high intelligence. For example, chimpanzees sometimes use stones to crack nuts.

Next to the primates, the most intelligent animals are the marine mammals, including whales, dolphins, and porpoises.

The *carnivores*, or flesh-eating animals such as dogs and cats, are next on the intelligence scale. Bears, lions, tigers, and wolves, although they have not been extensively tested, are thought to have intelligence equal to or near that of domestic dogs and cats.

Elephants and horses respond very well to commands and signals. Among the hoofed animals, the pig is considered the best problem-solver.

Rodents can be taught to tell one shape from another and solve simple problems. Birds such as ravens and pigeons can solve simple counting problems, and parrots and other "talking" birds can imitate human sounds very well.

Amphibians and reptiles are difficult to test and generally do not possess high intelligence. Some can be taught very simple skills, such as taking a pathway to a certain type of food. Fish have very good color vision and can be taught to swim toward certain colors and avoid others, sharks being the least intelligent fish.

Probably the "stupidest" animals are the *invertebrates*, animals without backbones. Although they can learn very little, some have been taught in laboratory experiments to avoid dangerous places.

Chapter Two

THE AMPHIBIANS: FROGS, TOADS, AND OTHERS

The word *amphibian* comes from the Greek *amphibios*, which means "living two lives." With some exceptions, amphibians live part of their lives on land and part in water. Scientists who study amphibians and reptiles are called *herpetologists*.

Along with reptiles, birds, and mammals, amphibians are vertebrates, animals with backbones. They are *ectothermic*, or *heterothermic*, meaning that their body temperature depends on the temperature of the environment around them. Ectothermic animals are often mistakenly referred to as being "cold-blooded." Because they cannot maintain a constant body temperature, ectothermic animals need a warm or moderate temperature to function. To survive cold weather, they must hibernate. *Aestivation* is a sleep similar to hibernation, but it occurs during hot weather, or in areas of the world where dry and rainy seasons alternate. Some toads and frogs, for example, hide away during the hot summer months, burrowing in mud or other cool, moist places. Sometimes they become active during a heavy rain but become dormant again as soon as the moisture dries.

ANURANS AND THEIR RELATIVES

There are about 3,200 species of amphibians in the world, making them the smallest of the major animal groups. Amphibians are classified into three major categories: *anurans*, *urodeles*, and *gymnophions*. Frogs and toads, or anurans, are the best-known and most numerous amphibians. Anurans can be found near all types of water except for the ocean, because salt water is generally poisonous to them, and they live everywhere in the world except Antarctica, New Zealand, and Greenland. There are about 2,700 species of anurans.

Salamanders and newts are known as urodeles (newts resemble salamanders, but are smaller). Urodeles look like lizards, with long, slender bodies and tails, but lack the scales, claws, and external ear openings of their reptilian cousins. The word *salamander* comes from the Greek *salamandra*, meaning "fire," because it was once thought that these small amphibians loved the warmth of the flames. Quite the opposite is true, however, and in fact urodeles are most often found living in moist, wooded areas. There are about 300 species of urodeles.

Gymnophions are the rarest amphibians and include only about 75 species. These strange, legless creatures resemble giant worms. Gymnophions are seldom seen, because they spend most of their lives underground, feeding on earthworms and carrion. Gymnophions can reach over four feet in length and are found in subtropical and tropical regions.

CHANGE OF LIFE

Amphibians go through a larval, or immature, stage in which their appearance differs markedly from their adult form. Anurans, for example, lay eggs that hatch into tiny, wriggling tadpoles. The tadpoles are shapeless at first, but soon develop flat, finlike tails. They gradually grow lungs and begin to develop stumplike legs. Finally, a little frog, still bearing a minuscule tail, emerges from the water. After several weeks, the tail gradually disappears and the frog assumes its adult form. This transformation from the larval to the adult stage is called *metamorphosis*, from the Greek words *meta*, meaning "change," and *morphe*, or "form."

FACTS OF LIFE

- The largest amphibian is the giant Japanese salamander, which can grow up to five feet long. At the other end of the scale are frogs that measure barely an inch.

- Like other amphibians, many urodeles secrete poison through their skins. The flesh and eggs of the California newt, also called the giant newt, are full of a lethal nerve poison so powerful that just one drop will kill 7,000 mice. The venom is not poisonous to humans, but handling one of these newts may cause a severe skin rash. The fire salamander, a black and yellow urodele found in the forests of Europe, protects itself by spitting out a noxious fluid. If this liquid reaches the eyes, it causes intense pain and temporary blindness.

- The tropical rain forest is home to 75 percent of all frog and toad species.

- Frogs and toads may look similar, but there are several differences. Toads generally have broader bodies and shorter, less powerful legs. Toads feel dry to the touch, while a frog's skin is moist and sometimes slimy. Toads are usually covered with warts, while frogs are smooth skinned. Frogs lay their eggs in a jellylike mass, while toads lay them in long strings.

- Many species of frogs and toads lay hundreds, sometimes thousands, of eggs. Only a fraction of these, however, will survive, because they are devoured by fish, birds, and even other anurans.

- The total body weight of anurans is composed of as much as 80 percent water (in humans, it is about 57 percent).

- Each male frog has its own distinct mating call.

- The common bullfrog can live for fifteen years. Other species of toads and frogs can reach the age of thirty. A bullfrog can jump nine times its own height.

- All toads have bulging poison glands around their heads. The most venomous of these creatures is the giant toad, or agua. Its flesh and skin are full of poison; a dog or cat that ingests one of these amphibians can die within an hour.

The agua (also called the cane toad) is the largest species of toad, sometimes reaching a length of nine inches, and can weigh up to four pounds. These large, wart-covered creatures are native to Central America, but they were imported to Australia, the West Indies, Hawaii, and other sugar cane–producing regions of the world to get rid of the beetles that ate the young, tender plants. While the toads did their job and devoured the pesky beetles, they also ate up everything else in sight, and in some parts of Australia they have become a bigger nuisance than the beetles ever were. In Queensland province in northeast Australia, there are so many giant toads that Aussies sometimes look out on their lawns and do not see grass, but a hopping, croaking carpet of toads.

● The water-holding frogs of Australia are used as a kind of hopping water hole for the desert-dwelling Koori people (formerly called aborigines). The Kooris squeeze the frog to get the water (supposedly clean) that comes from its bladder.

● Two thousand years ago, Roman wives used toad poison to kill their husbands.

● Frogs' legs are considered a delicacy in France, but they are also eaten in Asia. They are also growing in popularity in the United States. Bullfrogs, green frogs, and leopard frogs are the types that most often find their way to American dinner tables. In the West Indies, frogs' legs are known as "mountain chicken."

● The most lethal amphibians are the dendrobates, or poison arrow frogs, which live in the rain forests of Central and South America. Only about half of the hundred species of dendrobates, however, produce poison. Most of these brightly-colored frogs are tiny, no bigger than two inches. Scientists believe that the bright colors of the dendrobate warn potential predators that it is poisonous. The species that produces the most lethal toxin is *Phyllobates terribilis* (in English, this means "terrible poison arrow frog"). Just 0.00000007 of an ounce of the poison from this tiny golden frog may be enough to kill a man. These venomous frogs, however, are immune to their own poison; members of the same species often fight each other over territory.

The Chocos, one of the native peoples of the region, obtain the venom by spearing the frog and dangling it above a fire. The heat of the flames causes the skin glands to sweat, and the poison that is secreted is collected into a small container. Blow darts and arrows are then dipped into the poison. Once a monkey, jaguar, or other animal is scratched with one of the darts, the hunters follow it through the forest, waiting for it to die.

● Like snakes, anurans and most other amphibians shed their skins frequently in a process called *molting*. In summer, this can occur as often as every three days. In anurans, the process begins as a giant yawn. The frog or toad then twists, bends, stretches, and contorts its body in incredible ways to loosen the shedding skin. Finally, the creature pulls the skin completely off. You are not likely to find many frog, toad, or salamander skins lying around, however, because the animal usually eats it.

Amphibians and People

The great taxonomist Carolus Linnaeus called amphibians "foul and loathsome creatures." While it is true that most members of this group would not win any beauty contests, some amphibians are very helpful to man. Many types of anurans, for example, consume thousands of harmful insects every year. One species, the American toad, can eat eighty-six flies in 190 minutes. In 1987, a scientist from the National Institutes of Health in Washington, D.C. discovered that the skin secretions from African clawed frogs contain a class of antibiotics called magainins. The magainins *protect the frogs from the harmful bacteria found in the ponds and puddles where they live. Researchers think that magainins may be used in the future to treat burns and cystic fibrosis in humans.*

In recent years, scientists have become concerned about the shrinking number of amphibians. Some species have become greatly reduced in number and in some cases have become extinct. The decline in the number of salamanders, frogs, and toads began ten to twenty years ago, but only recently has the problem been studied by the scientific community. Some biologists believe that acid rain and snow may play a part in their demise, because amphibian skin absorbs toxic chemicals present in soil and water.

Chapter Three

BIRDS OF A FEATHER

Birds are members of the class Aves, from which we get our words *avian* and *aviary*. They are unique among animals in that they are the only ones that possess feathers. The glorious songs and beautiful plumage of many birds, as well as their ability to fly, have made them an object of fascination for centuries.

Ornithologists (biologists who study birds) believe that the ancestor of the modern bird was the *Archaeopteryx*, a creature that lived more than 140 million years ago. This great-grandaddy of all birds was about the size of a pheasant and, with its long, lizardlike tail, looked more like a reptile than a bird. From this gawky creature came more than 9,500 species of birds, ranging from the tiny bee hummingbird of Cuba, which grows to be only about two inches in length, to the mean-tempered ostrich, the world's largest bird, which can grow to be eight feet tall and weigh 300 pounds.

For centuries humans have envied the bird's ability to fly. Many of us have heard the Greek myth about Icarus, whose father, the inventor Daedalus, imprisoned on a remote island in the Aegean, fashioned two massive pairs of wings for himself and his son out of wax, string, and bird feathers. At first, the man-made wings worked beautifully, and the enthralled Icarus flew higher and higher, despite his father's warnings. Finally, the foolish boy flew so close to the sun that the wax on his wings began to melt. The wings fell apart, and before the eyes of his horrified father, Icarus fell to his death in the ocean.

It takes more than a pair of wings to fly, however. Even if human bodies were covered with feathers, we would still be earthbound. The bodies of birds contain several important modifications that help them to take flight. For example, most of their bones are nearly hollow, so that even large birds are relatively light (the mighty bald eagle weighs only about nine pounds). Large, strong breast muscles power their lungs, and an efficient respiratory system supplies plenty of oxygen to their cells during flight.

Birds are *oviparous*, meaning that they lay eggs. Egg-laying is another adaption for flight: A female bird about to produce young would be too heavy to fly if she carried her developing young inside of her, as mammals do.

Not all birds can fly, however. Penguins, rheas, ostriches, cassowaries, and kiwis are all flightless. Other birds, such as pheasants and chickens, can fly only short distances at low altitudes.

Birds are among the most versatile animals and can be found on every continent. There are about 100 billion birds in the world. They range in number from endangered species such as the whooping crane, whose population numbers in the hundreds, to Wilson's petrel, of which there are an estimated 100 million. Many birds, such as the trumpeter swan, for example, are monogamous.

Some birds, such as starlings and pigeons, are considered pests in certain areas of the country. Many others, however, perform an invaluable service by eating harmful insects or by consuming weed seeds. It has been estimated that a bobwhite can consume 15,000 such seeds a day.

Hark the Raven

Grip, Charles Dickens's pet raven, who was the inspiration for Edgar Allen Poe's poem "*The Raven*," was once the most famous bird in the world. The huge bird (eighteen inches long, with a wingspan of twenty-five inches) died after accidentally eating white lead paint 152 years ago. Grip was stuffed shortly after his demise and is now on display in the Rare Book Department of Philadelphia's Free Library.

Birds have also played a role in history. The sacred geese in the temple of Zeus are credited with saving Roman civilization from marauding barbarian tribes in A.D. 332 with their loud cackling. Although the invaders quickly killed the noisy birds, the geese were able to wake the city before any attack could be made.

A flock of birds was also partially responsible for Christopher Columbus's conquest of the New World. On October 7, 1492, Columbus was threatened with a mutiny of his crew while still some 720 miles east of the North American mainland. The sea-weary sailors were determined to turn the *Santa Maria* back to Spain. Sighting a flock of migratory land birds, Columbus was able to reassure the sailors that they were near the end of their journey. He turned the *Santa Maria* toward the southwest, followed the birds, and shortened his route to land by about 200 miles, making landfall at the island of San Salvador instead of on the mainland.

More recently, the crops of Utah's struggling Mormon settlers were saved from hordes of crickets by sea gulls. Since these birds are rarely seen so far inland, the Mormons saw this as a miracle, and in Temple Square in Salt Lake City there stands a monument to these birds, a tall, slim pillar on which are perched two golden California gulls.

From tiny, rainbow-hued hummingbirds to fierce, majestic eagles, birds are some of the planet's most fascinating creatures, as the following bits of bird lore illustrate.

FACTS OF LIFE

- The brilliantly colored red jungle fowl of southeast Asia, a species of pheasant, is the ancestor of all domestic chickens. From Asia it has spread into almost all regions of the world. It is believed that the bird was brought into the New World by the seagoing Polynesians, who carried the fowl to the Hawaiian islands. Today, there are about 3 billion chickens in the world.

- In the United States, the poultry industry is a $13 billion business. Americans consume about seventy-eight pounds of poultry every year. About 80 percent of the fowl eaten in this country comes from chickens.

- The domestic turkey descends from the wild turkey of Mexico. These turkeys were domesticated by the Aztecs and Incas, who used them both as a food source and as sacrifices to their many gods. The Spanish conquista-

A Murder of Crows

When is a flock of birds not a flock of birds? When it's a *murmuration* of starlings or a *watch* of nightingales. Here are some other unusual expressions used to describe birds in groups

- A *bazaar* of murres.
- A *siege* of herons or bitterns
- A *spring* of teal
- A *plump* of wildfowl
- A *cast* of hawks
- A *gaggle* of geese
- A *skein* of geese (flying)
- A *nye* of pheasants

dores introduced the birds to North America, and by the time of the first Thanksgiving in 1619, the bird was well established in New England and other parts of the country.

- Because flying uses up so much energy, birds eat more frequently than animals of similar size. Flightless birds, such as ostriches, have lower metabolisms than those that fly, so they feed on low-energy foods such as grasses and leaves. Flying birds, such as the wren, eat low-bulk, high-energy foods such as insects, seeds, nuts, fruits, and fish. The tiny hummingbird eats the equivalent of fifty to sixty meals per day!

- The highest-flying bird is the bar-headed goose. Some flocks of bar-headed geese fly over the world's highest mountain range, the Himalayas, at an altitude of more than 25,000 feet.

- The fastest avian diver is the peregrine falcon. The bird can swoop down on its prey at a speed of more than 200 miles per hour.

- The deepest diver in the bird world is the emperor penguin. They have been recorded at underwater depths of almost 900 feet.

- Did you ever hear the phrase "like water off a duck's back?" This saying comes from the fact that ducks and other waterfowl have waterproof feathers. Each feather is coated with oil, which makes water slide off them easily.

- There are several species of cassowary, relatives of the ostrich that live in the forests of Australia, New Guinea, and the nearby Pacific islands. These birds can reach five feet and weigh up to 120 pounds. Cassowaries can be dangerous because they have incredibly strong, three-toed feet with razor sharp claws. One kick from a cassowary can disembowel a man.

- Some birds, such as the black-necked swan, which is found in the lakes and ponds of southern South America, have legs set back far on their bodies, making it difficult for them to walk. Therefore, they spend most of their time in the water, rarely venturing onto land. Baby swans, called cygnets, often ride on the backs of their swimming parents.

MYSTERIES OF MIGRATION

About half the bird species of the world migrate to warmer climates in cold weather. Arctic terns migrate farther than any other bird. They travel about 11,000 miles each way between their breeding ground in the Arctic and their winter homes in the Antarctic.

Migration has puzzled and fascinated humankind for centuries. Our ancestors developed unusual and sometimes bizarre theories to explain the sudden disappearance of thousands of birds every year. Aristotle, for example, maintained that the European robin changed into the European redstart for the summer. An anonymous treatise published in London in 1703 put forth the theory that birds migrated to the moon for the winter, a trip that allegedly took sixty days. The barnacle goose, which is found on the tundras of northern Europe, was thought to hatch from barnacles in the sea. In reality, they nest in the Arctic, far from human eyes.

Birds sometimes fly thousands of miles during migratory flights. How do they find their way? Scientists think that many use the sun, stars, and landmarks such as mountains and streams as navigational markers. Other birds learn the migratory paths by following experienced leaders.

BIRDSONG AT MORNING

For centuries, poets have written about the beautiful songs of birds, seeing them as odes of joy or harbingers of spring. The actual purpose of a bird's song, however, is much more pedestrian: It is a way of proclaiming its territory to other birds and warning them to stay away. That the song may also attract a mate is of secondary importance to the singer.

All birds have voices. Some, such as the whooping crane, many species of geese, and the trumpeter swan, are capable of making very loud sounds. The magnificent trumpeter swan, found in the prairie wetlands and tundras of North America, has long vocal cords that enable it to make its startling cry. The loud duets of trumpeter swan pairs chase others from their territory and make the pair bond stronger. Other birds, such as turkey vultures, only grunt.

The beautiful, trilling songs we associate with birds are made by the *passerines*, or perching birds, a group that includes such familiar species as the robin, sparrow, and starling. About 60 percent of all bird species alive today are passerines.

Most birds sing only when they are searching for a mate or are setting up a territory; once these tasks are accomplished, they rarely sing. The European blackbird, for example, sings most in April and May; after July, it produces only call notes.

One of the most versatile songbirds is the mockingbird, which North American Indians called *cencontlatolly*, meaning "400 tongues." Although it is now illegal in the United States to keep wild birds as pets, at one time, mockingbirds were kept as cage birds because of their beautiful voices.

Perhaps the mockingbird's most amazing feat, however, is its ability to imitate other sounds. Not only does it copy the songs of other birds with uncanny accuracy, it also mimics man-made sounds, such as alarm clocks, dinner bells, whistles, and sirens. The Latin name of this bird, *Mimus polyglottos* ("many-tongued mimic") is a reflection of this unique skill. Although such birds as the mourning dove are natural singers, ornithologists think that others, including the mockingbird, may not be born with the ability to sing and must learn from experienced warblers.

COLOR, SIZE, AND COURTSHIP

Many birds are known for their breathtaking colors. In most species, it is the male that bears flamboyant plumage; the females are often dull in comparison. Nowhere is this color difference more striking than in peafowl. The peacock has become famous for its brilliant emerald and sapphire hues, while peahens are a drab brown. Young males, however, resemble the females and develop their beautiful plumage only when fully mature.

Female birds are often quite smaller than males. Female birds of prey, such as hawks, for example, are as much as 30 percent smaller than their mates. This difference in size is known as *sexual dimorphism*. In birds of prey, this size discrepancy is thought to reduce the risk of fighting during courtship, because birds more evenly matched in size would likely see each other as competitors for a territory.

Some birds engage in dramatic courtship rituals. Flamingos are known for their ritualized courtship displays, in which they often "march" in unison, doing "wing salutes" and other maneuvers. Sandhill cranes have been known to jump fifteen to twenty feet in the air during their mating season.

AVIAN SENSES

With a few exceptions, birds have the sharpest vision of any animal. It has been estimated that the eyesight of a

Pretty Poison

Scientists have recently discovered the first poisonous bird, the hooded pitohui (pronounced *pit-a-hooey*), found in the tropical forests of New Guinea. The flesh, skin, and feathers of this colorful orange and black passerine, which is about the size of a blue jay, contains a poison called homobatrachotoxin, a toxin previously found only in the poison arrow frogs of the Amazon basin. Just 100 milligrams of the bird's breast meat contains enough toxin to kill a mouse in twenty minutes.

Owls can turn their heads almost completely around. Courtesy of Zoological Society of Philadelphia.

sparrow hawk is eight times sharper than a man's. Unlike other animals, birds also have excellent color vision.

Birds' eyeballs, unlike man's, do not move in their sockets, so birds must move their necks to see objects in different directions. Many of us have seen robins and other birds with their heads cocked, as if they were listening to something, when actually what they were doing was moving their heads to *see* better.

The eyes of birds are the largest of any land animals. In many species, the eyes weigh more than the brain. Large hawks and owls have eyeballs the size of a man's. An ostrich's eye is about the size of a tennis ball.

Unlike humans, birds can look at the sun without damage to their eyes because of the presence of a *nictating eyelid*, a semitransparent membrane that is also found in the cat family (a vestige of the nictating eyelid can also be found in the inner corner of human eyes). This membrane helps to clean and protect the eye and also acts as kind of built-in pair of sunglasses, cutting down on glare. Birds are the only animals to close their eyes in death.

Birds also have excellent hearing. They can hear *infrasounds*—very-low-frequency sounds that human beings cannot discern. In nature, infrasounds include those made by thunderstorms, ocean waves, and earthquakes. This keen sense of hearing enables nocturnal hunters, such as owls, to pinpoint the slightest sound, for example, mice scuttling along the ground in near total darkness.

A BIRD'S FEATHERS

Feathers are extremely important to a bird—not only do they enable a bird to fly, they also preserve body heat. The feathers are made of *keratin*, the same substance human hair and nails are composed of.

How many feathers does a bird have? Naturally, the larger the bird, the more feathers. A ruby throated hummingbird has a count of 940 feathers, while songbirds such as robins and sparrows run between 1,100 and 4,600; a whistling swan has 25,000.

Some species of birds have been greatly reduced or even driven to extinction because of the demand for their foliage. Others, such as rheas and ostriches, can be shorn for their feathers without killing the birds. Ostrich feathers are favored by fashion designers for their dramatic appearance.

Birds spend many of their waking hours bathing in water or even dust, *preening* themselves in order to keep their feathers free of parasites and dirt. Some species engage in a behavior called *anting*, in which live ants are rubbed into the feathers in order to release formic acid, a burning substance that ornithologists believe may help repel mites and other tiny parasites. Other species have been seen to use beetles, orange peels, and even mothballs to preen. Still others, particularly starlings and members of the crow family, use smoke in their preening sessions. The bird will sit on a rim of a smoking chimney and, as the smoke curls around it, spread its wings as if anting. The bird then appears to take a beakful of smoke and rub it under one wing. Members of the crow family have even been seen "fire bathing," seemingly taking beaks full of fire and using them to clean their feathers. In England during the sixteenth and seventeenth centuries, crows, rooks, jackdaws, and magpies were called "firebirds" because of this habit. Sometimes they would perch on the thatched roofs of houses with glowing embers in their mouths, often setting the homes on fire.

FACTS OF LIFE

- Birds beat their wings at different rates of speed. Hovering hummingbirds may beat them sixty times per second. Owls use slow wing beats. Some large birds, such as vultures and condors, flap their wings very little; they seek out rising currents of hot air, called *thermals*, and circle in the sky for hours.

- Peafowl can become quite tame. When excited, they emit a strange cry that some people think sounds like a woman crying, "Help! Help!"

BIRD NESTS AND EGGS

A bird's egg contains a large yolk, which serves to nourish the developing chick. Some birds are *precocial*, meaning that they lay large eggs from which downy, well-developed chicks hatch. This group includes ducks and other sea birds. The chicks of precocial birds must find their own food soon after birth. Other birds, including most songbirds, are *altricial*, meaning that they hatch from small eggs and are blind, helpless, and naked at birth. Altricial birds are fed and warmed by their parents until they are old enough to survive on their own.

Eggs range in color from the delicate pale blue of a robin to the rough-grained black egg of an emu. A ruby-throated hummingbird lays an egg about the size of a pea; an ostrich's egg, on the other hand, is six to nine inches long and five to six inches in diameter. (A fertile ostrich egg can sell for $1,500.)

Ostrich eggs are dwarfed, however, by those of the elephant bird, or roc, which lived in Madagascar and became extinct in the twelfth or thirteenth century. This bird stood an incredible ten feet tall. The huge egg of the roc could hold two gallons of liquid and was 30,000 times bigger than the egg of the smallest hummingbird.

Being the smallest birds, hummingbirds naturally build the tiniest nests. Some are the size of half a walnut shell. The bald eagle builds the largest nest of any North American bird. One bald eagle nest found in Ohio was twelve feet deep and eight and a half feet across. It was estimated to weigh about two tons and was occupied continuously for thirty-five years, until it crashed to the ground.

Some birds, such as European cuckoos and American cowbirds, are parasites, laying their eggs in the nests of other species. Since the eggs of these parasitic birds hatch quickly, their chicks usually emerge well before the rightful young of the nest do. The parasitic chicks grow rapidly and often push out the other inhabitants of the nest, or eat so much food that the true young of the foster parents starve.

Some swallows and swifts secrete a sticky saliva, which they use to strengthen their nests. Some species of Asiatic swift build nests composed almost entirely of hardened saliva. The nests are gathered, cleansed, and used in making the famous bird's nest soup that is enjoyed in many Asian households.

Other nests used by man include those of the eider duck. The female eider duck plucks down from her own breast to form a large, fluffy ring around her eggs. Because eider duck down is very warm and strong, it is collected and used to make warm, high-quality sleeping bags and cold-weather clothing.

FACTS OF LIFE

- The honey guide of Africa lives largely on beeswax. They cannot get at the wax by themselves, however, so they perch near beehives and sing excitedly. Their calls attract honey-eating mammals, who open the beehives and eat the honey. The bird then feeds on the bee larvae and wax.

- Some birds act as "cleaners," removing parasites from other animals. The little white egret of the tropics sits on top of the water buffalo and removes ticks with its sharp beak. The Egyptian plover cleans the teeth of the Nile crocodile—without being eaten!

- While most songbirds live only about three or four years, a canary can live to be twenty-five, and an ostrich can reach the age of fifty.

- Parrots can live a very long time. The maharajah of Nawangar had a parrot that was 115 years old. The bird traveled with the Indian ruler in a Rolls-Royce and even had its own international passport.

QUIZ: FOR THE BIRDS

Test your knowledge of the world of birds by filling in the blanks from the list below. Correct answers can be found on page 187.

a. Flyways   b. Cormorant   c. Raptors   d. Cardinal   e. Brown pelicans
f. Albatross   g. Murres   h. Swallows   i. Golden plover   j. Owl

1. This seabird's wingspan can reach eleven feet. _____

2. In some Asian countries, this bird has been tamed and is used by peasants to help them catch fish. _____

3. This bird can turn its head almost completely around. _____

4. This is another term for birds of prey. _____

5. Legend has it that these birds always return to the mission of Capistrano on March 19, the Feast of St. Joseph. _____

6. The young of this species are very noisy, but the adults are virtually mute. _____

7. This songbird is the official state bird of seven states. _____

8. The eggs of these cliff-dwelling birds are tapered so that they will not roll from their high perches. _____

9. This small bird can fly nonstop from eastern Canada to South America, a 2,400-mile trip. _____

10. This term is used to describe established routes of migratory birds. _____

Chapter Four

FISH STORIES

The finned, aquatic vertebrates that comprise the superclass Pisces are among the world's most versatile animals. They can range in size from tiny guppies to the giant whale shark, the world's largest fish, which can grow up to fifty feet. Fish can inhabit the sapphire blue waters of the tropics or live thousands of feet below the surface in cold, dark waters where the sun's rays cannot reach. They can live in the frigid waters of the Arctic or in hot, bubbling springs where the temperature can reach 104°F. There are 30,000 species of fish, making them among the most numerous vertebrates on earth.

Fish often serve as food for other vertebrates; shore and ocean birds probably consume many more fish than man does. As wildlife, fish also provide enjoyment for millions of anglers; fishing is perhaps the world's most popular recreational activity.

They are the world's oldest vertebrates. Fossilized fish bones and scales have been found in rocks 400 million years old. The Devonian period, which occurred about 350 million years ago, has been called the "Age of Fishes" because of the bountiful fossil remains found in rocks from both the oceans and fresh water.

Most of these prehistoric creatures, of course, have become extinct. In 1938, however, a strange fish was found off the coast of South Africa.

Astonished *ichthyologists* (scientists who study fish) recognized the large blue fish as a coelacanth, a creature that was supposed to have died out millions of years ago. Increasingly rare, the coelacanths are the world's largest oldest living higher animals. Predating the dinosaurs by 200 million years, they have undergone so little change during the past thirty centuries that they have been called "machines for reading the past."

In terms of a natural resource, the value of fish cannot be overestimated. For hundreds of millions of people throughout the planet, fish are a major component of their daily diet, providing a much needed source of protein. The fishing industry is one of the largest in the world; hundreds of thousands of people depend on the bounty of the seas, rivers, and lakes of the world for their livelihood. Much of the world's food fish is caught in the continental shelf, which begins at the shoreline and continues seaward until the water is 100 fathoms (600 feet) deep. The global fish catch, however, fell from 100 million tons in 1989 to 98 million in 1991, largely because of overharvesting.

Fishing has played a central part in the U.S. economy for centuries. The Atlantic cod, a favorite food fish, stimulated the colonization of New England and helped foster the shipbuilding industry. In testimony to its role in American history, a large codfish of gilded pine was hung on the walls of the Massachusetts State House in 1784 as a memorial to the importance of the codfishery to "the welfare of the Commonwealth of Massachusetts." More than two hundred years later, the plaque still remains. In the United States today, fisheries represent a $46 billion industry. But overfishing has greatly decreased the population of the Atlantic cod, as well as of haddock and herring.

Fish are beneficial to man not only because they are a major food source, but also because they devour an enormous number of insects. One species, the mosquito fish, found in the southern United States, has been introduced to many of the warmer parts of the world where malaria, yellow fever, and other illnesses spread by mosquitoes are common. The mosquito fish help check the spread of these dread diseases by eating mosquito eggs. Other fish dine on *plankton* (microscopic plant and animal life), including diatoms.

Fish use gills instead of lungs to breathe. They extract oxygen from the water by taking it through their mouths, passing it through the gill chambers, and finally expelling it through openings in the side of the head. The lungfish, another holdover from primitive times, breathes by means of gills and a lung-like organ called a swim baldder, or gas bladder. There are six species: four in Africa, one in Australia, and one in South America. The South American and African varieties aestivate in mud during hot, dry periods, surviving off protein stored in their muscle tissues. They can survive for up to four years in this manner.

FACTS OF LIFE

- The butterfish, which is found in Atlantic coastal waters, molds its mass of eggs to resemble a ball of butter. It then guards the eggs in some cranny or empty seashell until the eggs hatch.

- The eggs of sea horses, which, with their equine appearance and curved tails, look quite unlike any other fish, are deposited by the female into a pouch on the underside of the male, where they remain until they hatch.

- The male Australian kurtus incubates its eggs on its forehead. Other male fish "guard" the eggs of their young. The male toadfish, found on the muddy bottoms of shallow water, viciously bites any interlopers while on nursery duty. Male Siamese fighting fish are so fierce while guarding their eggs that in their native Thailand that they are gambled on like gamecocks.

- Tilapias are African freshwater food fish. The male tilapia hatches eggs in its mouth. The eggs take about five days to hatch, and another six or eight days pass before the hatchlings are developed enough to live on their own. During this time, the fish lives on its stores of body fat.

SHARKS AND THEIR RELATIVES

Sharks, rays, and skates are among the most primitive fish; some of them have scarcely changed in 100 million years. Sharks have no bones. Their skeletons are made of cartilage (the same material that makes up our noses) hardened by lime.

Sharks have several rows of teeth. When one in the front row falls out or is lost, a tooth in the second row moves in to replace it. It has been estimated that during a period of ten years, a tiger shark may go through 24,000 teeth.

Because of hunting and habitat destruction, some sharks are in danger of extinction. In some parts of the world, sharks are also used as food, contributing to their decreasing numbers. Shark liver is very high in vitamin A, and an extract made from these primitive fish is even being touted as a cure for cancer. The soupfin shark, which is found in the Pacific Ocean, gets its name from the fact that its fins are used to make soup and other dishes in China and other Asian countries.

With a few exceptions (including the huge but harmless whale shark and the basking shark, both plankton eaters), sharks are predators that will eat walruses, sea lions, sea turtles, and each other. In one case, a shark even devoured a crazed elephant that had run into the ocean.

Others eat fish, seals, and walruses. Of the 350 species of shark, only 25 have been known to attack man. The most notorious of this group is the great white, the star of *Jaws* and its numerous sequels. Other sharks with a taste for human flesh include the hammerhead, lemon, bull, mako, sandbar, and tiger sharks. The tiger shark is called the "garbage can shark," because it has been known to swallow license plates, car parts, and paint cans.

Barracuda, in particular the great barracuda, have been known to attack swimmers, but these fish are less dangerous than sharks.

The rays and skates, cousins to the shark, are fish with strange flattened bodies that move in smooth, rippling motions. The harmless Atlantic manta ray can grow up to twenty feet across. Stingrays have whiplike tails with poisonous, barbed stingers that can inflict a painful wound. In some parts of the world, the tails have been used as whips and the barbed stingers for spear tips.

FACTS OF LIFE

- The ocean is divided into several layers, each which is populated by different varieties of fish. The *euphotic zone* which begins at the surface of the water and goes down to about 500 feet (150 meters), is a region of warmer waters where sunlight penetrates. The euphotic zone is home to such fish as the marlin, flying fish, and anchovy. The *mesopelagic zone*, between about 500 feet (150 meters) and 3,300 feet (1,000 meters), is inhabited by a vast assortment of fish, including bluefin tuna and barracuda, as well as other sea animals such as squid, octopuses, and prawns. Sunlight penetrates part of this region, to about 650 feet (200 meters). The bottom layer of the ocean, between 3,300 and 10,000 feet (1,000 and 3,300 meters), is called the *abyssal* or *bathypelagic* zone. This is a region of near-freezing water, where no light penetrates. Many of the fish in this zone have luminous organs that help them find their way in the darkness of these depths. Other fish of the abyssal region have no light organs and live in total darkness. Bathypelagic fish include the angler fish and brotulid.

- Some fish, including the barracuda, mackerel, and tuna, are *pelagic*, meaning that they live near the surface of the water. Other fish, such as catfish, sea robin, and flounder, live near the bottom. Light cannot reach below 1,500 feet, so the fish, and other aquatic animals, live in total darkness.

Deadly Denizens of the Deep

Many of us have heard about the ferocious, flesh-eating piranhas of South America. Of the twenty species of this fish, however, only five are actually carnivorous, and some are mild-mannered enough to live in home aquariums.

Less well known but deadlier than the piranha is the Australian stonefish, which lives in the Red Sea, the Indian Ocean, and off the northern coast of western Australia. This warty creature injects its poison through sharp spines on its back. Because of its dull reddish brown color it is easily mistaken for a rock. The stonefish's poison can cause convulsions, paralysis, and death. An antidote exists, but treatment lasts many months and is not always successful.

The pufferfish family includes about one hundred species. One variety, the death puffer, contains a poison called *tetrodotoxin*, or TTX, which is 275 times more deadly than cyanide.

Despite this danger, death puffer is eaten in Japan, where it is called *fugu*. Japanese chefs are specially trained to cut away the poisonous parts, but every year, about twenty Japanese die from fugu poisoning.

- Fish cannot see well. They can, however, hear and have a well-developed sense of balance and taste.

- The flying fish does not actually fly; it glides through the air above the surface of the water for short distances with the aid of winglike fins and a strong tail. How far they go depends partially on how fast the wind is blowing.

- There are some species of parasitic fish, perhaps the most unusual of which is the dwarf male angler fish. The jaws of the male fuse with the skin tissues of the female to receive nourishment from the female's blood; in exchange, the male acts as a sort of swimming sperm bank, always available to fertilize the eggs.

- Fish come in a wide range of colors. The most colorful varieties live in the coral reefs of the world's tropical waters. Such species as the parrotfish and angelfish come in brilliant shades that dazzle the eye. Scientists think that these flashy colors may help protect the fish by confusing their enemies. Many fish that live in shallow water, such as the sturgeon, are silvery with bright markings. Deep-sea fish (those that live below 100 fathoms, or 600 feet) are often colored a bright red. Below 200 fathoms, fish tend to be black or dark brown in color and possess luminous organs that allow them to see in the dark. The glassfish has flesh so transparent that its internal organs are clearly visible through its flesh.

The Salmon's Incredible Journey

One of the most amazing odysseys in the animal world is undertaken by the Chinook or king salmon. These fish go on a perilous journey lasting many months just to spawn, or lay their eggs, in the waters of their birth.

After hatching, the baby salmon swim to the Columbia River, which rises in the Rockies and flows through southeastern British Columbia and much of the Pacific Northwest. Feeding on plankton, they make their way to the open sea, gradually turning predator as they mature and consuming smaller fish such as herring. The king salmon makes a

Spawning salmon have been known to leap upstream in their desperate struggle to reach the waters of their birth. Photograph by G. Haknel. Courtesy of U.S. Fish & Wildlife Service.

700 mile journey through the Pacific to beyond the Queen Charlotte Islands of British Columbia before it turns back, gripped by the urge to spawn.

How do these fish find their way home? Like birds, fish have a very keen sense of smell, and the salmon are able to zero in on their home streams by recognizing their distinct odor—if the salmons' nostrils are plugged, they will lose their way. Only a tiny percentage of the vast shoal that started on the journey ever makes it; their ranks are decimated by disease, fishermen, birds of prey, and hungry bears.

The determination of these fish is amazing. They have even been known to jump upstream rapids on their journey. Those that reach their goal die shortly after spawning.

QUIZ: SOMETHING FISHY

Test your knowledge of the world of fish with the following multiple-choice questions. Answers can be found on page 187.

1. This is another name for the California sardine.

   a. wrasse   b. pilchard   c. tarpon   d. quillback

2. This fish is the largest of the minnows.

   a. mackerel   b. batfish   c. carp   d. bonefish

3. In the classic Italian book *Pinocchio*, the little wooden boy was actually swallowed by one of these, not a whale.

   a. flounder   b. dolphin   c. paddlefish   d. dogfish

4. This primitive fish kills other fish by attaching itself to their bodies, making a wound, and sucking out their body fluids.

   a. lamprey   b. stickleback   c. triggerfish   d. mullet

5. The milt (sperm) and roe (eggs) of this fish are poisonous.

   a. ladyfish   b. whitefish   c. smelt   d. gar

6. These small fish, which live in the open ocean at about 500 feet, possess luminescent organs that make them glow in the dark.

   a. hatchetfish   b. ladyfish   c. catfish   d. needlefish

7. An angler's delight, these silver game fish of the Atlantic can reach fifteen feet in length and weigh more than 1,000 pounds.

    a. quillback   b. tarpon   c. chub   d. stonecat

8. This tasty fish is a member of the herring family.

    a. shad   b. tuna   c. flounder   d. cod

9. These are tropical eels.

    a. perches   b. bluefish   c. morays   d. crappies

10. The black roe of the female of the European species of this fish are sold as caviar.

    a. catfish   b. sturgeon   c. flying fish   d. mullet

11. Which of these fish are *not* members of the mackerel family?

    a. tuna   b. albacore   c. bass   d. bonito

12. This aggressive fish, although not particularly large, has been observed attacking schools of smaller fish, seemingly just for the sport of it.

    a. bluefish   b. perch   c. bass   d. grunt

13. This famous food fish is found mainly in the Gulf of Mexico.

    a. red snapper   b. smelt   c. salmon   d. haddock

14. Finnan haddie is lightly smoked:

    a. halibut   b. red snapper   c. haddock   d. mullet

15. Which of these fish is a member of the sunfish family?

    a. hake   b. bass   c. greenling   d. blenny

Chapter Five

SPINELESS WONDERS: THE INVERTEBRATES

T he earthworm slithering across the sidewalk after a rainstorm, the crab scuttling sideways along the beach, the monarch butterfly spreading its orange and black wings to the sun—as different as they may look, they all have something in common. They are invertebrates, or animals without backbones. They range in size from the mysterious giant squid to tiny beetles only millimeters long and can be found in every part of the world. It has been estimated that 99 percent of the world's creatures belong to this group.

CREEPERS AND CRAWLERS: THE ARACHNIDS

Spiders, scorpions, mites, chiggers, and ticks are small, insectlike animals that belong to the class Arachnida. The arachnids are part of the great phylum Arthropoda, which also includes the crustaceans, insects, the Diplopoda (millipedes), and Chilopoda (the centipedes). Arthropods are characterized by a hard, protective coating called an *exoskeleton*.

Spiders are the best-known arachnids—and probably the most unpopular. The well-known nursery rhyme "Little Miss Muffet" illustrates the fear and loathing many people (including the author) hold for these eight-legged creatures. But despite their creepy appearance, most spiders are quite harmless.

Although all of them are venomous, inflicting their poison by means of a pair of hollow fangs, only 30 or 40 of the 50,000 or so known species, are dangerous to man. Many spiders are actually quite beneficial, because they devour millions of harmful insects ever year.

For the record, there really was a "Miss Mouffet." Her father, the sixteenth-century physician Thomas Mouffet, believed that spiders had healing properties when eaten. It is no wonder that the poor girl became upset at the sight of one of the little beasties. Here are some more facts about spiders and their creeping, crawling cousins.

FACTS OF LIFE

- One of the most unusual arachnids is the horseshoe crab, which is not a crab at all. This animal is not used as food by man, but the female of the species lays hundreds of thousands of eggs, which are a valuable source of nourishment for shorebirds and other creatures.

- A scorpion's sting is at the end of its tail. Before it is about to attack, it makes a warning noise by rubbing its claws against its legs.

- A scorpion's sting can be fatal, but of the twelve varieties known in the United States, only two are dangerous to man. According to the American Association of Poison Control Centers, there were 6,765 *reported* cases of scorpion bites in the United States in 1991, none of them fatal. Most scorpions live in warm climates, though some species can be found in cold, wet areas.

- Most spiders have eight eyes although some have six. They generally have very poor eyesight, however, and many of them are nearly blind.

- The world's largest spider, the South American *Theraphosa leblondii*, is the size of a dinner plate.

- In southern Italy in the fifteenth to seventeenth centuries, a large wolf spider called the tarantula, after the port city of Taranto, was said to have bitten a great many people. The victims of this spider cried, screamed, and leapt about uncontrollably, launching into a frenzied dance. Whether this was a symptom brought on by the poison or by an attempt to purge the body of it is unclear, but whatever the case, the creature lent its name to a lively peasant dance called the tarantella.

- Some larger species of tarantula regularly dine on small birds. The spider injects its poison into the unfortunate creature, and then it's bye-bye, birdie.

- Because of their low metabolism, many spiders can live without food for over a year.

- Since spiders are incapable of digesting solid particles of food, they inject a poison into their prey with their fangs. Their digestive liquids turn their prey's body into a kind of "soup," which they then eat.

- All spiders are cannibals.

- All spiders spin silk with the use of organs called *spinnerets*, which are located in the abdomen. A spider's web serves not only as a means of trapping unwary insects but also as its home. Spiders leave their webs only when food is scarce or to mate.

- When most of us think of spider webs, the familiar circular structures immediately come to mind. Not all spiders weave webs of this type, however. Some webs are in the form of dense sheets, while others have a random, tangled appearance.

- Spider silk is very fine, but amazingly strong. A spider can be a thousand times heavier than its own web. Many attempts have also been made to use spider silk in textiles, with little success. One American zoologist found that it took 415 spiders to get enough silk for one square yard of material, half the amount obtainable from an equal number of silkworms.

- Not all spiders spin webs. The trapdoor spider digs burrows and manufactures "doors" out of soil particles cemented together with saliva and bound up with silk. When a predator approaches, the spider holds the door "closed" with its fangs.

- Probably the world's most poisonous spider is the Australian funnel-web, which digs its den in people's gardens. The venom of this spider can kill a person in less than two hours. Fortunately, an antivenom for this spider's bite was developed in 1980.

The Black Widow

In the United States, there are five species of spiders with bites that are poisonous to man: the brown recluse, the sac spider, the brown widow, the red-legged widow, and the famous black widow, the most poisonous of the lot, which earned its name from the fact that the female sometimes kills the male after mating. Scientists believe that only the female's bite is dangerous to man. The black widow likes dark, quiet places and in the days before modern plumbing was fond of hiding in outhouses, where it often spun webs across toilet seats! This spider is found in every state except Alaska and Hawaii.

Although the female black widow is only about one-and-a-half inches long (the male is about a fourth of this size), its poison is said to be fifteen times more powerful than that of a rattlesnake. The black widow spider bears a red mark in the perfect shape of an hourglass on its abdomen; because of this it is sometimes called the "red mark" or "hourglass spider."

Like most spiders, however, it is shy and elusive and will usually bite only when disturbed. Deaths from spider bites are relatively rare; there have been fewer than one hundred known fatalities from black widow bites in the last two hundred years. With effective use of antidotes, the mortality rate from black widow bites has dwindled even further. Shock, particularly to young or elderly people, is the main cause of death in many cases.

THOSE CRUSTY CRUSTACEANS

Crustaceans are invertebrates with numerous jointed legs. The word *Crustacean* comes from a Latin word meaning "hard shell," and these animals are characterized by a tough exoskeleton that protects their soft bodies. Crustaceans, lobsters, crayfish, shrimp, and crabs are considered delicacies in many parts of the world, including the United States. Other members of this family include barnacles, water fleas, and wood lice.

Many of us have become acquainted with crustaceans on our dinner plates, but there is much more to this group of animals than meets the palate.

FACTS OF LIFE

- Barnacles will attach themselves to anything, including ships, the wood pilings of wharves, and even whales. Once they affix themselves to something, they stay there for the rest of their lives and can be extremely difficult to remove. Barnacles that attach themselves to ship hulls impede water flow and may increase the ship's fuel cost by as much as 40 percent. Solutions containing copper compounds are often used to destroy these animals, but scientists are researching the use of natural toxins from marine sponges to impede barnacle growth.

- Some crustaceans, such as the water flea, may be less than one millimeter long (about one-twenty-fourth of an inch). The largest crustacean in the world is the giant spider crab of coastal Japan. When its claws are out-stretched, it measures twelve feet.

● Many crustaceans, such as crayfish and crabs, have the ability to regenerate new limbs if one is lost. Lobsters can even detach one of their claws at will.

● A female lobster is called a hen or chicken. A lobster hen can lay 100,000 eggs at a time. Most of these, however, will end up as food for other marine life.

● In the United States and Canada, about 44,000 tons of lobsters are caught every year.

● Like shrimp, lobsters have ten legs. Eight of them are used for walking, and the other two have developed into huge, powerful claws that are capable of giving a wicked pinch. For this reason, the lobsters' claws are wedged closed or held closed with a rubber band when they are taken to market. Lobsters are dark green when alive; they turn red only when they are cooked.

● A few crustaceans, such as the spiny lobster, migrate. These animals live in the shallow coastal waters off Florida and in the Caribbean, and when the first autumn storm brings an abrupt drop in the water temperature, they head for warmer waters. Migrating about thirty miles south each fall, they cover as much as ten miles a day, walking single file in groups that can number up to sixty.

THE INSECTS: BUTTERFLY, BEETLE, AND BEE

Insects are the most numerous creatures on earth. There are about one million insect species, more than all the plant and animal species combined. Scientists discover 7,000 to 8,000 new kinds of insects every year, and it is believed that there may be from 1 to 10 *million* insect species still undiscovered.

The sheer number of insects on earth is mind-boggling. *Entomologists* (zoologists who study insects) estimate that the average number for each square mile of land equals the total number of people on earth. One scientist estimated that there are *twelve insects* on earth for every human being!

In terms of adaptability, the class Insecta is the most successful of all the groups of animals. They can be found in all types of environments, from the burning sands of the Sahara to the frigid wastes of the Antarctic to teeming urban areas. In the New York City area alone, there are 15,000 insect species.

They can dwell in dark subterranean chambers or in the snow-capped Himalayas. One insect, *Helaeomyia petrolei*, even lives in pools of crude petroleum.

Many of our encounters with insects are unpleasant. Insects such as locusts and termites cause billions of dollars of damage every year, and mosquitoes, fleas, and flies transmit serious and sometimes fatal diseases. The little black ants that spoil a picnic, bees and wasps that inflict painful and sometimes dangerous stings, and annoying mosquitoes that buzz and bite have caused many people to think of insects as nothing but pesky "bugs" to be swatted, stomped, or sprayed.

But other insects, such as the praying mantis, devour millions of harmful pests annually. The tiny, colorful ladybug is another beneficial insect. In California in the late 1800s an insect called the cotton cushiony scale ravaged California's lemon and orange groves. Citrus farmers introduced ladybugs into their groves, and within two years the harmful scales were under control.

Without insects we would not have important products such as shellac, beeswax, honey, or silk. Millions of acres of plants would go unpollinated, drastically affecting our food supply, and many species of birds, reptiles, fish, and mammals that depend on insects for nourishment would vanish. Humans could probably survive without insects, but it would be in a world drastically different from the one we now inhabit.

Insects have been on earth for at least 400 million years, struggling, adapting, and surviving. It has been said that they are humankind's only rivals for control of the globe. Instead of going to the dogs, the world may be going to the bugs. Perhaps it is wise to learn as much as we can about these creatures.

FACTS OF LIFE

- The world's largest insects are the giant goliath beetles of Africa, which can grow up to four inches. And atlas moths can have a wingspan of ten inches. At the other end of the scale, fairy flies measure less than one-hundredth of an inch, making them small enough to pass through the eye of a needle.

- Insects come in a wide variety of colors. Those in tropical climates tend to be more brilliantly hued than those in temperate regions, where insects tend to be brown and gray. Insects of arctic and alpine regions are often hairy and dark: Hairiness prevents heat loss, and dark colors promote heat absorption from the sun.

- Insect blood is very different from human blood, being a combination of blood and lymph called *hemolymph*. It contains no red blood cells and is colorless, pale yellow, or greenish, the color being largely determined by the food the insect eats.

- Many of us refer to all insects as "bugs." True bugs, however, have several important characteristics in common, including piercing, sucking mouthparts and two pairs of wings.

- In many countries, insects are enjoyed as food. Locusts (which are high in protein) have been eaten since antiquity. In some parts of Mexico, the egg cases of an insect called the water boatman are made into cakes. In South Africa, termites are roasted and eaten by the handful, like pretzels and popcorn. And everyone knows that a bottle of tequila is not authentic without that yummy little agave worm lying at the bottom!

- Dragonflies cannot walk at all, but they can fly very quickly, forward, backward, straight up and down. Or they can hover in the air, almost still, like tiny, brilliantly colored helicopters.

Bothersome Bugs

Only about one percent of insects can be classified as harmful to man, but this small group causes an estimated $7 billion worth of damage annually. Termites gnaw on wood; cabbage butterflies feed on cabbage, broccoli, and related crops; gypsy moths strip the leaves away from thousands of acres of trees; migrating locusts (a swarm of locusts can number in the *billions*) devastate acres of crops every year.

Other insects cause disease. The common housefly is not only annoying, but also dangerous. Flies enjoy feeding on carrion, garbage, feces, and just about anything else disgusting. They can transmit such diseases as typhoid, cholera, dysentery, and even tuberculosis. One fly, dissected after a meal, was found to contain six *million* bacteria in its body. The fly transmits this bacteria when it spits up material from its last meal to soften up its food.

Just as deadly as the housefly is the tsetse fly, which carries parasites that cause the dreaded disease known as sleeping sickness. It is estimated that sleeping sickness yearly kills 10,000 people, as well as countless cattle, on the African continent. Drugs have been developed that can cure this disease, but, unfortunately, only about 20 percent of the people infected with sleeping sickness have access to them.

Mosquitoes are also a type of fly. Throughout the world, there are about 2,400 to 3,000 mosquito species, with more than 100 types in North America alone. These tiny, buzzing creatures transmit such diseases as malaria and yellow fever, which affect millions every year. Mosquitoes have caused more deaths throughout history than all human wars combined. Entomologists are always searching for new ways, including the use of pesticides, to combat these destructive insects.

In some instances, however, pesticides used in insect control have had serious and long-lasting effects on the environment. One pesticide, dichloro-diphenyl-trichloro-ethane (better known as DDT), which was widely used in the 1960s, ran off from the soil into streams, rivers, and other waterways and thereby affected the water supply. This pesticide is retained in the tissues of both animals and humans for years and has serious effects on wildlife. For example, it caused the shells of birds' eggs to become so fragile that they broke almost as soon as they were laid. The populations of such species as the brown pelican were decimated, and only recently have they began to make a comeback. The Environmental Protection Agency banned this chemical in 1972, but it is still used in other countries.

The Social Insects

Social insects, such as termites, bees, ants, and some wasps, live in organized colonies. The nests of ants and termites may include a million individuals. Each insect in these colonies has a specific job, from the queen, whose only duty is to lay eggs, to workers, soldiers, and nurses, who look after the young. In bee, ant, and wasp colonies, all the workers are females. The male's only job is to mate with the female, after which he dies. Termite colonies do, however, have a permanent reproductive male called (you guessed it) a king.

Termites are among the best engineers in the animal kingdom. Their giant nests are constructed of mud mixed with the saliva of the workers, which hardens like concrete when it dries. Termites of the species *cubitermes*, which is found in tropical rainforests, build a nest that looks like a stack of umbrellas; heavy rains easily run off these sloped structures. Other species of tropical termites build hills that can be taller than a man!

There are more than 80,000 species of ants. Perhaps the most dangerous are the fire ants, which traveled from Brazil (probably via ship) into the southeastern United States and as far north as New Jersey. These tiny insects deliver a very painful sting. In the United States alone, 67,000 to 80,000 people must seek medical care after being bitten by these aggressive ants. They also

Bug Off!

Here is a recipe for an insect repellant for home gardeners who want to avoid using pesticides:

In a blender, food processor, or food grinder, grind together four fresh hot chili peppers, four onions, and two whole bulbs of garlic (remember to use gloves when handling the chili peppers). Place the ground vegetables in a deep bowl or pot and add enough water to cover the vegetables by approximately one inch. Allow to stand for twenty-four hours. Strain through cheesecloth, saving the liquid. Add enough water to the strained liquid to make one gallon. This can be used as a general-purpose insect spray over the entire garden. It is also said to discourage four-footed nibblers.

devastate crops, kill birds and other small animals, and have even been known to destroy cattle.

Ants are probably the most sophisticated of the social insects and live in highly organized colonies. Some ant colonies have "slaves" that are captured by raiding other anthills. They also capture aphids, tiny insects that suck the nectar from plants. "Dairy farmers" in the ant colonies keep "herds" of aphids. By stroking the aphid's body, the ants stimulate the flow of a sweet substance called "honeydew," which the ants then eagerly lap up.

Honeybees are not native to either North or South America. The first beehives were brought to the United States by colonists in 1621. The Native Americans called bees "white man's flies."

Honey is made from *nectar*, a watery solution of sugars, plus a little protein and salts, which is secreted by flowers. The bees (it is the workers of the hives that collect the nectar and manufacture honey) can fly up to three miles from their hive to collect pollen and nectar. Bees make honey in order to feed on it during the winter, when there are few flowers in bloom. Honeybees do a "dance" to signal to other bees where food is located. A dance performed in a circle indicates that food is close to the hive, while a "waggle" dance, done in the form of a figure eight, means that the food is farther away. In a good year one beehive can produce about eighty-eight pounds of the sweet, sticky syrup. The beekeeper must replace the taken honey with sugar or the bees will starve. American beekeepers produce 250 million pounds of honey every year.

Male bees, called drones, are basically useless. One in a thousand gets to mate with the queen. A queen bee can lay 2,000 eggs a day. In the fall, the worker bees, all females, chase the drones from the hives because they eat too much during the winter. Soon after leaving the hive, the drones die.

FACTS OF LIFE

● You can set a watch by bees in a buckwheat field. They quit working promptly at 11 A.M., as the dew dries up and nectar flows less readily.

● If the queen bee dies, the pitch of the bees' buzzing changes. Beekeepers describe it as "a low, mournful hum."

Attack of the Killer Bees

In October 1990, the first swarm of "killer bees" reached Hidalgo, Texas, from Brazil, where they had accidentally been released in 1957. More correctly called Africanized bees (they are a hybrid of Brazilian and Tanzanian species), they are smaller than the European bees kept by American beekeepers. They are, however, also more aggressive and apt to swarm faster and chase their victims farther than their more docile cousins do. They also sting more (twenty-four stings per second as compared to four stings per second for European bees) and produce less honey.

The first documented death from an attack of the "killer bees" in the United States took place in July 1993, when an eighty-two-year-old farmer received forty stings from bees living in an abandoned house in Rio Grande City, Texas, not far from the Mexican border. The bees have reached as far north as Arizona, where they have killed dogs and terrified residents. So far, scientists do not know how to stop them.

Ultimately, nature may have the last word. European bees survive harsh northern winters by hibernating. African bees are not used to doing this and may succumb to colder weather. If they don't, well, that's another story.

Butterflies and Moths

Butterflies and moths belong to the order Lepidoptra, meaning "scale wing." These insects get their bright colors from the thousands of tiny scales on their wings. There are 200,000 species in this order, and 12,000 species of moth and butterfly in North America alone.

How can you tell a moth from a butterfly? Moths are usually drab in color, while butterflies are more brightly hued. There are exceptions, of course, such as the metallic moth of Papua, New Guinea, which comes in dazzling iridescent shades of red, blue, and orange. Butterflies fly during the day, whereas moths are active at night or at dusk (in German, moths are called *Nachtschmetterlinge*, or "night butterflies"). Moths have chubby, hairy bodies;

those of butterflies are slender and hairless. Butterflies rest with their wings upright, whereas moths hold them flat. Butterflies also have knobbed antennae; moths have featherlike or plain ones.

Because most moths and butterflies do not tolerate cold weather well, they must hibernate or migrate during the winter. The North American monarch, well-known for its beautiful orange and black coloring, gathers in huge clouds and flies south to spend the winter in tropical or subtropical regions.

Monarch caterpillars feed on milkweed, which contains natural poisons. This gives the adult butterflies an unpleasant taste, and they are avoided by birds and other insect-eating animals.

FACTS OF LIFE

- Butterflies have good color vision and can detect color patterns on each other and on plants that the human eye cannot see.

- The brilliantly colored wings of South American morphus butterflies, particularly of the species *Morpho cypris*, are often used in jewelry and novelty items. Only the males are used, however, because the females are much duller in color. So many of these butterflies are caught for this purpose that some biologists fear that they may become an endangered species.

- The saddleback caterpillar of the tropical Limacodid moth has poisonous spines on its back, which can cause skin irritation when touched.

The Story of Silk

One of the most important species of moth is Bombyx mori. *From this small insect comes one of the world's most beautiful fibers, silk. Because of its beauty, silk has been called "the queen of fabrics" and has been admired and coveted for centuries. Cleopatra is said to have owned at least one silk dress.*

The story of the silk trade is one of intrigue, romance, and mystery. Silk cultivation, or sericulture, *is one of the world's oldest industries. The first silk was produced in about 2640 B.C. in China, where the Chinese Empress Hsi Ling Shi gave her royal patronage to the budding industry. For many years, this empress was venerated in China as the "goddess of silk."*

But for more than 3,000 years, the secrets of silk production were zealously guarded by the Chinese, and anyone who dared reveal them was put to death. In about A.D. 300, a clandestine mission from Japan suc-

ceeded in penetrating China, and the spies were able to obtain silkworms. They also brought four Chinese girls to Japan to teach them the art of silk-making.

Legend has it that the silk industry spread to India, now a major silk producer, when a Chinese princess was betrothed to an Indian prince. When the bride went to India, she carried silkworm eggs and mulberry seeds in her elaborate headdress. From India, sericulture spread into Persia and central Asia, and then slowly spread to the Mediterranean countries.

Constantinople became a center of silk manufacturing when two Persian monks sent by Emperor Justinian I to China in A.D. 552 succeeded in bringing back a small supply of silkworms concealed in their hollow canes. During the Renaissance, France, Italy, and Belgium became centers of silk manufacturing. Surviving examples of fabrics woven during this time reveal a skill and artistry that have rarely been equaled.

Although some parts of the silk industry have become automated, much of the labor is still done by hand, as it was centuries ago. Silkworms are raised under carefully controlled conditions (not all silkworms live in captivity; the slubby tan silk called tussah is produced by silkworms who live in the wild and feed on oak leaves). The hairy silk moth, which, in contrast to the beautiful fabric it produces, is a drab brown creature, lays 300 to 500 eggs. After the eggs hatch, the baby silkworms are fed on a diet of mulberry leaves. Their appetites are enormous: they eat every two to three hours. It takes about 485 pounds of chopped mulberry leaves to produce two pounds (about one kilo) of raw silk.

After the silkworm is done gorging itself, it spins its cocoon, which takes about three days. The insect inside the cocoon is destroyed, usually by placing the cocoons in a hot oven. The cocoons are then soaked in hot water to dissolve the

Flights of Fancy

Just as hummingbirds are attracted to sugar water, butterflies seem to like certain types of flowers, including snapdragons, zinnias, asters, and salvia. The Burpee Company sells a collection of seeds which it says will attract butterflies, as well as hummingbirds, to your garden. To order a free catalogue, call 1-800-888-1447, or write the Burpee Company at 300 Park Avenue, Warminster, PA 18991-0001.

Made in the U.S.A.

Numerous attempts have been made since colonial times to raise silkworms in the United States, but without much luck. One of the more successful efforts was that of an African American woman, Ruth Lowery of Huntsville, Alabama, in the mid-nineteenth century. Using silkworms given to her by her father, she was able to spin silk and even produce silk garments. This Alabama-grown silk was of such high quality that it won prizes in international fairs.

The city of Huntsville presented Miss Lowery with a mulberry tree in order to provide nourishment for her silkworms. Her early death, however, ended the industry that had had such a promising beginning.

gummy substance, called sericin, that holds the long filaments together. The silk filaments are then unreeled in one long, continuous strand. Each cocoon produces a continuous filament measuring from 2,000 to 3,000 feet.

Today, China and Japan are the world's leading producers of raw silk, followed by Brazil, India, and South Korea. The United States leads the world in the manufacture of finished silk products.

For centuries, the exclusive fabric houses of Italy and France, sometimes using looms hundreds of years old, created the luxurious silks used by the world's top designers. In recent years, however, Asian countries, particularly Korea, have started to produce fabrics that rival European silks in quality, and at a lower cost.

THE MOLLUSKS

Like crustaceans, mollusks have soft, squishy bodies. Most of them, such as snails, have hard shells that protect them; others, such as octopuses and cuttlefish, have shells *inside* their bodies. Slugs, snails, and whelks are *univalves*, meaning that they have one shell. Clams, oysters, mussels, and scallops are *bivalves*; their two shells are held together by a hinge. The scallop's muscular hinge is used as food—it is the only part of the animal that is eaten.

Like the crustaceans, many mollusks, including scallops, oysters, clams, conches, and mussels, are considered delicacies. The first oyster "farms" were developed by the ancient Romans, who used these tasty mollusks as an aphrodisiac. Female oysters are even more prolific than lobster hens, laying some 500 million eggs a year. Today, however, many of the world's oyster beds are in danger, not only from natural predators, but also from pollution.

Shellfish Alert

Shellfish lovers beware: Eating raw or undercooked oysters, mussels, clams, or whole scallops can be hazardous to your health. According to the Centers for Disease Control and Prevention in Atlanta, a microscopic organism called *Vibrio vulnificus,* found in warm sea waters, accumulates in the flesh of shellfish. Cooking destroys the bacteria.

The Food and Drug Administration (FDA) estimates that about 5 to 10 percent of mollusks coming to market are contaminated with the *Vibrio* bacteria. A healthy person who ingests a small amount of the bacteria usually won't be harmed, as stomach acid destroys most of these organisms, and the few that manage to survive are quickly neutralized by the body's immune system. Illness can occur, however, when the bacteria are ingested by people with health problems that weaken or damage the immune system, such as diabetes or HIV infection. When the bacteria multiply in such persons, fever, diarrhea, chills, and vomiting can result. Although the cases total fewer than one hundred nationwide, the mortality rate is 45 to 60 percent. In Florida, nine people who consumed contaminated oysters died between April and December of 1992. Mollusks should be eaten *only* if they are thoroughly cooked. *Never* eat raw shellfish.

FACTS OF LIFE

● Pearls come from Pacific pearl oysters, which are not used as food. Most pearls today are cultivated; natural pearls are very rare and expensive.

The Cephalopods

Cuttlefish, squids, octopuses, and nautiluses are called *cephalopods*, which are characterized by prominent heads and strong, muscular tentacles.

Cuttlefish are found in most waters, except those surrounding the Americas. The cuttlefish has a spongy, chalky internal shell, rich in lime, that is used to feed canaries, parrots, and other cagebirds. The cuttlefish can hide from its enemies by producing a dark brown pigment called sepia, which was used as an ink in ancient times.

Octopuses have eight arms. There are about one hundred species of octopus, the smallest of which is a tiny species, found in the Indian Ocean, that measures about one inch, while the largest is the giant octopus of the Pacific Ocean, which can weigh as much as one hundred pounds and measure twenty feet.

Like chameleons, octopuses can change color. Their skin contains cells called *chromatophores*, which contract or expand, allowing for rapid color change. If an octopus climbs into an empty shell, it turns pink; if it crawls

Pretty but Deadly

The blue-ringed octopus, which lives in the tropical waters near Australia and Indonesia, is the only octopus whose bite is dangerous to humans. This colorful little creature, which has blue circles on a purplish brown body, injects its victims with a large dose of TTX, the same poison found in the death puffer. This potent toxin can kill a human being in a few hours.

among rocks and seaweed, it will turn gray or green. An angry octopus turns dark red.

FACTS OF LIFE

● Octopuses have good memories and learn quickly. They can learn simple tricks and solve problems. For example, if an octopus is given a glass jar with a crab inside, it takes the top off the jar with one of its eight arms.

● Octopus can make interesting and amusing pets. They enjoy being stroked and can learn to play games such as tug-of-war. Some octopus even seem to develop an attachment to their caretakers.

The Giant Squid: A Real-Life Sea Monster

For centuries, sailors have told stories of enormous sea monsters with long tentacles and sharp, parrotlike beaks. Norse sailors called this creature of the deep a kraken, from a Scandinavian word meaning "stunted tree." With its writhing tentacles, the kraken was said to resemble a tree torn up from its roots. The fantastic stories told by seafaring men were thought to be just myths until the 1800s, when documented sightings of the giant squid proved that such a creature did indeed exist.

The giant squid is one of the world's strangest and most mysterious creatures. Since none of them has ever been caught alive, most of what is known of them has been through studying dead or dying specimens. The biggest giant squid on record was found in New Zealand in the 1930s and measured fifty-seven feet long, but there is evidence that some may be even larger.

These ten-armed monsters are found in cold waters at depths below 3,000 feet, near the ocean floor. They have been spotted alive off the northern coasts of Canada, Scandinavia, and northern Japan, as well as off the coasts of New Zealand and South Africa.

The greatest number of sightings of this elusive mollusk occurred during the 1870s, when many of these animals were washed up on the beaches of Newfoundland. Their stomachs were empty, suggesting that the squids had died from starvation. Giant squid sightings have become rarer, and some scientists feel that this huge mollusk is dying out.

Some of the toothed whales feed on giant squids. Ferocious battles between sperm whales and giant squids occasionally take place on the surface of the water and have been observed from ships. Sperm whales are sometimes seen bearing scars on their heads from these skirmishes.

Giant squids have been known to attack ships, but there is no record of their ever having sunk one. There is evidence, however, that, given the chance, the giant squid is a man-eater, as the following tale illustrates. During World War II, a British ship was sunk in the north Atlantic. As the ship's freezing survivors clung desperately to a bobbing life raft, one of them felt something grab his leg. Like a vision from a nightmare, a giant squid rose swiftly, and while his comrades looked on in helpless horror, the squid wrapped its tentacles around the screaming sailor and pulled him to a gruesome, watery death.

STARFISH, SPONGES, AND OTHER SEA DWELLERS

At the New Jersey State Aquarium in Camden, a special display allows visitors to handle marine creatures, including sharks and eels. One of the most popular of these living exhibits is a starfish. Visitors are surprised to learn that these attractive, docile-looking creatures are actually voracious carnivores and are not fish at all, but along with sea urchins, sea cucumbers, and sand dollars, belong to a group of animals called *echinoderms*, meaning "spiny skins." The echinoderms are the only phylum whose members are all marine dwellers.

Most starfish have five arms, but others can have more than forty. Like lobsters and crabs, if a starfish loses an arm, a new one will grow in its place. If one is cut in half, each half will become a new starfish.

Starfish feed on mollusks and crustaceans. In some areas, they are a serious threat to oyster and clam beds. The starfish does not swallow; it eats by turning its stomach out through its mouth and placing it on top of its prey, whereupon the latter is dissolved by the starfish's digestive juices.

The sea cucumber, a purplish brown creature covered with warts, has an unusual way of defending itself. When attacked, it throws out sticky threads from its mouth, which entangles its enemies and allows the sea cucumber to

Strange Ship of the Sea

One of the oddest medusas is the Portuguese man-of-war, which is found in warm waters around the world. The man-of-war was given its name by medieval sailors who thought it resembled a Portuguese sailing vessel. It looks something like a strangely shaped balloon with twenty to thirty long, dangling strings. It is not one animal, however, but a colony of as many as a thousand polyps. The "balloon" part, also called a float, is actually one overgrown polyp full of gases that help keep the man-of-war afloat; the "strings" floating underwater are actually tentacles that are covered with as many as 750,000 stinging cells each. The tentacles, which can reach fifty feet, will sting anything they touch, including unwary swimmers and scuba divers. The man-of-war's sting is not fatal to humans, but can cause intense pain, shock, and unconsciousness.

make a quick getaway. In China, the sea cucumber is called a *trepang* and is considered a potent aphrodisiac.

Sponges

Simpler in structure than the echinoderms are the sponges, which belong to the phylum Porifera, meaning "pore bearer." There are about 5,000 species, ranging in size from a few inches to four feet. They are primitive animals possessing only two layers of cells, with no heads or internal organs. Because they rarely move and have such primitive body structures, early scientists identified them as plants.

Live sponges look quite different from those seen in bathrooms. They come in a variety of shapes and colors, and those in the oceans tend to be brighter in color than those found in fresh water. Some sponges, such as the Venus's basket, are quite beautiful.

Nowadays, most of the sponges we use in our homes are synthetic, but for many years, sponges were important commercially. Today, most bath sponges are caught in the waters of the Mediterranean.

The Coelenterates

Medusas, sea anemones, and polyps belong to the phylum Coelenterata. Like the mollusks, coelenterates all have soft bodies. Many of them have poisonous tentacles that are capable of inflicting painful stings. In 1991, there were 578 reported exposures to these creatures in the United States; 121 of them required care at a medical facility. None of the stings, however, proved fatal.

Medusas are transparent or come in pale shades of blue, purple, or red. The medusas got their popular name of jellyfish because if they are left in the sun, their bodies, which are about 95 percent water, will soon resemble a shapeless mass of clear jelly.

With their petal-like tentacles, anemones are sometimes called "the flowers of the sea." Found in all the waters of the world, many of the 1,000 species come in gorgeous shades of pink, red, purple, blue, or gold and have exotic names such as strawberry anemone, marvelous sea anemone, and dahlia anemone.

The anemones' beauty is deceptive, however, because, like the man-of-war, they have tentacles that are covered with stinging cells. Like starfish, sea anemones are carnivores, eating mollusks, crustaceans, plankton, and fish. They catch their prey with sticky strings fired from cells located on the tentacles called *spirocysts*. Like an insect in a spider's web, the hapless shrimp or crab is entangled in the sea anemone's strings. Sea anemones are able to move but usually stay in one place, anchoring themselves to surfaces with a sticky substance that comes from the underside of the animal.

Although the anemone's poison is fatal to small sea animals, the small, brightly colored clownfish sometimes makes its home inside the anemone, cleaning it and sometimes sharing its food. One or more clownfish may live in a single anemone, but if a strange clownfish comes by, it will be poisoned and eaten.

The tiny polyp, a relative of the sea anemone, forms a covering of lime around itself in order to protect its soft, vulnerable body. Coral, a limestone, is made from the skeletons of millions of these tiny animals. These simple creatures have built thousands of miles of reefs on which hundreds of islands have been formed.

There are about 5,000 species of coral known. Only about half of them, however, build reefs. Reef-building coral, known as *madrepore*, thrives in water whose temperature stays between 77°F and 85°F. Above 96°F, reef-building corals die. Some of the most beautiful coral reefs are located in the Florida Keys, the Caribbean, and the Indian Ocean.

Coral reefs are also home to thousands of plants and animals. Many of the world's reefs, however, are in danger. The Florida Keys coral reef could be irreversibly damaged by the year 2000, due to coral disease that may be related to warmer sea temperatures and nutrients from human waste that foster the growth of harmful algae.

Floating Death

The deadliest of the medusas is the sea wasp, a transparent creature also known as the fire medusa. They can be no bigger than a grape or as large as a head of cabbage. Whatever their size, they are deadly—the poison from a fire medusa can kill a person in about five minutes.

Chapter Six

OF MEN AND MAMMALS

It is hard to believe that animals as different as the tiny hog-nosed bat, which tips the scale at two grams (less than an ounce), and the mighty blue whale, which weighs as much as two hundred elephants, have anything in common, but they do. They are both members of the class Mammalia.

Of all the major animal groups, this is the one that most sparks our interest. Not only are they the most versatile and diverse of all animals; they have been crucial to human survival for centuries. Horses, camels, llamas, and even elephants have served as pack animals. Cows, pigs, and other animals are important sources of food, and their skins provide clothing. Domestic dogs and cats have become friends and companions to millions. Perhaps we feel a special kinship with mammals not only because they are important to us in so many ways, but also because we are mammals too, members of the group called primates.

There are 4,000 species of mammals, making them the smallest group of animals after the amphibians. But what this group lacks in size, it makes up in diversity. Mammals can live in almost all environments, including scorching deserts, mile-high mountains, and even the deep waters of the ocean.

Some groups of mammals, such as the order Rodentia, have hundreds of species; others include only a few. The order Proboscidea, for example, includes only two members, the African and Asian elephants.

Some animals, such as the Norwegian rat, are *cosmopolitan*. This does not mean that they are readers of the popular women's magazine; it refers to the fact that they can be found in many locations throughout the world. Others, such as the lemur, which lives only in Madagascar, are said to be *endemic* to that area, meaning that they can be found nowhere else in the world.

Which characteristics make a mammal a mammal? For one thing, with the exception of the monotremes, they all give birth to live young. This trait is not unique to mammals, however; other animals, including some species of fish and reptiles, also do this. Like birds, they are *homoiothermic*, which means that the animal regulates its temperature by means of mechanisms inside its own body. The body temperature of most mammals remains relatively constant; most cannot tolerate a drastic change in this vital sign without suffering harmful effects.

All mammals have a four-chambered heart. They also have hair on their bodies. This may take the form of the thick, luxurious fur of a Persian cat, a horse's long, coarse mane, or, in the case of a whales and dolphins, a few scattered hairs located on the head. Other characteristics of mammals include large, well-developed brains, three bones in the inner ear, and teeth that are modified to perform a variety of functions.

The word *mammal* comes from *mammae*, the Latin term for the mammary, or milk, glands. All mammals produce milk and nurse their young. Most mammals suckle their young from nipples on the abdomen, near the hind legs (this may sound strange, but think of where a cow's udder is and you will get the picture). Only humans, primates, elephants, and bats have nipples on the chest.

Mammals can be divided into three broad groups: the monotremes, the marsupials, and the placentals. The monotremes and marsupials are the most primitive mammals, both possessing some reptilian characteristics, while the placentals—of which man is a member—are the most advanced.

THE MONOTREMES

When specimens of the newly discovered species *Ornithorhynchus anatinus* arrived in Europe in the late eighteenth century fresh from Australia, scientists at first thought they were victims of an elaborate hoax. With its soft brown fur, large, ducklike bill, and powerful webbed feet, the duck-billed platypus was like nothing the world had ever seen.

The scientists of the day debated over how to classify the creature. It had hair and nursed its young, but laid soft-shelled eggs similar to those of a reptile. The platypus had a soft brown *pelage*, or coat of fur, like many other mammals, but built a nest of grass and leaves and incubated its eggs, like a bird. The strange animal nursed its young, but at the same time possessed a cloaca, a tube through which the genital, urinary, and fecal products passed, another characteristic of reptiles. And unlike other mammals, its body temperature was subject to considerable fluctuation. After much debate, it was decided that the duck-billed platypus was indeed a mammal, but of the most primitive type.

The duck-billed platypus is a monotreme, one of only two representatives of the order Monotremata. This bizarre animal is endemic to eastern Australia and Tasmania, where it lives near freshwater streams, ponds, and rivers. With its powerful webbed feet, it is a good swimmer and is capable of holding its breath under water for one full minute. It feeds on plants and small aquatic animals. Platypuses have no teeth; food is crushed between horny plates located under the bill. The female does not have nipples like other mammals; she feeds her young with milk that simply seeps through porelike openings in her abdomen.

The duck-billed platypus is unique in that the male has a poisonous spur located under its hind feet, making it one of the world's few venomous mammals. The spur is used for defense and helps in the capture of small prey (other poisonous mammals include some species of shrew and the closely related solenodon, both of which secrete poisonous saliva that paralyzes their prey).

There are two species of echidna, or spiny anteater: the short-beaked variety, which is found in Australia and New Guinea, and the long-beaked species, which lives only in New Guinea. These monotremes resemble porcupines. Like the duck-billed platypus, echidnas lay eggs. When attacked, the echidna rolls itself into a prickly ball, and any animal foolish enough to attack it will get a mouthful of spines.

THE MARSUPIALS

When the first Europeans reached the land that was later to be called Australia, in 1629, they were amazed by the sight of a large creature with enormous feet, short arms, and a huge, muscular tail that bounded through the grass with incredible leaps. Puzzled, they asked the Koori native who served as a guide what the animal was. The man shrugged and said, "*Kangaroo*," a Koori word meaning "I don't know." The explorers, however, thought that the man had replied with the Koori term for this strange beast, and the name kangaroo is still used for this animal today.

The kangaroo belongs to the order Marsupialia, a group of animals that gets its name from the *marsupium,* or pouch, where the immature young of these animals develop. The largest kangaroo, and biggest living marsupial, is the red kangaroo, which can stand seven feet tall and weigh up to 200 pounds. The grey kangaroo, or forester, is slightly smaller, and as its name implies, lives in forests and woodlands. Of the 251 living marsupial species, 170 are native to Australia and its adjacent islands.

Although marsupials are much more highly developed than the primitive monotremes, they have small, simple brains and are not as advanced as the placental animals. Their unique characteristic is their method of reproduction.

Female kangaroos, which are called does (the males are called boomers), depending on the species, produce a single ovum every four to six weeks. If the egg is fertilized by the male kangaroo's sperm, the egg, now called a *zygote,* begins to divide inside the mother's body. After five to six weeks, the embryonic kangaroo is ready to be born. As the birth approaches, the doe finds a quiet, safe place and cleans and licks her pouch and belly. This may help her offspring find its way to the pouch by smell.

The newborn kangaroo, or joey, is only 0.75-inch (18 mm) in length and weighs less than one ounce. The tiny, hairless animal, with the aid of forelimbs equipped with strong claws, drags itself through the fur of the mother's belly to the safety of the pouch, a journey that takes about two minutes and is accomplished entirely without assistance from the doe. The joey attaches itself to one of four nipples inside the pouch, which swells sightly so that the young animal cannot easily lose hold of it. The young joey does not even have to make the effort to suck; the mother kangaroo pumps milk into its mouth by contractions of her stomach wall.

Once in the pouch, the joey remains there for about 300 days in the grey kangaroo and about 235 days in the red kangaroo. At the end of this time, the joey is large enough to live outside its mother but is suckled by the doe for an additional six months or so.

When a kangaroo joey is too large to ride in the pouch any longer but still stays with its mother, it is called a young at heel. Even a well-grown joey, however, does not soon forget the safety and security of its mother's pouch. When threatened, it will hop headfirst into the pouch, turning itself around as its mother leaps away from danger.

Both male and female kangaroos travel in large groups called mobs. Boomers fight each other for leadership of the mob, leaning back on their strong tails and kicking with their rear feet or "boxing" with their forelimbs.

Kangaroos, of course, are the best-known marsupials, but there are others.

FACTS OF LIFE

- The Virginia opossum is the only marsupial native to the United States. Despite its name, it is found throughout Mexico and Central America to Costa Rica. The Virginia opossum's fur is long and thick, but other parts of its body are more delicate; in the northern part of its range, portions of the ears and tail are often lost to frostbite.

- Female opossums have a well-developed pouch and bear an average of seven young per litter. The young opossums are carried on their mother's back. When threatened, both males and females will feign death, or "play possum."

- The yapok, or water opossum, which lives in southern Mexico to northern Argentina, is the only truly aquatic marsupial. An expert swimmer and diver, it burrows into stream banks, where it builds a nesting chamber just above the water level. The female yapok's pouch can be closed by a sphincter muscle surrounding its edge, making it waterproof for the young carried inside while the mother swims.

- The Tasmanian devil is a powerful animal about the size of a small dog. It earned its name because of its fierce temper. It was once found in Australia, but now lives only in Tasmania, an island off the coast of Australia. It is known for its shrill, blood-curdling cries.

- The sugar glider, a small, gray opossum, is one of the few social marsupials, living in small groups in the trees. It gets its name from its fondness for the sweet sap produced by certain eucalyptus trees.

- The greater glider of Australia's eucalyptus forests is a squirrel-like creature with a gliding membrane stretching from its wrist to its ankle. It lives high in the forest, where it leaps from tree to tree. The gliders can jump as much as 120 feet.

- There are fifty-eight species of kangaroo, which are divided into two groups. The first group, the macropods, (which means "big foot") includes the kangaroos, wallabies, pademelons, quokkas, and wallaroos, all of which are large animals with huge feet and large hind legs. The second group, the potoroids, are much smaller than the macropods and includes the rat kangaroos, betongs, and potoroos. One of the most unusual potoroids is the burrowing boodie, the only kangaroo that lives underground.

- The Tasmanian pademelon, also known as the red-bellied wallaby, depends on sound rather than on sight for protection. When it hears something approach, it thumps its feet on the ground.

- The smallest kangaroo is the musky rat kangaroo, which weighs only one ounce. The rat kangaroo is the only kangaroo that produces twins; all the others bear only a single offspring.

- Tree kangaroos can hop like other kangaroos, but they are also good tree climbers. They use their strong claws to grip the bark of trees and their long tails for balance. Matschie's tree kangaroo of northern and eastern New Guinea can leap from trees as high as fifty-five feet.

- Animals that hop on just their hind legs, like kangaroos, are said to ricochet. Both feet leave the ground and land at the same time. The red kangaroo can jump six to eight feet high (although four to five feet is more typical) and can cover up to twenty-five feet in a single leap. The red kangaroo usually hops along at about eight miles per hour, but can attain short bursts of speed of thirty-five to forty miles per hour.

The Koala: Teddybear of the Treetops

Next to the kangaroo, the koala is perhaps the best-known symbol of Australia. Despite its cuddly bearlike appearance, the koala, which lives in the eucalyptus forests of Queensland and New South Wales, is not even remotely related to these large carnivores.

Koalas are mostly arboreal, spending much of their time in eucalyptus or gum trees. The koala is what is known as a specialized feeder, meaning that it eats only the leaves of the eucalyptus tree. Eucalyptus is the source of eucalyptus oil, which is used in many medicines, including cough medications. (For this reason, koalas often smell like cough drops.) There are hundreds of varieties of eucalyptus, but most koalas eat only about thirty-five kinds. Some koalas are even pickier and eat only two or three varieties. Like squirrels, koalas store leaves in their cheek pouches until they are ready to eat them.

The word *koala* is a Koori term that means "one who doesn't drink." Koalas get almost all the water they need from the gum leaves they eat, because eucalyptus leaves are two-thirds water. They especially enjoy the tender bases of the leaves, which may contain more sugar.

Koalas have poor eyesight, but can hear very well and also have a keen sense of smell. During certain seasons, eucalyptus leaves contain prussic acid, a

The koala spends most of its time in trees. Photograph by Ron Singer. Courtesy of US Fish & Wildlife Service.

fatal poison. The koalas can smell the poison and avoid the leaves during these times.

Koalas are sexually mature at about three to four years of age. They mate in December, which is summertime in Australia. The newborn koala is tiny, measuring only three-fourths of an inch and weighing about a half gram. Like the kangaroo joey, the pink, hairless creature must make the perilous journey to its mother's pouch entirely unaided, where it remains for about six months. In the wild, the defenseless young koalas have a high mortality rate, because they are preyed upon by dingoes, owls, and even some large lizards. Koala cubs like to ride on their mothers' backs, even when they are almost grown.

Koala females usually bear only one cub at a time. Male koalas may have a harem of several females. They add new meaning to the term "deadbeat dad," because they completely ignore their offspring, even though they may live in the same tree.

Until about 1930, koalas were extensively hunted for their soft, brownish gray fur. In 1924 alone, over 2 *million* skins were exported. Aware that the koala might become extinct if the slaughter was allowed to continue, the Australian government made the hunting of koalas illegal in 1930.

The koala is still in danger, however, primarily because the great eucalyptus forests where they make their homes are being cleared to accommodate Australia's growing population. In response, the government has created preserves where koalas and other species can live in peace.

Koalas can also be successfully bred in captivity. In 1976, Australia sent six young koalas to the United States in honor of America's Bicentennial. A breeding program began in the San Diego Zoo in the same year, and over the next thirteen years, forty cubs were born. The San Diego cubs were loaned to other zoos and animal parks for breeding purposes, and it appears that the koala will continue to survive, at least in captivity.

THE PLACENTALS

This group includes the vast majority of mammals living today. Of the three groups, the placentals have the most efficient means of reproduction. Their young stay inside the bodies of their mothers for a much longer gestation time than marsupials, giving them protection during the most vulnerable period of their lives. The gestation period of the placental mammals varies from fifteen days for the golden hamster to almost two years for the elephant.

There are so many types of placental mammals that it would take a book three times the length of this one to list them all. We will explore some of the more interesting groups, starting with the aardvark, an animal that is literally in a class by itself.

The Aardvark: One of A Kind

Aardvark is the name of the only living representative of the order Tubulidentata. With its beady black eyes, rough, leathery brown skin, and long, tube-shaped snout, it is one of the world's strangest-looking creatures.

The aardvark, whose name means "earth pig" in Afrikaans, lives in the savannahs of sub-Saharan Africa, where it builds intricate tunnels that can stretch for hundreds of yards. It uses its powerful claws to dig into anthills and termite mounds, where it uses its eighteen-inch tongue to scoop up these insects for the aardvark equivalent of a gourmet feast.

The aardvark can grow fairly large; males can weigh up to 200 pounds.

Like a Bat Out of . . .

In the year 1770, the British explorer Captain James Cook made a historic trip to Australia, a mysterious island that few Europeans had ever seen. His ship, *The Endeavor*, was in need of repairs, so he landed on a beach on the eastern coast of the island. As the work on the hull progressed, he sent one of his men, a trustworthy and level-headed sort, to search for fresh water to drink. Less than an hour later, the man came running back, screaming that he had seen Satan himself in the shape of a flying monster! The captain quickly organized a search party to look for the winged demon and found that it was a huge bat, what the Australians now call a flying fox.

Mice With Wings: The Bats

Bats are the only mammals that can fly, and this has made them the object of fear and fascination for centuries. There are nearly 1,000 species throughout the world, making them the largest group of mammals after the rodents. The world's smallest mammal, and tiniest bat, is the Kitti's hog-nosed bat, which weighs less than a penny and is about the size of a bumblebee. Discovered in Thailand in 1973, this little creature is already close to extinction, because it has been killed in large numbers to provide trinkets for the tourist trade.

The flying foxes, of which there are 67 species in India, Australia, and Asia, are the largest bats. The giant flying fox, which is found in Java, is about eighteen inches long and has a wingspan of five feet.

Bats belong to the order Chiroptera, which comes from two Greek words meaning "hand" and "wing." They are divided into two suborders: the Megachiroptera, literally, the "big bats," which eat fruit, and the Microchiroptera, or "little bats," which eat insects. These two terms are somewhat misleading, because there are some small bats among the Megachiroptera and some fairly large specimens among the Microchiroptera.

The megabats are found only in Asia, Africa, and Australia; there are none in North or South America. The microbats are found throughout the world. All bats found in the United States belong to the latter group.

Like those of birds, the bodies of bats are modified for flight. The wings are formed by elongated finger bones, over which is stretched a very thin membrane of skin that arises from both sides of the body (in microbats, this membrane extends across the legs down to the feet). The bat's thumb, which ends in a powerful claw, is free of this membrane and is used for hanging, crawling, and manipulating objects.

Along with spiders, bats are some of the world's most misunderstood creatures. Because of their nocturnal habits and strange, grotesque appearance, some people are afraid of them. And to many, there is just something *weird* about bats, something unnatural. Perhaps it is those leathery wings, or their rodentlike bodies. (People have long associated bats with mice, even though the two are not even remotely related. In fact, the German word for bat is *fledermaus*, or "flying mouse"; in French, the bat is called a *chauve souris*, or "bald mouse"). But whatever the case, it appears that many agree with the poet Theodore Roethke, who wrote:

> *For something is amiss or out of place*
> *When mice with wings can wear a human face.*

Some of the *frugivorous*, or fruit-eating, bats do cause damage to crops. And the blood-drinking vampire bats of South America can cause disease and death, although they rarely bite humans. But generally speaking, most bats are quite harmless. They are timid creatures that avoid people and bite only in self-defense. There are millions of bats in the world, but they are so elusive that many of us may never see one outside of captivity.

Going Batty

Austin, Texas, calls itself "The Bat Capital of America" because of the thousands of Mexican free-tailed bats that emerge from beneath the Congress Avenue Bridge for their nightly insect runs. Meanwhile, back at the James R. Eckert Bat Cave Preserve, which millions of the free-tailed bats use as a maternity cave, the Nature Conservancy of Texas presents "bat talks" four times a week. The Eckert cave, which is located northwest of Austin in Mason, Texas, is open from May 1 to October 31. For more information, contact Bat Conservation International at (512) 327-9721, or the Austin Visitor's Bureau at (800) 926-2282.

Many will be surprised to learn that some bats are beneficial to man, devouring millions of harmful insects every year. It is estimated that one little brown bat (*Myotis lucifugus*), a common species in the United States, can catch 500 or more mosquitoes in an hour, or one every seven seconds.

The fruit-eating and nectar-feeding bats play an important role in the dispersal of seeds and pollination of tropical plants such as figs, avocados, mangoes, and many more. The flowers of the durian fruit, a cash crop worth $112 million annually, are pollinated almost entirely by one species, *Eonycteris spelaea*, a cave-dwelling, nectar-eating bat. (Although durian fruit smells like rotting meat, this unsavory aspect does not prevent it from being a delicacy in Southeast Asia.)

Bat dung, or guano, is used as a

nitrogen-rich fertilizer in many developing countries. Because many bats return to the same caves year after year, huge quantities of it accumulate. The bat guano from Khao Chong Pran cave in Thailand is "mined" by Buddhist monks, and proceeds from its sale are used to support a monastery and school.

FACTS OF LIFE

● Most bats live twelve to fifteen years, but some can survive as long as thirty.

● Most of us think of bats as being dark in color (remember those paper bats you made out of black construction paper for Halloween?), but in fact they come in colors. The pallid bat has cream-colored fur, while the Indian flying fox has reddish brown fur. Other bats are yellow, gray, or even spotted. Albinism is also found in bats.

● Bats can fly as fast as 60 miles per hour and as high as 10,000 feet.

● Not all bats are night creatures; some are diurnal. The Indian flying fox is commonly seen during the daylight hours roosting in large, noisy colonies, also called camps, high in the trees.

Bat Habits

Many bats, including the pipistrelle and the big brown bat, are social animals, living in large groups in caves. These colonies can be huge. Bracken Cave in Texas has a colony of Mexican free-tailed bats that has more than 20 *million* individuals. Destruction of habitat, and use of pesticides, however, has decimated many bat colonies.

Bats hibernate in caves where the temperature ranges between 40°F and 48°F, although some opt for caves where the temperature hovers near freezing. Several different species of bats may hibernate in separate areas of the same cave.

As the bats sleep, their body temperature drops from about 104°F to as low as 32°F, and their breathing rate goes from 200 breaths a minute to a low of 23. During hibernation, the bats live off their body fat, and by the end of the winter, they are very thin and must feed immediately after their sleep.

Other bats migrate. The Mexican free-tailed bat travels up to 900 miles south into Mexico to spend the winter.

Bats generally give birth to one offspring, called a pup, each year. Some bats have twins, and the big brown bat has been known to bear triplets. When mother bats go searching for food, they often leave their pups in bat "nurseries" with other bat babies.

Bats make good mothers and have been known to "rescue" their pups from perilous situations. In one instance, a bat mother followed a man who had caught her pup, and landed on the man's shoulder. When the startled man dropped the little bat, the mother took her pup, flew away with it, and began to nurse it.

Night Vision

We have all heard the phrase "blind as a bat," but actually no healthy bat is blind. Some species, such as the flying foxes, have large eyes and relatively good eyesight. Most bats, though, do have poor vision. Despite this handicap, they can find their way around on the blackest of nights (even owls, known for their superb night vision, cannot see in *total* darkness).

How do they do this? The answer lies in the bat's oversized ears. Bats use a form of sonar (**s**ound **n**avigation **r**anging) called *echolocation* to "see" at night. As the bats fly, they give off a series of high-pitched clicking noises that bounce off objects in the bat's path and return echoes to the animal. By analyzing these "sound pictures," the bat is able to pinpoint the exact location of the object, its size, speed, and direction of movement.

Human beings cannot hear sounds above 20 kilohertz (kHz). Most of the noises bats make are in the range of 20 to 60 kHz, and therefore are inaudible to our ears (scientists use a small hand-held instrument, called a *bat meter*, to detect these sounds). Some species, however, including two that live in the southwestern United States, do make sounds that are within the range of human hearing. Others, including the so-called gleaning bats of the tropics, emit high-pitched sounds, above 200 kHz. More than 80 percent of bats use echolocation; some species, including most of the flying foxes, do not.

The Vampire Bat: Blood for Breakfast

Bats feed on other things besides insects and fruit. Some eat fish, frogs, and even other bats.

Perhaps the most notorious members of the order Chiroptera, however, are the three species of vampire bats, including the common vampire bat, the hairy-legged vampire, and the white-winged vampire bat. The common vampire is a medium sized bat that ranges from Mexico to Chile, northern Argentina and Uruguay, and Trinidad. Neither the common nor the white-winged vampire bat ventures into the United

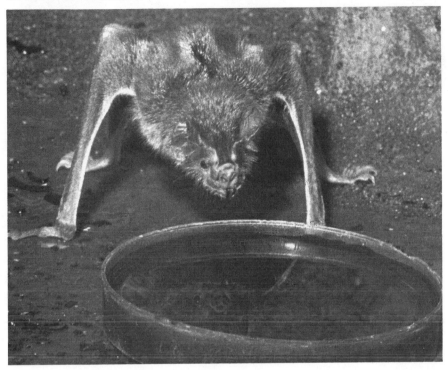

A vampire bat prepares to take a sip of what looks like water—or is it?
Courtesy of the Zoological Society of Philadelphia.

States, but the hairy-legged vampire ranges from Val Verde County in
Texas to southern Brazil.

   Vampire bats feed on the blood of any homoiothermic animal they
can find, including wild and domestic animals, even birds. (Dogs, however, are rarely bitten, because with their excellent hearing, they can pick
up the high-frequency sounds the bats make as they zero in on their prey.)
Cattle, though, seem to be their favorite. The vampire bat has large,
razor-sharp incisors that it uses to cut a small wound in a cow's neck. It
can hover in the air without a sound, landing on its victim, or can walk
up to the animal on its long hind legs. The bat then slices the animal's
skin and laps up the blood by means of a "drinking straw" that is
formed under the bat's tongue and in its lower lip. An anticoagulant in
the vampire bat's saliva causes the blood to flow easily. Vampire bats
often attack the same animal night after night, weakening and eventu-

ally killing it. A vampire bat can drink its own weight in blood in one night. Vampire bat mothers nurse their young, but sometimes they feed them regurgitated blood.

Human beings occasionally become victims of vampire bats. The bats prefer to bite their human prey on the cheeks, nose, finger, or other juicy and accessible body parts. Because the anticoagulant keeps the victim's blood flowing, a child bitten by two or three of these creatures can die from loss of blood.

The major threat from these bats, however, is the fact that they carry paralytic rabies and other serious diseases (other species of bats in the United States can also contract rabies, but they usually do not live long enough to transmit the disease). Whole herds of cows have been wiped out by these creatures.

Chapter Seven

THE CARNIVORES

To a large extent, scientists classify mammals by the characteristics of their dentition, or the structure of their teeth. Mammals, including humans, have different kinds of teeth that perform different functions: incisors located at the front of the jaw for biting, long pointed teeth at the corners of the mouth for stabbing, and flat cheek teeth in the back of the mouth (called molars and premolars) for chewing.

Animals in the order Carnivora, or meat-eaters, possess teeth called *carnassials,* which are specially adapted shearing blades to cut up meat in guillotine fashion. The carnivores can be found in all parts of the world, including the Arctic and Antarctic. They include 34 varieties of aquatic animals, called the *pinnipeds,* a group of carnivores which includes seals and walruses, as well as 239 species of land-dwelling and semiaquatic meat eaters known as *fissipeds.* Many familiar species, including our domestic dogs and cats, are fissipeds.

THE BEAR FACTS

The members of the family Ursidae, better known as bears, are the largest living terrestrial carnivores. Although they are classified in this group, with the exception of the polar bear, many of them are *omnivores,* eating both flesh and vegetable matter. A few species are almost entirely vegetarian. The diet of the

American black bear, for example, consists of 90 percent plant matter. The bear family is a small one, including only eight species. There are bears on every continent except Africa and Australia.

The smallest bear is the sun bear of southeastern Asia; it weighs less than 150 pounds and stands about four feet tall. The largest is the polar bear, which can stand over eight feet tall and weigh about 1,100 pounds. The enormous polar bear is found across the Arctic Ocean on sea ice and along the Arctic coastlines of Norway, Canada, Russia, and the United States. It is the most carnivorous of all bears, subsisting almost entirely on seals and fish. An excellent swimmer, it paddles with its front legs only.

The brown bear is found in North America, Europe, and Asia and is the most diverse of all bear species—it can be found in deserts, rain forests, mountains, and even the Arctic tundra. In the Pacific Northwest, brown bears enjoy dining on spawning salmon. Despite its name, the brown bear comes in a wide range of colors, including cream, reddish brown, gray, and dark brown. Some brown bears, especially older ones, are almost black. The Kodiak bear, which is found only in Alaska, is a variety of brown bear. The Kodiak rivals the polar bear in size. The grizzly bear was once thought of as a separate species ("Ursus horribilis, meaning "horrible bear") but scientists now recognize that it is also a type of brown bear.

Like its cousin the brown bear, the American black bear has a misleading name; its color can range from black to brown to almost white. Many black bears in the western part of the United States, including those in Yellowstone National Park, are brown. Unlike the brown bear, which can live in a variety of habitats, the black bear is rarely found outside of woodlands.

The Asiatic black bear can be found throughout Asia. It is also called "the moon bear" and can be recognized by the distinctive white V on its chest. The Asiatic black bear is more aggressive than other bears.

The sloth bear, with its long, shaggy black fur, looks different from other species of bear. It gets its name from its ability to hang upside down from tree branches, like a sloth. It is sometimes called the "honey bear" because of its love of the sweet, sticky stuff. The sloth bear lives in tropical dry forests of India, Sri Lanka, Nepal, Bhutan, and Bangladesh. It has a tubelike snout that it uses to suck up termites, like a vacuum cleaner. This is the only species of bear to carry its young on its back. Although it moves slowly, like a sloth, it can be dangerous when surprised at close range.

The spectacled bear is South America's only species of bear. It is found from Colombia to northern Argentina and lives high in the mountains above 14,000 feet. It earns its name from the masklike white markings around its eyes. The spectacled bear is a good climber and sometimes even sleeps in trees.

Bedtime for Bruins

Contrary to popular belief, bears do not actually hibernate during the winter. In the autumn they eat enormous amounts of food—gaining up to one hundred pounds—and then fall into a state of extended inactivity, spending the winter in caves, tree hollows, or similar enclosures. This state is called winter dormancy. Although their body temperature does not change, their oxygen intake is reduced to one-half its normal amount and their heart rate decreases from forty beats per minute to ten. They do, however, leave their dens on warmer days.

The little sun bear is also called the Malayan bear. It gets its name from its habit of basking in the sun for hours. Of all the bears, this is the most agile climber. Sun bears are found in the tropical forests and woodlands of southern China, eastern India, and Borneo and Sumatra. They are popular pets in many Asian countries, and their flesh is also eaten.

FACTS OF LIFE

● Bears give birth to one to three cubs, which are no bigger than rats when they are first born. It takes two to four weeks for them to open their eyes. The little cubs stay with their mother for about a year before venturing out on their own.

Bears in Trouble

Unfortunately, some species of bear, especially those native to the Asian nations, are rapidly disappearing. This is because their body parts and fluids, including gallbladders, paws, fat, spinal cords, blood, and bones, are widely used in Asian folk medicine as remedies for complaints ranging from baldness to rheumatism. Many of these remedies, of course, are completely useless, but bear bile has been found effective in treating certain liver and gallbladder diseases in humans. Although a synthetic version of the bile is available at a fraction of the price, purists prefer the real thing.

Sadly, poachers have taken to slaughtering bears in other nations, including the United States, for their body parts. Recently an 800-pound black bear, one of Canada's largest, was found dead in Riding Mountain National Park. Its gallbladder had been cut out.

To meet the demand for bear bile, wildlife farms have sprung up throughout Asia, including China and North and South Korea, where live bears are kept and "milked" for their bile. A tube is implanted in the gallbladder and the bile is extracted through it. This, of course, prevents the bear from being killed, but whether or not it is a humane prac-

tice is open to question. Wildlife writer Judy Mills, one of the few west-
erners to observe this practice, writes in International Wildlife, *a publi-*
cation of the National Wildlife Federation, "The milking itself did not
appear to be painful. But the bear went berserk during the procedure,
wildly digging at the floor of its cage like a dog trying to dig through
dirt. . . . The bear continued to growl and snap its jaws, and the owner
locked it once again in the darkness of the milking shed."

The Giant Panda

In 1869, the French Jesuit missionary and naturalist Pére Armand
David wrote in a letter to the Museum of Natural History in Paris: "I
see a fine skin of the famous white and black bear, which appears to be
fairly large. It is a very remarkable species . . . it must constitute an
interesting novelty for science."

The "famous white and black bear" that David was referring to, of
course, was the giant panda. With its shoe-button eyes (the panda's eyes
are actually quite beady; it is the large round patches around them that
make them look so large), roly-poly body, and dramatic black and white
coloring, the giant panda is one of the world's most familiar and fasci-
nating animals. The panda appears on the logo of the World Wildlife
Fund, and it has been called "China's national treasure."

Like the duck-billed platypus, the giant panda posed a dilemma for
Victorian naturalists. While it closely resembled an ursid (the Chinese
called the panda beishung, *or "white bear"), it had a skull and digestive*
system very similar to that of a raccoon. At first, the giant panda was
placed in the raccoon family, but later studies, including analysis of
complicated molecular data, confirmed that the giant panda is indeed a
member of the bear family.

Giant pandas live in south central China, near Szechwan province,

Kissing Cousins

The lesser, or red, panda was discovered about forty years before
its more famous cousin. Closely
resembling a raccoon, it is about
the size of a large cat. Like the
giant panda, the lesser panda is
fond of bamboo.

a wet, cold, humid region where
snow stays on the ground from
October to May and the tempera-
ture rarely goes above 50°F. In the
wild, the panda's primary food is
bamboo (they sometimes eat more
than twenty pounds a day), but they
will also eat small mammals, birds,
and fish. They are too slow moving
to catch larger game.

Pandas can grow to be about five or six feet in length, and can weigh from 165 to 300 pounds. The front paws have six fingers. The sixth, which is an extension of the wrist bone, works like a thumb. Using these fingers, the panda can peel the outer shell of the bamboo plant to reach its juicy inner core. They spend about twelve hours a day eating bamboo.

Pandas are nearsighted, but they can smell and hear very well. They are shy, timid animals but, when provoked, can inflict a nasty gash with their sharp claws.

Pandas are generally solitary animals, except for the mating season, when small groups of two or three may be formed. Pandas usually give birth to one cub, although they can have twins and even triplets. Panda mothers, however, can take care of only one cub every two years, and if a second panda baby is born, it is usually abandoned.

The first giant panda to reach North America alive was Su-lin (meaning "something very cute"), who was bought by the Brookfield Zoo in Chicago. Almost four decades later, to commemorate Richard Nixon's visit to China, a pair of pandas, Ling-Ling ("the tinkling of small bells") and Hsing-Hsing ("a bright star") were given to the National Zoo in Washington, D.C. (in return, the U.S. gave the Peking Zoo two musk oxen). The two pandas were the zoo's most popular attractions until Ling Ling died of natural causes in 1993.

At the present time, Hsing Hsing is the only panda in an American zoo. The San Diego Zoo had planned to bring two pandas, a male and a female, to the zoo for at least three years. The zoo spent $1 million on its panda project, including a gift shop stocked with panda dolls, T-shirts, and other souvenirs. In exchange for the pandas, the zoo was to pay the Chinese government $1 million a year, money that was to go toward preserving panda habitat.

In June 1993, however, the U.S. Fish and Wildlife Service prohibited the zoo from importing the bears. Interior Secretary Bruce Babbitt stated in a letter to the zoo that the U.S. government was concerned that "the People's Republic of China may not be doing enough to conserve wild pandas" and that "bringing the pandas to the San Diego Zoo might generate irresistible pressure for the capture and export of pandas."

Despite the fact that China has protected the panda since 1939, scientists believe there are only about 1,000 or so left in the wild. Habitat destruction and periodic "die offs" of the bamboo that the giant pandas feed upon have decreased their numbers.

Giant panda Hsing-Hsing, munching bamboo at the Smithsonian's National Zoo, seems unaware of the sad plight faced by other members of his species in the wild. Photograph by Jessie Cohen. Courtesy of the National Zoological Park, Smithsonian Institution.

Poachers are also a major threat. Although anyone caught killing a panda is severely punished (in May 1993, two farmers in the southern city of Guangzhou were shot by a firing squad for selling three panda skins), even the death penalty has not proven to be much of a deterrent in this impoverished nation where one panda skin can fetch tens of thousands of dollars on the black market.

Pandas are major attractions at the few zoos that have them, and the zoos rake in thousands of dollars through increased attendance and souvenir sales. The Chinese government also makes money from "rent-a-panda" deals. Japan's Adventure World Zoo recently paid $10 million for a ten-year loan of one male and one female panda.

Ironically, the panda's popularity may be contributing to its demise, because panda "rentals" disrupt the breeding of this animal. Pandas reproduce poorly in captivity, mainly because the male pandas come into heat only once a year, and in zoos, this time usually comes when the females are unreceptive. Panda cubs born in captivity also have a high mortality rate. All the cubs produced by Ling-Ling and Hsing-Hsing died, succumbing to pneumonia and bacterial infections. An exception to this sad rule are the pandas at Mexico City's Chapultepec Zoo. These pandas have given birth successfully five times over two generations in the last decade. Chapultepec Zoo now has six pandas, the largest collection outside of China.

What can be done to save the giant panda? In December 1992, China's State Council approved a $52.6 million panda conservation plan that will double the number of antipoaching patrols and increase the number of panda preserves. Panda lovers around the world are hoping that these plans will succeed, so that "China's national treasure" will be preserved for generations to come.

THE CANINE FAMILY

The Wolf That Came In From the Cold: *Canis familiaris*

The dog was the first animal to be domesticated, some 10,000 to 15,000 years ago. Scientists believe that the ancestor of the dog was the wolf.

The descendants of these wolves, the members of species *Canis familiaris*, have guarded our homes, pulled carts, wagons, and sleds, and saved us from treacherous waters, earthquakes, and avalanches. They have been used to herd sheep, cattle, and other grazing animals (the kelpie, an Australian sheep dog with a bit of dingo blood, keeps track of his charges by running along the sheeps' backs). In some countries, dog hides have even been used to make clothing and their flesh has been eaten.

Dogs have also been used extensively in battle. In World War II, Germany had an army of 200,000 trained dogs, mostly German shepherds, guarding the Nazi concentration camps. The Americans also used dogs, particularly on the Japanese-held Pacific islands where they were used to flush out snipers and search for wounded G.I.'s in the steaming jungles.

Perhaps the most inhumane employment of dogs was by the Red Army. The Soviets trained dogs to expect to find food under ammunition wagons. They then attached TNT charges to the backs of the dogs and sent them toward enemy lines, exploding the charges as the poor creatures advanced.

But most of all, dogs have been our companions and friends. They have the capacity to make us smile and laugh, and even cry. Over the centuries, humans and dogs have forged a bond that few animals can equal.

There are approximately 400 million dogs in the world today, encompassing 500 breeds and countless mixtures. There are 7 to 8 million dogs in France, 5 to 6 million in Germany, and 4 million in Italy. The United States, however, leads the pack with 52.4 million.

Dogs do not have good eyesight and probably see only in shades of black, white, and gray. But their hearing is so sharp that a dog can hear a wristwatch ticking from thirty feet away. Their sense of smell is among the keenest in the animal kingdom; it has been estimated that it is forty times sharper than a human's!

The canine ability to sniff out odors indiscernible to the human nose sometimes is amazing. Take the case of Snag, a black female Labrador retriever who had been abandoned by her owners. As is often the case with unwanted pets, she was about to be "put to sleep" when she was rescued by the Texas Border Patrol. Snag was recruited to work in the department's drug enforcement unit, sniffing out drugs such as cocaine and marijuana that smugglers attempted to bring from Mexico into the United States. Her biggest "haul" came when she

Going to the Dogs

The Dog Museum in St. Louis is described as the first fine arts museum devoted to dogs. Located in an 1853 Greek Revival mansion, the museum includes paintings, sculpture, artifacts, and a library, all related to the domestic dog. The Dog Museum publishes a newsletter, Sirius, and offers memberships. For more information contact: The Dog Museum of America, Jarville House in Queeny Park, 1721 South Mason Road, St. Louis, MO 63131. (314) 821-3647.

helped discover thousands of bags of cocaine, with a street value of almost $800 *million* that had been hidden in an empty propane tanker. For her efforts, Snag was featured on a box of dog biscuits (the canine equivalent of appearing on a box of Wheaties) and was featured on the true crime show, "America's Most Wanted." Health problems forced her to give up her work, and she now has a second career as a companion to her former handler and his family.

Domestic dogs exhibit an astounding variety of color, size, and temperament. The tallest dog is the Irish wolfhound, which can reach three feet at the shoulders and six feet standing on its hind legs (this breed actually died out one hundred years ago, but was "reconstituted" by breeding Great Danes, deerhounds, and mastiffs). The smallest is the tiny chihuahua, which rarely weighs over five pounds.

Dogs range from common varieties such as the poodle and German shepherd to species such as the Levesque, an ancient French hunting dog, and the American Hairless Terrier, the rarest dog in the world (only seventy are thought to be in existence). And of course, we cannot forget the millions of All American Mutts, who are as loved and valued by their owners as the most expensive show dogs.

The Manhattan-based American Kennel Club (AKC), founded in 1884, keeps records of more than 34 million purebred dogs in its files, dating back to 1878. The name of the dog's sire (father) and dam (mother) and other pertinent information are recorded. The AKC recognizes 134 breeds. The latest breeds to be sanctioned by the AKC are the Chinese crested terrier and the American Eskimo dog. Some breeds, such as the Jack Russell terrier, are popular in England and other countries, but are not officially recognized by the AKC.

Each breed of dog is assigned to one of seven groups, which are basically categorized according to the purpose for which the breed was developed. These include the sporting, hound, working, terrier, toy, nonsporting, and herding groups. There is also a "miscellaneous" class for dogs who do not quite fit into any specific category.

The Academy Awards of the doggy set is the Westminster Dog Show, which is held every February in Madison Square Garden in New York City. Here, over 2,000 purebred dogs are narrowed down to 134 "Best in Breed" and, finally, 7 "Best in Group" winners. One of these "magnificent seven" will go on to win the coveted title of "Best in Show."

The table lists the most popular dogs in the United States as of 1991.

America's Top Twenty

Ranking	Name of Breed	Number of Dogs Registered Per AKC Figures
1	Labrador Retriever	105,876
2	Cocker Spaniel	98,937
3	Poodle	77,709
4	Rottweiler	76,889
5	German Shepherd	68,844
6	Golden Retriever	67,284
7	Beagle	56,956
8	Dachshund	48,713
9	Chow Chow	45,131
10	Shetland Sheepdog	44,106
11	Miniature Schnauzer	42,404
12	Shih Tzu	39,503
13	Pomeranian	41,034
14	Yorkshire Terrier	39,772
15	Dalmatian	30,225
16	Chihuahua	29,860
17	Boxer	26,722
18	Lhasa Apso	23,543
19	Siberian Husky	23,436
20	English Springer Spaniel	21,342

Like hemlines, fashions in dogs come and go. Millie, who occupied the White House during the Bush years, sparked an interest in English springer spaniels, taking the Number 20 spot formerly held by the doberman. When Millie gave birth to her first litter, requests for the presidential pups poured in from all over the country.

Movies can also spark an interest in a particular breed. For a brief period, the French mastiff, or "dogue (rhymes with "vogue") de Bordeux" was popular, having first been introduced to the American public in the hit film *Turner and Hooch,* where Tom Hanks (Turner) plays a perfectionist cop who unwillingly inherits a very untidy dog (Hooch). Suddenly, the dogue de Bordeux was in demand, until it was discovered that it required a great deal of exercise (it is definitely not an apartment dog) and has a tendency to bite.

The Most Dangerous Dogs

Each year, 3 million people are attacked by pet dogs—almost 60 percent of them are children. Many of these attacks do not result in serious injury, but from 1990 to 1992, there were forty-one documented dog bite fatalities. The breeds involved included:

- 17 pit bulls
- 6 German shepherds
- 5 chow chows
- 5 malamutes
- 4 huskies
- 4 wolf-hybrids
- 2 akitas
- 2 rottweilers
- 1 Doberman

However, today's "hot dog" can quickly fall out of favor. A perfect example is the Doberman pinscher, who was number 2 on the AKC's 1979 list. The Doberman's popularity took a nose dive in the 1980s, perhaps because this breed, particularly the male, is aggressive and can be difficult to control if not properly trained. The Doberman's registration figure has dropped by 73 percent, and they are now number 29 on the 1991 list.

The chow chow and the rottweiler were the fad dogs of the 1980s. The rottweiler, however, is slowly being replaced by the Akita, called the "yuppie puppy" because of its popularity with upscale types. Some dog experts believe that the dalmatian and bichon frisé, a Franco-Belgian breed whose name means "curly lap dog," will be *the* dogs of the nineties.

The border collie, a sturdy breed that was developed to herd sheep, is also undergoing a surge in popularity, largely because of a controversial 1994 book by Stanley Coren entitled *The Intelligence of Dogs: Canine Consciousness and Capabilities.* This book, which ranks the intelligence of 133 breeds, rates border collies as the brainiest dogs, followed by poodles, German shepherds, golden retrievers, and Doberman pinschers. The five dumbest breeds, according to Coren, are in descending order, the borzoi, chow chow, bulldog, basenji, and Afghan hound. (Coren doesn't bother to rate what many dog experts feel are often the longest-lived, healthiest, and most intelligent of all dogs—mutts.)

Many dog experts view the trend toward "fad dogs" as a harmful one, as overpopularity can be detrimental to a breed. Overpopularity can lead to careless breeding, resulting in genetic defects. For example, the dalmation, an ancient breed whose striking coloration has made it a favorite with magazine and television advertisers, are often deaf or ill-tempered, and because of genetic diseases, are frequently short-lived.

It's A Dog's Life

It has often been said that each year of a dog's life is equal to seven years of a human's; however, this is not quite true. Here is a chart showing a more exact relationship between dog and human ages:

Dog's Age	Human Equivalent
2 months	14 months
6 months	5 years
8 months	9 years
12 months	14 years
18 months	20 years
2 years	24 years
3 years	30 years
4 years	36 years
5 years	40 years
6 years	42 years
7 years	49 years
8 years	56 years
9 years	63 years
10 years	65 years
11 years	71 years
12 years	75 years
13 years	80 years
14 years	84 years
15 years	87 years
16 years	89 years

QUIZ: WILD DOGS OF THE WORLD

The dog family includes not only the familiar domestic breeds, but also a large number of wild relatives. Match the name of the animal with its description. Answers can be found on page 187.

a. Hyena *b.* Coyote *c.* Paraguayan fox *d.* Jackal *e.* Bush dog *f.* African hunting dog *g.* Red fox *h.* Dhole *i.* Arctic fox *j.* Dingo

1. Closely related to the wolf, it is found from Central America to Alaska.

2. They were brought by the Kooris to Australia 4,000 years ago.

3. This nocturnal animal feeds on carcasses.

4. In the winter, its fur is white, but in the summer it changes color.

5. This Asian species feeds on large mammals, including deer and water buffalo.

6. Although it closely resembles a canine, it is not a member of the dog family.

7. This stocky, aggressive animals often lives in deserted armadillo dens.

8. This dog sometimes feeds on prey while it is still alive.

9. Like a possum, this animal has been known to play dead when threatened.

10. More than one color phase can be found in the litters of these common canids.

CRY WOLF

Who's afraid of the big bad wolf?
The big bad wolf
The big bad wolf
Who's afraid of the big bad wolf?
La la la la la!

Throughout history, *Canis lupus* has been painted as a villain. From nursery stories such as "The Three Little Pigs," "Little Red Riding Hood," and, of course, "The Little Boy who Cried Wolf" to medieval accounts of werewolves and nineteenth-century pioneer stories of howling wolves descending on helpless travelers and devouring them alive, this large canid has been the object of fear and hatred.

Before the coming of the Europeans, wolves were common throughout the northern hemisphere, living just about anyplace except the deserts and tropical jungles. The first settlers brought their prejudice against wolves with them from the European continent, and at the same time, as populations grew and the food the wolves depended upon, such as bison, elk, and deer, were killed off by humans, the animals took to killing livestock.

The first bounty on wolves was set in 1630 in the Massachusetts Bay colony. Ten shillings was paid for each wolf killed. Through the centuries, wolves were shot, poisoned, and trapped to such an extent that by the 1960s, they had been exterminated throughout most of their original range.

In the 1970s, however, people became aware of the importance of ecosystems and how each individual within an ecosystem contributes to our lives. Wolves are important predators who help control the population of such animals as deer, elk, moose, and musk oxen. And as scientists began to study wolves in the wild, one thing became very clear: Wolves have more to fear from humans than we have to fear from them. They are by nature very shy animals that avoid people whenever possible. Wolves are also intelligent, highly social creatures that live in close-knit family groups and mate for life.

There are two types of wolf in the United States. The largest is the gray, or timber, wolf, which is also the biggest member of the canine family. Gray wolves can weigh up to 175 pounds and measure nearly six feet from nose to tail. They are usually a grizzled gray, but can be black, silver, or brown; in the cold Arctic regions, they are often white. Gray wolves were once found throughout North America and in South and Central America but are now limited to sections of Canada, the upper Midwest (Minnesota, Michigan, and Wisconsin), and a few scattered areas in the western United States. A smaller version of this animal, the European gray wolf, could once be found in every country on the continent, but now lives only in small areas in southern and eastern Europe.

The rarer, smaller red wolf once ranged from Pennsylvania to Texas. Despite its name, the red wolf is not actually red; it can be tan, cinnamon, gray, or even black. These wolves suffered the same type of treatment as the gray wolf, however, and except for a few that have been reintroduced into the wild, most are now found only in zoos.

Wolves live in complex family groups called *packs*, which number from two to ten animals. Each pack is led by a dominant male and his mate, called the alpha pair. Every member in the pack has a rank. Each wolf knows its place, and any that challenge the alpha pair are likely to be expelled from the pack. Only the alpha pair breeds, and they are also responsible for keeping the pack together, deciding when and where to hunt, and how to defend the group against enemies.

Each breeding pack has its own territory, which covers from 30 to 150 square miles. The wolves mark their territories by urinating and defecating in specific locations.

Wolves communicate by howling (they do not, however, howl at the moon). A wolf's howl can be heard up to six miles away. Sometimes the entire pack will howl in unison. They also communicate by whimpering, growling, and barking like domestic dogs.

In 1988, six red wolves were reintroduced into the Alligator River National Wildlife Refuge in eastern North Carolina, and the population there has slowly grown. Wildlife biologists hope to continue placing both timber and red wolves in areas where they were once abundant, including Yellowstone Park. This plan has met with opposition, however, from ranches and farmers, who fear that the wolves will prey on livestock.

Wolves in the 'Hood

Because wolves are handsome and intelligent and closely resemble domestic dogs, some people have assumed that they make good companion animals. Most wildlife experts, however, discourage people from keeping wolves as pets, because they are just not suited to domestic life. They howl, tear up furniture, yards, and houses and are often aggressive toward other animals and, many times, people.

Wolves will readily mate with dogs, and the resulting offspring are also attractive, intelligent animals. It is not wise, however, to keep wolf-hybrids as pets either; they tend to be unpredictable and, like their full-blooded wolf cousins, can be very aggressive and sometimes vicious.

In the Philadelphia area recently, a two-year-old boy was mauled while reaching through a fence to stroke a wolf-hybrid. The child's arm became badly infected, and the life-threatening infection spread throughout his entire body. Thousands all over the Delaware Valley hoped and prayed for the toddler's recovery. The child lived, but his arm had to be amputated, and the animal was later destroyed.

Despite growing reports of such incidents, some people insist on keeping wolf-hybrids, and even purebred wolves, as pets. While on a visit to the Fort Greene section of Brooklyn several years ago, I came upon a man sitting on the steps in front of a well-kept brownstone, accompanied by a huge, beautiful white "dog."

"What a pretty dog!" I said. "What's his name?"

"It's a she, and her name is Dag," the man answered.

"What kind of dog is it?"

"It's not a dog. It's a wolf," he replied nonchalantly.

"Aw, c'mon," I answered. "That's no wolf!"

The red wolf, like the timber wolf, has been hunted nearly to extinction. Photograph by Curtis Carley. Courtesy of U.S. Fish & Wildlife Service.

"Sure it is," he said.

I peered closely at the "dog." Yes, there *was* something wolflike about those huge paws and those golden-brown eyes that watched my every move. But surely, no one would be so foolish as to keep a wild animal in the heart of the city—or would they?

"Wanna hear him sing?" the man asked. Before I could reply, he leaned close to the animal's huge head. "Sing for me, Dag," he commanded. "Sing!" And then, the "dog" raised her head and let out an eerie howl that rose above the sounds of traffic and children playing and laughing on the busy city street.

BIG CATS, LITTLE CATS: THE FAMILY *FELIDAE*

> *Tyger, tyger, burning bright*
> *In the forests of the night,*
> *What immortal hand or eye*
> *Could frame thy fearful symmetry?*

> —William Blake

Visit a zoo at any given time and chances are that you will find, along with the primates, that the big cats are among the most popular animals, for humans have been fascinated by the cat family for centuries. The lion, leopard, and William Blake's "tyger" have all become symbols of grace, strength, and majesty. Even *Felis domesticus*, the cat that we share our home and hearth with, has a bit of the king of the beasts in him as he stalks through the grass, looking for mice.

As animals go, the cat family is a fairly small one, encompassing only about forty species. They are divided into four groups. The members of the genus *Panthera*, which include the lion, leopard, tiger, and jaguar, catch their prey by stalking, leaping on them, and killing them with a swift bite to the neck. For this reason, they are sometimes called the leaping cats. Members of this group are also distinguished by their loud roars, which are made possible by flexible connections in their throats. Like domestic cats, they have retractable claws.

The cheetah is also a big cat. Unlike the members of the genus *Panthera*, however, cheetahs kill their prey, which includes fast-moving animals such as the gazelle, by running after them at great speeds instead of stalking and leaping on them. The cheetah also differs from the other big cats in that its claws are only partially retractable. This is one of the reasons the cheetah is placed in a class by itself, as is the clouded leopard.

The fourth group, which consists of twenty-eight species, includes our familiar house cat, as well as the cougar and smaller wild cats such as the ocelot, bobcat, and lynx. The smaller cats have bony connections in their throats instead of flexible ones and cannot roar, but they do purr.

The Big Cats

The big cats are found throughout the world, except in Australia, New Zealand, Madagascar, and the Arctic and Antarctic. They are a versatile group, being as much at home in the cold, snowy wastes of Siberia as they are in the hot savannahs of Africa. More species, however, are found in warmer climates than in cold ones.

Sadly, many of the big cats are in serious danger of extinction. Take, for example, the tiger, which has been ruthlessly hunted for its magnificent striped coat. The ancient kings, moguls, and maharajahs of Asia have always hunted tigers for sport, but these cats did not become seriously endangered until the arrival of the British in the eighteenth century. In India, English shooting parties would sometimes kill forty to fifty tigers in a single *day*; from 1800 to 1900, there were 100,000 tigers killed in this one nation alone. Over 1,000 a year were killed in the early part of this century, until by the 1920s, only about 100,000 of these magnificent creatures were left in all of Asia.

In 1970, when the worldwide population of tigers had plummeted to 5,000, a massive conservation drive was started, which included the establishment of preserves in some Asian countries. Despite severe penalties, poaching of these animals continues (in some Asian countries, tiger paws, bones, and even penises are highly prized ingredients in folk medicine), and scientists fear that some species, including the Bengal tiger, may become extinct in the wild during the next twenty-five years. As tigers are secretive animals, it is difficult to obtain an exact count; estimates of the total tiger population range between 5,000 and 6,000 animals. There are more tigers in captivity than in the wild.

Fortunately, tigers can be bred successfully in captivity, but it would be indeed unfortunate if the "fearful symmetry" of this beautiful creature, or of any of the big cats, were to disappear from the wild forever.

Lions

The lion is the most familiar of the big cats, and the most abundant. Twelve thousand years ago, lions had the largest range of any mammal besides man, roaming through Africa, Europe, the Middle East, the Americas from Alaska to Peru, and Asia as far north as Siberia. Through the centuries, however, because of human influence and climate fluctuations, the lion's range has been reduced to sub-Saharan Africa and a small population in the Gir forest of northwest India.

Lions are known for their distinctive manes. Only males, however, possess them. The young lions start growing them at about three years of age. The mane tends to be longer and thicker in harsher climates. Male lions are much larger than females and can weigh more than 500 pounds.

King of the Beasts

Majestic and powerful, lions have fascinated humans for centuries. In 1720, a lion was exhibited in Boston. The animal caused a sensation, as it was the first of its species to be seen in the young nation. About 100 years later, the emperor of Morocco presented then-president Andrew Jackson with a lion. Jackson, however, didn't know what to do with it, and asked the advice of Congress. The lion was ultimately sold.

Lions are very strong. They can break a zebra's neck with one blow of their massive paws. They are also very fast and have been known to attain speeds as great as 40 miles per hour for short distances.

Lions are the only social animals in the cat family, living in groups called *prides*. A pride can number anywhere from three to thirty individuals, but usually includes about a dozen members. The lionesses in a pride are usually related as sisters, daughters, or aunts. Unlike most other female animals, lionesses will suckle another lion's cubs and have been known to "adopt" the young of lionesses who have been killed.

Although they are significantly smaller than the males, lionesses are responsible for initiating about 80 percent of the hunting in a pride, and they teach the young cubs to hunt. Far from being liberated females, however, they wait until the males have eaten their fill and then get the remains.

FACTS OF LIFE

● Lions in captivity have sometimes been mated with other species. A cross between a male lion and a female tiger is called a *liger*, while the offspring of a male tiger and a female lion is called a *tiglon*. The less common union of a lion and a leopard produces a *leopon*, an animal with a small mane and spots!

● In 1928 white lions were spotted in South Africa. The next recorded sighting was not until 1975 in the Timbavati Game Reserve in Kruger National Park. In 1993, the Philadelphia Zoo became the first in the nation to exhibit white lions—two females named Jezebel and Vinkel. The white lions are snow white as cubs, but gradually darken to a beautiful cream color. They are fully accepted by other members of the pride, but their unusual coloring makes them an easy target for enemies.

● White lions, which are extremely rare in the wild, are not albinos. They are leucistic, meaning that they lack pigment in their hair and skin, but, unlike albinos, they do have color in their eyes (Vinkel and Jezebel have pretty amber eyes). Their white coloring is the result of a combination of two recessive genes.

Tigers

The tiger is the largest of the big cats. They live throughout Asia, including India, Sumatra, Java, and China. There are no tigers in Africa. About 60 precent of the wild tiger population lives in India.

There were originally eight subspecies of tiger, but today, just five remain. The largest is the Siberian, or Amur tiger, of which there are only about 200 left. The Siberian tiger can weigh up to 600 pounds. The smallest species is the Javan tiger. The South China subspecies, which is down to around 50 animals, is the rarest tiger, and the most abundant is the Bengal (about 2,000 remain in the wild). Most of what we know about tigers is based on studies done on the latter species.

Tigers are solitary animals, generally coming together only to mate. They are not totally antisocial, however, and are generally aware of who their tiger neighbors are in a given area. Upon meeting them, they will sometimes exchange a friendly greeting, rubbing heads or flanks, and then go their separate ways.

Tigers are very wary of man. They make an unusual noise that sounds something like *pok-pok-pok*. Tigers use this noise to warn others of their presence.

Occasionally, they will attack and eat humans. These man-eating tigers are rare and almost always are animals that are old, injured, or ill and must seek slower prey that is easier to catch. Studies show that less than 3 percent of the tiger population will become man-eaters.

White tigers like "Simita" were once prized by the maharajahs of India for their beautiful pelts. Photograph by Bill Hoffman. Courtesy of the Zoological Society of Philadelphia.

Unlike most other cats, tigers seem to enjoy the water and are good swimmers. In harsh climates, such as that of Siberia, they can accumulate up to two inches of fat under the skin.

Beautiful and rare, white tigers have dark (but not black) stripes on a white background and brilliant sapphire-blue eyes. They are neither albinos or leucistic, but a variation of the more common black and orange tiger. The unusual coloring is the result of a dominance of white genes similar to those found in white domestic cats. Once fairly abundant in the State of Rewa in India (today called Madhya Pradesh) white tigers were especially valued as trophies. The maharajahs of Rewa killed hundreds of them over the years and they were almost extinct by 1950.

In 1960, a white tiger named Mohini ("the enchantress") was purchased by an American for $15,000. Mohini, the first white tiger to leave India, was presented as a gift by the buyer to the National Zoo in Washington, D.C.

Mohini became one of the zoo's main attractions and produced many cubs over the years, some white, some orange. Today, Mohini's descendants can be seen in several zoos throughout the world.

Leopards and Jaguars

There are two types of true leopard: the common leopard and the snow leopard. The common leopard lives in the wooded grasslands of Africa and southern Asia. They are probably the best tree climbers among the big cats and can scale a vertical tree with amazing ease. They are solitary animals who hunt at night.

The rare and beautiful snow leopard, or *ounce*, lives in the high mountains of Central Asia, where it feeds on wild goats, deer, and marmots. It is believed that there are only about 5,000 of these big cats left.

The black leopard, sometimes called the black panther, is most common in the forests of Southeast Asia. This animal has darker spots on its coats that are difficult to see. Both tawny and black leopards can occur in the same litter. Bagheera, the black panther who befriends Mowgli in *The Jungle Book*, was a black panther. Leopards were once tamed and used to hunt game in India.

In much of South America, *el tigre* does not refer to the familiar striped feline, but to the jaguar. The name means "the wild beast that can kill its prey in a single leap." Once found from the southern United States to Argentina, the jaguar now can be found only as far north as Mexico. It resembles a leopard, but is larger, stockier, and not as agile. Jaguars are not good tree climbers and prefer to hunt at ground level or in the water. They rarely roar.

Like tigers, jaguars are good swimmers and enjoy catching fish. Forest jaguars, which are darker than those that dwell in the grasslands, have even been known to kill crocodiles. Like tigers, they have been known to attack and kill humans when no other food is available.

The Clouded Leopard

The clouded leopard, which is not a true leopard, is one of the world's rarest animals. It is found in the evergreen forests of India, Myanmar (formerly Burma), Indochina, Borneo, Sumatra, and Taiwan. The clouded leopard has a beautiful coat with dark rosettes and ovals on a brownish yellow background. This animal also occurs in a melanotic form. It is an excellent tree climber and has the ability to move along horizontal branches upside down. Clouded leopards do not roar. Little is known about their habits, but in captivity, clouded leopards are playful and have developed affectionate relationships with their keepers.

Cheetahs

Besides their partially retractable claws, and the way they catch their prey, cheetahs differ from other members of the genus *Panthera* in that they do not roar, but instead make a variety of noises including birdlike chirping sounds. With their long, lean, streamlined bodies and small heads, they also look different from the other big cats.

Cheetahs were once found throughout Africa and India, where they were trained to hunt game. They have been extinct in India, however, since the 1950s and today live mainly in Namibia and Zimbabwe in southern Africa. There are only about 15,000 cheetahs left in the world today.

The cheetah is the world's fastest land mammal, reaching speeds up to 70 miles per hour. It can reach 60 mph in about three seconds from a standing start (a 1991 Corvette takes four and a half seconds to accelerate to this speed). If cheetahs were human, they would break all Olympic records; they can run a quarter mile in only twenty seconds! Cheetahs are sprinters rather than marathoners, however. They can maintain such speeds only for about 500 yards and must rest afterwards.

Cheetahs are not social animals, but sometimes a group of three or four males will form what is called a *coalition*. The coalition may be permanent, or may exist for only a few months. The members of the coalition will not allow any other male cheetahs into their territory and have been known to kill intruders.

Hyenas and cheetahs are bitter enemies. Lions and cheetahs are also adversaries. Lions will sometimes kill a whole litter of cheetah cubs, though they rarely eat them (one of the reasons only 50 percent of cheetah cubs make it to adulthood). The lean, lanky cheetah is no match for the powerful lion and will usually flee rather than put up a fight.

QUIZ: WHAT AM I?

Here are some species of smaller wild cats that you may not be familiar with. Try to guess what they are. Answers can be found on pages 188–189.

1. I am the largest of the small cats and can be found in the western and southeastern United States, as well as in Mexico and Central and South America. I am called by many names, including "painter," and "catamount." I am very strong and can kill and drag prey up to seven times my own weight. When the first European settlers saw me, they thought I was a lion, but could not understand what had happened to my mane! *What am I?*

2. I live throughout South America and can also be found in Texas. I am small, weighing anywhere from ten to twenty pounds, but I am a swift and silent hunter. I come in three colors, black, reddish brown, and gray, and all three shades can be found in the same litter. *What am I?*

3. I have a beautiful reddish brown coat that blends in well with the African savannahs and Asian deserts I call home. At one time, I was used to hunt birds and rabbits. In Turkish, my name means "black ears." *What am I?*

4. Although I am principally a forest dweller, I can also live in grass and scrublands from Arizona to Argentina. I like to swim and climb, and sometimes I hunt in pairs with others of my species. Because of the stripes around my neck, they call me *el tigrillo*, or "little tiger," in Mexico. I have been hunted nearly to extinction for my gorgeous coat. *What am I?*

5. I live on the savannahs of sub-Saharan Africa. With my long legs and spotted coat, I look a bit like a miniature cheetah. I have been hunted for both my fur and my flesh, and because I sometimes like to feast on domestic poultry, I am considered a pest and my numbers are dwindling rapidly. *What am I?*

The Little Cats

God made cats so that man may have the pleasure of caressing the tiger.

—*Indian Proverb*

The world can be divided into two groups. There are those of us who idolize, adore, and worship cats, considering them creatures of great charm and personality. Then there is the second group, which consists of people who wonder why the other half idolizes, worships, and adores a creature who spends eighteen hours of the day sleeping and the remainder engaged in (a) ignoring you; (b) staring vacantly into space; (c) shredding your sofa; (d) upchucking assorted greenish foamy substances on your carpet; (e) harassing, torturing, and devouring various helpless creatures twenty times smaller than it; and (e) making you sneeze.

Much to the dismay of cat-haters everywhere, however, America's ailuromania, or love of cats, shows no sign of abating. The United States has more cats than any other country in the world. And in 1985, for the first time in American history, cat ownership outstripped dog ownership. There are about 54.6 million cats in this country, as compared to 52.4 million dogs, which means that there is about one cat for *every five people*!

The number of households owning dogs (34.7 million) is actually *greater* than the number of households owning cats (27.7 million). This discrepancy is explained by the fact that many cat owners have more than one cat.

The Cat Fancier's Association (CFA) recognizes 33 breeds of cats, among them a rare breed known as the Bombay, which, despite its exotic name, was actually developed in St. Louis. According to the CFA, the most popular purebred cat in the United States today is the Persian, with 56,847 registered with the Association as of 1989. Next comes the Siamese, with 3,710, the Abyssinian (2,669), Maine coon cat (2,449), and Burmese (1,206). No one knows for sure how many pedigree cats there are in the country. As is the case with dogs, however, the vast majority of the cats in the United States are mixed breeds, known in cat show parlance as moggies. One cat expert estimates that as many as 90% of all cats in the United States are moggies.

There are several periodicals devoted to cats, veterinarians with practices devoted solely to cats, and shops specializing in cat paraphernalia (the Philadelphia area alone has three such stores). We spend $21.5 million a year on cat food and $295 million on cat litter, not to mention the big bucks dished out for scratching posts, catnip mice with cute felt ears, little plastic balls with bells inside them, and other toys that are played with for a day or so and then discarded under the living room couch to collect dust bunnies.

The popularity of cats can be illustrated by Socks, Chelsea Clinton's black and white moggie. Socks's move into the White House marks the first time in many years that a Demo*cat* has replaced a Re*pup*lican as First Pet.

Here is the scoop on Socks: Yes, he is neutered; no, he does not give interviews; and his favorite pastime is curling up and sleeping in a drawer. For the record, Socks has a sister in Arkansas named Midnight, whose human is a staunch Republican. The Clintons, fearful that the homesick tomcat will head back for the green hills of Arkansas, keep Socks on a leash when outdoors, but despite this restraint, he has managed to catch a fair number of squirrels.

Lifestyles of the Rich and Furry

Do you have a cat, dog, bird, monkey, chicken, or other companion animal you want the world to know about? Have he/she/it listed in *Who's Who of Animals: Biographies of Great Animal Companions*. The 1,200 entries include the usual dogs and cats, as well as iguanas, ferrets, pythons, and a miniature kangaroo. For more information, write: "Who's Who of Animals," Companion Publishing, 2708 Hillsborough Road, P.O. Box 2820, Durham, N.C. 27715.

Anyone writing to him—Socks gets mail at the rate of one hundred letters per week—will get a handsome postcard with The Whiskered One's photograph on it that says "I'm proud to be your First Cat".

For the cat lovers out there, here are some delightful facts about our feline friends. For the other half of humanity, here are some things about cats that you did not care to know and would never bother to ask.

FACTS OF LIFE

- Humans are plantigrade, meaning they walk on their heels and toes; but cats walk only on their toes.

- Cats almost always land on their feet if they fall a short distance. Cats that have fallen from greater heights in fact, do not always do this and can sustain serious injuries. A pregnant cat named Pat, however, was dumped off a bridge in Portland, Oregon, and survived the 205-foot fall.

- Dog food should not be fed to a cat, as it lacks taurine, a substance that is necessary to ensure a cat's good health. Feeding a cat a continuous diet of dog food can make it go blind.

- Domestic cats are descended from *Felis silvestris*, a small wild cat.

- Contrary to popular belief, Socks is not the first presidential cat. Theodore Roosevelt had a cat named Slippers. Slippers would disappear for days and weeks at a time, but somehow always managed to show up just before big state dinners.

- Cats, including the big ones, have about forty more bones than humans do and a very flexible spine. This is why cats are so agile.

- Cats go wild over catnip, but a lot of them like garlic, too. Garlic does not have the same effect on them, however, as catnip does, though some pet owners swear that cats and dogs fed on garlic have fewer fleas.

- Chinese peasants can tell the time by looking at their cat's eyes—the pupils are narrowest at noon.

- Cat owners tend to be better educated than dog owners.

- Cats cannot see in total darkness, but their night vision is about six times better than a human's. This is because they possess an extra layer of reflecting cells, called the *tapetum ludicum*, which absorbs light. It is these reflectors that shine in the dark when the cat's eyes are caught in the glare of a headlight or streetlamp.

- White cats with blue eyes are often deaf.

- Cats have three eyelids.

- Chatham Island in the Pacific is overrun by thousands of feral cats that live on fish. Every one of the cats is black.

- In the northeastern United States, cats often have six or seven toes on one paw.

- The cat is so fastidious (or empty-headed, depending on your point of view) that it spends 30 percent of its waking hours grooming itself.

- At the Anderson House Hotel in Wabasha, Minnesota, guests can reserve a "four-legged, fur-person bed warmer."

Sad Facts

According to the Doris Day Animal League, 25 percent of pets are destroyed by the time they reach two years of age. Every year 12 million animals are placed in shelters; at least 25 percent of them are purebreds. Only 25 percent of lost dogs and 2 percent of lost cats are reunited with their owners. Among the most commonly abandoned animals are Rottweilers, Shar peis, and Vietnamese pot-bellied pigs.

- You may get a frog in your throat, but a Frenchman gets a *chat*.

- A cat's hearing is among the sharpest in the animal world. A cat can recognize its owner's footsteps from hundreds of feet away.

- The average life expectancy of a cat has nearly doubled since 1930, from eight to sixteen years. Males lives an average of thirteen to fifteen years; females, fifteen to seventeen. The oldest cat on record was Puss, who died in 1939, just one day after celebrating his thirty-sixth birthday.

Some Famous Cat Lovers . . .

Benjamin Franklin

Daniel Boone (he had a pet cat named Bluegrass.)

Abraham Lincoln

George Washington

Albert Einstein

Mark Twain (he wrote, "A home without a cat may be a perfect home perhaps, but how can it prove its title?")

. . . And Cat Haters

Julius Caesar

Adolf Hitler

Johannes Brahms

William Shakespeare

Napoleon ("The Little General" was so afraid of cats that the mere mention of them made him tremble.)

Dwight D. Eisenhower ("Ike" hated cats so much that he reportedly ordered any stray feline found on the White House grounds shot.)

- Towser, a tabby in charge of rodent control at a Scottish distillery, had captured 23,000 mice by the time she was twenty-one (an average of three mice a day).

- Tiger and Samantha are the most popular names for pet cats.

- Cats purr at twenty-six cycles per second, the same frequency as an idling diesel engine.

- Cats have had up to nineteen kittens per litter, but litters are usually small.

- A cat is not considered a senior citizen until it is ten years old.

- A cat's ears contain twenty tiny muscles and can rotate through 180 degrees, allowing for a wide variety of "ear expressions." For example, cats prick their ears to show other cats there is something going on of interest. Ears held slightly back show uncertainty, while fully flattened ears indicate anger or fear.

- Each cat has a "home range," which consists of the total area that it routinely travels. For rural cats, the home range can encompass as much as sixty acres.

- The ancient Egyptians venerated cats so much that the penalty for killing one, even accidentally, was beheading. When a cat died, the whole family shaved their eyebrows in mourning. Cats were often mummified and buried with their owners, along with mummified mice so the dearly departed had something to munch on in the afterlife. The Persians used

Aspirin Alert

Aspirin should *never* be given to cats except under a veterinarian's supervision, because it can be fatal to them. If you think your cat, dog, or other companion animal has been poisoned, you can call the National Animal Poison Control Center (NAPCC) at (800) 548-2423 (there is a per-case charge, so have your VISA, MasterCard, Discover, or American Express card ready).

this Egyptian idolatry of cats to their advantage over 2,000 years ago. When at war with the Egyptians, they rushed into combat holding cats in their arms. The horrified Egyptians were afraid to strike, lest they injure one of the precious animals. Needless to say, the battle ended in a *cat*astrophic defeat for the Egyptians.

● Feline fortunes declined from about the years 1400 to 1700, when the cat was thought of as a "creature of the devil" throughout Europe. Cats, particularly black ones, were persecuted, tortured, and killed. Many were destroyed in mass burnings; the French town of Metz was known for these catkillings.

● Rome has more homeless cats per square mile than any other city in the world.

● Not all cats hate water. One breed, the Turkish Van, is often referred to as the "Turkish swimming cat" because of their fondness for playing in warm, shallow pools and streams. These cats, which are creamy white with orange markings, take their name from the isolated region around Lake Van in southeast Turkey, where they have been bred for more than one hundred years.

● Cats deprived of tryptophan, a substance found in milk, eggs, and poultry, become insomniacs.

● Unplanned parenthood: The largest recorded number of kittens born in a lifetime to a single female is 420!

● Cats lose more hair in the summer because light makes them shed. Electric light and light from a television set count, too.

THE PINNIPEDS

Seals, sea lions, and walruses are known as *pinnipeds*, a word meaning "wing or fin-footed." Some of these carnivores are equally at home in the water as they are on land. Other species, such as the elephant seal (of which there are two varieties—the Northern and the Southern) rarely come to land, spending 85 to 90 percent of their time at sea. Pinnipeds can be found all over the world, but most of them dwell in cold waters; the monk seal is the only species that dwells in warm waters. Today, there are about 20 million pinnipeds throughout the world.

Pinnipeds can be divided into three groups. The first, Phocidae, includes what are called the true seals. The true seals lack a visible external ear, having only small holes on the sides of their heads. The family Otariidae, which includes fourteen species, consists of fur seals and sea lions. These pinnipeds have small external ears and, for this reason, are sometimes called eared seals.

The family Odobenidae includes just one animal, the walrus. Walruses differ from other pinnipeds in that both males and females have long tusks. Like the true seals, they lack an external ear. Male pinnipeds are called bulls, the females are cows, and their offspring are pups.

How do the true seals differ from fur seals and sea lions? Generally, the true seals spend more time in the water and dive more deeply than the latter two groups of pinnipeds. When true seals move across rocks and beaches, they travel by contractions of their powerful belly muscles, making them resemble huge, fat caterpillars. Sea lions and fur seals, however, actually "walk" on land with a clumsy, waddling gait. They can move fairly quickly—some sea lions can run as fast as a person!

The bodies of all pinnipeds are streamlined for life in the water. In addition to their reduced ears and webbed flippers, they have a thick layer of fat under their skin, called *blubber*. This blubber helps protect their bodies from heat loss and also stores food energy.

Many pinnipeds were nearly driven to extinction by overhunting. Although they have been harvested by the Inuits (formerly known as Eskimos), Aleuts, and other native peoples since the Stone Age, they took only what they needed to survive from the vast pinniped *rookeries*, or breeding grounds.

Walruses were an especially important animal to the Inuits. No part of the walrus was wasted. The huge animal's tusks were used to make smooth, durable slide runners and carvings, and the intestines were fashioned into rain parkas. The tough hides, split in half, were made into coverings for small boats called *oomiaks*, which are still in use today. The air sacs became drums and food containers, while the meat, flippers, and internal organs were used as food. Even the animal's stomach contents were eaten. A walrus's stomach can contain as much as 108 pounds of shelled clams, which the Inuits cleaned and ate as a special treat.

All this changed with the coming of the Europeans in the eighteenth and nineteenth centuries. The first victims were hooded and harp seals, which were killed for their skins and oil. Walruses gave ivory and fur seals were especially coveted for their beautiful, glossy pelts, which were made into warm, soft coats.

Huge numbers of pinnipeds were slaughtered to satisfy the seemingly insatiable demand for their fur, oil, and other products. In the Gulf of St. Lawrence, 4,000 walruses were killed in 1765 alone; by 1800, this species had completely disappeared from the region. From 1800 to 1801, seventeen ships from Britain and the United States harvested 112,000 Antarctic fur seal skins. Considering that most of these animals give birth to only one pup at a time, and that many young pinnipeds die before reaching adulthood, it was clear that their populations could not withstand such pressure for long. By the turn of the century, many of the world's pinnipeds were on the verge of extinction.

In 1972, the U.S. Congress passed the Marine Mammal Protection Act, which placed marine mammal conservation under the jurisdiction of the federal government. This Act forbade the taking or importation of marine mammals or products made from them except under special, limited conditions. For example, native peoples are permitted to harvest whales, seals, and walruses at subsistence levels.

Although some pinnipeds, such as the shy Mediterranean monk seal, are still in danger, others have made an encouraging comeback. The world's walrus population, for example, which had dwindled to 40,000 in the 1920s, was estimated to be 250,000 in 1990.

FACTS OF LIFE

- Pinnipeds are long-lived animals, often reaching twenty years of age or more.

- Pinnipeds feed on fish, squid, or shrimplike animals called krill. Leopard seals enjoy dining on penguins, devouring the flesh from the clumsy birds in about five minutes. Some pinnipeds, especially walruses and sea lions, feed on the pups of other pinniped species. Stellar's sea lions devoured up to 6 percent of the pups of northern fur seals on one Alaskan island.

- The smallest pinniped is the ringed seal. They weigh about 150 pounds and are about four and a half feet long.

- The largest pinniped is the southern elephant seal. The bulls can be as long as twenty-one feet and weigh almost 7,000 pounds!

- Male pinnipeds are often much larger than the females. The bull northern fur seal can be nearly seven feet in length and weigh 600 pounds, but the female is only about 80 percent of the length and 20 percent of the weight of the male. This seal also differs from the female in that it has a huge, bulbous nose, which increases in size during mating season.

- Seals are excellent divers. The Weddell seal, which lives on the ice of the south polar seas, can go down as far as 2,000 feet (about 600 meters). In comparison, an experienced human diver can dive only 30 feet or so without mechanical aids. Weddell seals can stay underwater for 73 minutes. The champion diver among the pinnipeds, however, is the elephant seal. One elephant seal cow was recorded making a dive of 4,125 feet, more than four-fifths of a mile! The cow took only about seventeen minutes to go down to this depth and seventeen minutes to return to the surface.

- The California sea lion, a large animal with a handsome chocolate brown coat, is the pinniped most commonly seen in circuses and zoos. These intelligent, gregarious animals are easily tamed and trained and have an impressive array of vocal sounds. They are also excellent acrobats; one California sea lion can climb a ladder while balancing a ball on its nose.

- Next to elephant seals, walruses are the largest living pinnipeds. The scientific name of the walrus, *Odobenus*, means "tooth walker." Walrus tusks are actually giant canine teeth. Walruses often use their tusks to anchor themselves as they climb out of the water onto the ice. The tusks of a male walrus can reach three feet in length.

MEERKATS, MONGEESE, AND OTHER SMALL CARNIVORES

When we think of the word *carnivore*, we think of large animals such as bears, wolves, and the big cats. This family, however, also includes many smaller animals, including mongooses, raccoons, and weasels.

The Herpestids

Mongooses and related animals, such as meerkats and lisangs, all belong to the family Herpestidae. There are about thirty species of mongoose, located most-ly in Africa and India. The best-known member of this family is probably the fictional hero of the Rudyard Kipling story, the mongoose named Rikki-Tikki-Tavi. In this tale, Rikki-Tikki-Tavi becomes famous for killing two vicious cobras.

Mongooses were imported from their native India into Jamaica, Hawaii, Australia, and other countries to help control rodent populations. But they killed more than snakes and rodents; they also killed small animals of all types, including poultry and native birds. For this reason, the mongoose is consid-ered a pest in some parts of the world. They can be imported into the United States only with a special permit and must be kept in captivity.

The meerkat is a small, noisy mongoose that lives in large colonies, often in association with other mongoose species, or sometimes even with ground squirrels and small rodents. In its native South Africa, the meerkat is often tamed and kept as a pet.

The dwarf mongoose, which tips the scale at about two pounds, is the smallest member of this family. Despite its small size, it is very aggressive and can inflict a nasty bite.

The Mustelids

The family Mustelidae (meaning "musk bearer") includes such animals as weasels, skunks, badgers, ferrets, and otters. These long, slender animals often possess musk glands that can emit powerful odors. There are more than sixty species of mustelid spread throughout the world except in Australia and Antarctica. The smallest member of the weasel family is the least weasel. The tiniest carnivore in the world, it measures about ten inches long. The largest mustelid is the wolverine, which lives in Scandinavia, northern Asia, and North America.

Mustelids are placed in five subfamilies: the true weasels, which include minks, ermine, ferrets, martens, skunks, and wolverines; the honey badgers; badgers; the skunk family; and the otter.

FACTS OF LIFE

●   The wolverine is also called a glutton, which gives you some idea of what its appetite is like. A ferocious little animal that resembles a miniature bear, it has been known to kill animals many times its size, including reindeer! Its fur has the unique ability to shed ice crystals and once was used by the Inuits as a trim or lining for the hoods of parkas.

- The ratel, or honey badger, lives in Africa and southwestern Asia. It gets its name from the fact that it loves honey and will sometimes tear into a hive with its powerful claws, eating the honey as well as the bees. Its tough hide makes it almost invulnerable to the bees' stings.

- Otters are intelligent, playful animals that often live in family groups. Sea otters are among the elite group of animals that use tools, breaking open the shells of oysters and other mollusks with rocks. Baby otters often ride on their mothers' stomachs while the mother swims on her back. In India and Bangladesh, fishermen train smooth-coated otters to herd fish into nets.

- There are several species of skunk, including the familiar striped variety, the spotted skunk, and the zorilla, which is found in Africa. Skunks are actually omnivores, eating berries, seeds, fruits, and grasses as well as insects and even mice. These animals are known for the amber-colored oil they can eject when threatened; this liquid is made mainly of sulphur and is luminous at night. The striped skunk, which is found everywhere except in desert areas, can spray its "perfume" ten to fifteen feet and the mist can reach three times as far. They can spray five to six times in a row. This foul odor can be smelled up to a mile away. Skunks, however, usually give some sort of warning such as "handstanding" on their front feet, before spraying. How do you remove that awful odor once you have been "skunked"? Many people suggest a good rinse of tomato juice to wash away the smell.

The Procyonids

The procyonids are small animals that are fond of climbing trees. The most familiar member of this family is the raccoon, which is found from southern Canada to Panama. It has also been introduced to parts of Europe.

Many people think that raccoons "wash" their food before eating; however, what they are actually doing is wetting their paws to increase their sense of touch as they knead and tear at their food, feeling for inedible material.

Raccoons are highly intelligent, adaptable creatures that can be found living in suburban areas and even large cities. They are fond of raiding garbage

The Kinkajou is a cousin to the raccoon.
Courtesy of the Zoological Society of Philadelphia.

cans for food scraps. Some become quite tame. Despite their cuddly appearance, however, raccoons can be vicious and can also carry rabies.

The coati, a relative of the raccoon, is a small animal with a pointed snout that live in the southwestern United States and as far south as Argentina. Male white-nosed coatis are solitary, but the females roam in noisy bands numbering up to twelve individuals, including their young. Although the coatis in these groups are unrelated, the females nurse and groom each others' young and cooperate in searching for food and chasing away predators.

The kinkajou lives in the tropical forests of Mexico and South America. It has a prehensile tail like a monkey's, which it can use to wrap around tree branches.

The Viverrids

Civets and genets belong to the family Viverridae. This group also includes exotic-sounding animals such as the binturong, fossa, and fanaloka. Civets and genets resemble cats, with lithe, lean bodies that are patterned with stripes or spots. In some countries in Europe, the genet is used to control rodent populations. The African civet produces a strong-smelling substance in its anal glands; the musk is used in perfumes to make them last longer.

Chapter Eight

FLIPPER AND FRIENDS: THE CETACEANS

Whales, dolphins, and porpoises belong to the order Cetacea. *Cetacea* comes from two words: the Greek *cetus* and the Latin *ketos*, which both mean "whale."

Cetaceans range in size from dolphins measuring five feet long to the mighty blue whale, the largest living animal. There are seventy-six species. Some of them, such as the blue whale, are very rare; others, like the friendly bottlenose dolphin, are fairly common.

Cetaceans are found in every ocean of the world and several rivers. Like those of pinnipeds, the bodies of cetaceans are modified for life in the water. Cetaceans have a layer of blubber underneath their skin that insulates them from the cold. There are no hindlimbs, and the forelimbs have developed into flippers. Like the true seals, cetaceans have no external ears. Most of them have a *dorsal fin* located on their backs to help them glide smoothly through the water, and a flattened tail that is divided into two flukes.

The nasal openings, called *blowholes*, are located at the top of the head. The blowhole can be rectangular, **S**- or crescent-shaped, or a crosswise slit. When cetaceans surface for air, they must first breathe out. The *blow*, or spout, is the name given to the cloud of moist vapor that is blown off as the animal empties its lungs.

A whale's blow consists of fine oil droplets that come from its sinuses and a detergentlike substance from the lungs. The blow leaves a greasy film on anything it touches. Sailors aboard the old whaling ships avoided touching the blow, because they believed that it burned the skin and caused blindness if it got into their eyes. The blow has a foul odor that smells like a combination of bad fish and old oil. Whales have such terrible breath that sailors once believed that a whiff of it could cause brain disorders!

The order Cetacea is further divided into two suborders: the Mysticeti, or baleen whales, and the Odontoceti, or toothed whales. There are three families and ten species of mysticetes, all of which have horny triangular plates called baleen instead of teeth. The baleen helps them strain small fish and tiny animals called zooplankton from the water. The right, rorqual, and gray whales belong to this group. The mysticetes have two blowholes.

There are six families and sixty-six species of odontocetes. Odontocetes have anywhere from 2 to 260 teeth, but only have one set in a lifetime. In some members of this order, the teeth remain buried in the gums of all individuals except adult males. Dolphins, porpoises, white whales, and sperm whales are all odontocetes. These whales have a single blowhole.

DOLPHINS AND PORPOISES

Dolphins and porpoises live in all but the coldest waters of the world and can dwell anywhere from the deep waters of the oceans to great rivers like the Amazon and Ganges. Most of the dolphins we are familiar with live in coastal waters.

Porpoises are generally smaller than dolphins and have short, blunt snouts instead of the long, sharp "beaks" that characterize dolphins. The major difference between dolphins and porpoises, however, is in their dentition. Dolphin teeth are shaped liked small cones, and porpoise teeth resemble little shovels (in this section "dolphins" will be used to refer to both dolphins and porpoises). There are about forty dolphin and six porpoise species. Porpoises are members of the family Phocoenidae, and marine dolphins are members of the family Delphinidae.

Most dolphins are large, ranging in length from six to nine feet and weighing between 200 and 400 pounds. The smallest dolphin is the franciscana, which is about four feet long and weighs only 45 pounds.

The biggest dolphin is the killer whale, or orca. A full grown male orca can be about thirty-one feet long and weigh a whopping nine tons. Orcas can be recognized by their distinctive black and white coloring and mouthful of large, pointed teeth.

Orcas are fierce carnivores, preying on penguins, seals, and even fish. They will roam up to sixty-eight miles per day in search of food. Orcas are the only cetaceans that feed on homoiothermic animals. They have even been known to attack the enormous blue whale. The sight of these animals attacking whales gave them the name "whale killer," which later was reversed to "killer whale."

Orcas, however, do not attack humans. In captivity, they are quite gentle and can be taught to perform, even allowing humans to ride on their backs.

Because of their high intelligence and humanlike characteristics, dolphins are among the world's most beloved animals.

FACTS OF LIFE

- Bottlenose dolphins are found in the coastal waters of the continental shelf as well as the open sea. This is the species of dolphin most of us are familiar with (Flipper was a bottlenose dolphin). Like orcas, they are friendly, intelligent animals that can be taught to perform an impressive array of tricks.

- Other whales besides the orca, including the pilot whale, are actually dolphins. They are called "whales" only because they are larger than most dolphins.

- The spotted dolphin can jump twenty feet above the surface of the water. Other dolphins can perform similar acrobatics; the spinner dolphin gets its name from its ability to leap from the water and spin in the air. This playful animal sometimes makes seven or more complete turns in a single leap.

- Dolphins are long-lived animals, sometimes reaching forty years of age.

- Dolphins can hear well, but they have no sense of smell and little sense of taste.

- Like bats, many dolphins use echolocation to find food, especially in murky waters where visibility is poor. They can be amazingly accurate; a blindfolded bottlenose dolphin can distinguish a 2½-inch ball from one 2¼ inches in diameter from a distance of five feet.

- Like other cetaceans, dolphins lack vocal cords. But they make a variety of sounds, including clicking noises and whistles. Dolphins have a complex system of air channels and cavities in their heads that are connected to their blowholes. By some process not quite understood, air circulating through these channels seems to make the sounds. Dolphins have a bump, called a *melon*, on the front of their heads. This is filled with fatty tissue and oil that carries sound well. The melon also helps focus the clicks into a narrow stream of sound.

- Dolphins can make very loud noises. Scientists think that these noises can be loud enough to stun or even kill their prey.

- There are several species of river dolphins, among them the susus, which live in the Ganges and other Indian rivers. They have very small eyes and are almost blind. Susus catch their food by echolocation. They are the only dolphins to swim on their sides, feeling their way along the murky river bottoms with their fins. Susus are among the rarest species of dolphins. Because of pollution and habitat destruction, it is estimated that there are only several hundred left.

- The boutu, which lives in South America's Orinoco and Amazon rivers, is also called "the pink dolphin" because of the beautiful coral color of its skin. The source of this pinkish cast is probably the blood vessels right under the surface of the skin. Boutus in captivity tend to darken when placed in clear water.

- Like susus, boutus are in danger of extinction. Many fishermen consider them competitors for fish and shoot them on sight; others are caught in gill nets. There is also a market for the dried eyeballs and sexual organs of boutus, which are valued as aphrodisiacs in Brazil.

Dolphins and Humans: A Special Relationship

Many dolphins are friendly toward humans. Pelorus Jack was a Risso's dolphin that lived in New Zealand in the early nineteenth century. This dolphin used to greet steamships as they sailed across the outside of Pelorus Sound in Cook Strait and "hitch" rides on their bow waves, which are formed at the front of the ship as it passes through the water. A special order was issued in 1904 to protect the dolphin from being shot or harpooned. The playful dolphin inexplicably disappeared in 1912, after almost twenty-five years as a friendly and familiar sight in the New Zealand waters.

Another famous dolphin was Opo, who appeared in Hokianga Harbor, New Zealand, in 1955 near the little town of Opononi. A female bottlenose, she liked to swim and play with humans and give children "horseback rides." If one of the children became too rough, however, she would indignantly swim away and slap her tail against the water in protest. A sign near the beach read, "Welcome to Opononi, but don't try to shoot our Gay Dolphin." When Opo died, her body was pulled to shore and buried in a marked grave covered with flowers.

There are also many stories about dolphins who have rescued humans

Nets of Destruction

Dolphins like to swim over schools of yellowfin tuna. This was not a problem when tuna fishermen used traditional hook and line methods to catch fish. In the late fifties, however, the tuna industry began to switch to more efficient methods of catching fish, including gill netting. Gill nets are large panels, sometimes stretching for miles, that are hung vertically in the water. Fish can swim partway through the mesh, but are snagged by their fins or gills when they try to back out of the nets.

Gill and other types of nets (including purse seine nets, which can be closed like a change purse when full) enabled fishermen to catch much more fish, but, unfortunately, they also trapped other species, including dolphins. The number of dolphins caught in the nets is enormous. In Sri Lanka, it has been estimated that from 15,000 to 40,000 dolphins, representing over a dozen different species, may die each year in net fisheries. In 1990, the American public became aware of the problem, and leading tuna companies such as Starkist announced that they would no longer purchase tuna from fisheries that used gill nets.

Thousands of dolphins, however, still perish every year in fishing nets, especially in many developing nations where fishermen are reluctant to switch to less efficient, but less destructive, methods.

from danger. In May 1978, four people were lost in a thick fog off the coast of South Africa. They were safely guided through the dangerous waters by four dolphins, which nudged their boat along to safety. The Imagren, a fishing people who live on the edge of Africa's vast Sahara desert, use bottlenose and Atlantic humpbacked dolphins to help them catch mullet. Experienced fishermen can spot a passing mullet school by the slight change it causes in the ocean's color. One of them wades into the ocean and begins to violently beat the waters with a stick. Attracted by all the commotion, dolphins soon appear, racing toward the beach. The dolphins "herd" the mullet into a small area, and the fishermen surround the frightened fish with nets. The Imagren have been known to catch more than two tons of fish within a half hour with the help of the dolphins.

WHALES
The Baleen Whales

The suborder Mysticeti includes the right whales, gray whales, and rorquals (the blue, fin, sei, Bryde's, and minke whales). The mysticetes can be identified by the thin, fibrous plates of baleen that hang from their upper jaws inside the mouth. The whales skim krill and other small ocean animals through the baleen, sometimes eating tons of these creatures in a single feeding.

The length, number, and texture of baleen plates varies according to the species. The baleen of bowhead whales is the longest; it can be fifteen feet in length. The baleen of most other species is less than three feet. Most whales have 200 to 400 baleen plates, but the gray whale has only 140 to 180.

Baleen ranges in color from creamy white to blackish brown. Some species have coarsely textured baleen; others, such as the sei and southern right whales, have fine, almost silky baleen.

Baleen was once called *whalebone,* but it actually consists of a protein called keratin, the same substance that our nails and hair are made of. It was once softened, trimmed, and shaped into products such as whip handles, umbrella ribs, stiffening for collars, and the rib-crushing corsets that were the mainstay of early-nineteenth-century fashion. The huge demand for baleen, as well as the oil from these whales, drove some species to the point of extinction.

Like Captain Ahab in *Moby Dick,* these majestic cetaceans have captured the imagination of human beings for centuries. But today we know much more about whales than Herman Melville did.

FACTS OF LIFE

- There are four species of right whale: the southern right whale, which lives only in the Southern hemisphere, the Northern right whale, which lives exclusively in the Northern hemisphere, the bowhead whale, and the pygmy right whale. Right whales are full of oil, have long, finely textured baleen, and are curious and unafraid of ships. They also float when dead, qualities that made them the "right" species for early whalers to hunt. Today, right whales are among the rarest of cetaceans. Their population, which was estimated at 100,000 before commercial whaling, is only about 4,000 today.

- Whales can sometimes be seen *breaching* (jumping from the water and then crashing back onto the surface with a mighty splash) or *flippering* (beating the water with their tails or flippers). When one whale starts this kind of behavior, others often follow suit.

- Right whales can produce moans of 160 to 230 kHz and belches of 500 kHz (remember that humans cannot hear sounds above 20 kHz).

- The gray whale, which is about forty feet long and weighs from twenty-eight to thirty-eight tons, undertakes the longest migration of any mammal. Each October, when the breeding season begins, they travel from Alaska to Baja California—a 15,000-mile round trip. The whales arrive in the warm Mexican waters in January and stay there for a few months to breed.

- Gray whales are the only whales to feed on the ocean floor. They dine on small crustaceans attached to seaweed.

- Gray whales were often called "devil fish" or "hard heads" by whalers because they were so protective of their calves. They were known to ram ships in order to defend their young.

Big Blue

The rorquals are baleen whales that can be identified by their streamlined bodies, pointed heads, and small dorsal fins. They also have throat grooves, or pleats, that extend to the belly. This family includes the largest whale, the blue, as well as the minke, the smallest. The sei whale is the fastest whale in the ocean. A long, slender whale, it can cruise at ten to twelve miles per hour. The minke whale, one of the smallest cetaceans, grows to a length of about thirty feet. With 900,000 minkes in waters around the world, it is one the most plentiful whales in the world.

On the other hand, there are only about 10,000 blue whales left in the entire world, about one-fifth of the prewhaling population. The blue whale is the biggest animal that ever lived on earth. How big is big?

FACTS OF LIFE

- A blue whale can weigh 200 tons and can grow to over ten feet in length. A newborn blue weighs 7 tons!

- A blue whale's tongue weighs as much as an elephant. The largest dinosaur that ever lived weighed thirty to thirty-five tons; a blue whale weighs three to five times as much.

- A blue whale's heart weighs half a ton. The animal needs such an enormous organ to pump its 7 tons of blood through its 150-ton body. A whale's heart pumps very slowly, about nine times a minute, as compared to seventy-five times a minute for humans.

- The blue whale's mouth is twenty feet wide.

- Ironically, the blue whale, the world's largest animal, feeds on zooplankton, the world's smallest. A ninety-ton blue whale eats four tons of zooplankton a day.

● Besides being large, the blue whale is also noisy. The 180-decibel whistle produced by the blue whale is the loudest animal sound ever recorded. It equals the noise made by a navy cruiser traveling at normal speed.

Song of the Humpback

The humpbacked whale's scientific name, "Megaptera novaeangliae, meaning "winged New Englander," refers to the whale's whitish flippers, which are one-third the length of its body. Its common name comes from the way it humps its back prior to diving. Because they are relatively slow moving and tend to stay close to shore (qualities that made them targets of early whalers), humpbacks are favorites of whale watchers in Alaska and Hawaii. There are about 12,500 humpbacks in waters surviving from a prewhaling population of 125,000.

Humpbacked whales are known for their "songs." These "tunes" are made up of a distinct sequence of different noises, ranging from deep groans, moans, loud roars, and sighs to shrill squeaks and chirps. All humpbacks in the same area sing the same song, and each year's song is slightly different from that of the year before. Humpbacks from different waters sing different songs. Only the male humpbacks, however, sing. It is believed that they sing to warn off other males and to attract females.

The humpbacks' songs last up to ten minutes. The "winged New Englanders," however, would never win any Grammy awards, because they repeat the songs over and over again for hours at a time, like a record when the needle sticks! A 1970 recording of cetacean noises, however, Songs of the Humpback Whale, *has sold more than 100,000 copies.*

The Toothed Whales

The sperm whale is the best known odontocete. They get their names from the organs in front of their heads that contain spermaceti, a golden, waxlike substance that was once used to make a variety of products; spermaceti is so named because early whalers thought it was coagulated sperm. Sperm whales are the largest of the toothed whales. They can grow to be fifty-nine feet long and weigh up to forty-five tons. Females are significantly smaller, growing to be about thirty-nine feet in length. The most famous whale in fiction, Moby Dick, was a white sperm whale.

Sperm whales are the deepest divers among the whales. They can dive to depths of 1.75 miles and stay underwater for up to two hours. Sperm whales feed on giant squids, which can be as big as the whales themselves. Another whale by-product, *ambergris*, a waxy substance that develops in large, foul-smelling lumps in the whale's intestine, was once extensively used in perfumes.

Another odontocete, the beluga whale, or white whale, was once called the "sea canary" by whalers because of the high-pitched, birdlike sounds they make. Young belugas are bluish gray, but the adults are a beautiful creamy white. Belugas are found in deep, icy Arctic waters, but occasionally they make their way to the Yukon and St. Lawrence rivers and have even been sighted in the Rhine. Recent studies have shown that many of the belugas of the St. Lawrence are afflicted with bladder cancer, ulcers, and other diseases that are probably caused by toxins from the region's polluted waters.

The narwhal is related to the beluga. It is found in very cold arctic waters. Narwhals are unique in that they possess two teeth embedded in the upper jaw. In the male, the left tooth grows though the upper lip and forms a left-handed spiraling tusk that can weigh twenty pounds and reach nine feet. For this reason, the narwhal was once called "the unicorn whale."

The Yankee Whalers—Giant Killers of the Deep

When the Pilgrims first dropped anchor in a Cape Cod harbor on a frosty December day in 1620, they were amazed at the whales that swam around their ship, the Mayflower. *"If we had instruments and means to take them we might make a rich returne, which to our great grief we wanted," one of them later wrote. "We might have made three or foure thousand pounds of Oyle." Such a grand sum would have paid their emigration debts down to the last penny, with plenty left over.*

The Aleuts and other native peoples have hunted whales for centuries, but the Basques were the first people to hunt whales on a large scale. Starting in the twelfth century, they pursued the right whales in the Bay of Biscay, an inlet of the Atlantic between the western coast of France and the northern coast of Spain. They hunted them so ruthlessly that by the sixteenth century, the right whales had all but disappeared from this area. The Basques then built larger boats and sailed to the western North Atlantic as far as Newfoundland in search of whales, teaching the Dutch and other peoples how to whale along the way.

The American colonists wasted no time in catching up with their Basque predecessors. By 1664, Plymouth's Secretary Randolph was able to report to London that "the new Plymouth colony made great profit from whale killing." Although whales were hunted as far south as Long Island, New York, and Cape May, New Jersey, the cradle of "offshore whaling" was New England. Watchtowers were built from Puritan Cape Cod to

*Quaker Nantucket, and when a right whale was spotted, the wooden
whaling boats took off in hot pursuit of them. The whales were harpooned, dragged to shore, and cut up and boiled down to obtain their oil
and baleen. One large right whale could yield up to two tons of baleen
(top quality whalebone plates sold for a whooping $7.60 a pound) and
twenty-five tons of oil. If a whaleboat could capture just one large right
whale, it would pay for all the costs of the voyage, plus make hundreds of
thousands of dollars in profit. One whaling vessel made $850 dollars in
profit for every $500 invested.*

*The whaling industry changed forever on a stormy day in 1712,
when one Captain Christopher Hussey was blown out to sea. Far away
from land, the crew came upon a huge pod of sperm whales. They killed
one of the slow-moving cetaceans and towed it back to land. Not only
did the huge whale yield oil from its melted-down blubber, its enormous
head could produce up to a ton of the precious spermaceti, which was
used to make polishes, waxes, and fine candles (Nantucket's candle facto-
ry turned out 389 tons of sperm candles every year). The stinky, grayish
ambergris, used as a fixative in expensive perfumes, could be sold for $20
an ounce.*

*Besides ambergris and oil, other parts of the sperm whale could be
used. The liver was used to manufacture vitamins (one whale liver can
yield up to five pounds of vitamin A), and the tendons were used for tennis racquets strings and as catgut by surgeons to sew up wounds. Whale
skins were made into shoes, bicycle saddles, and suitcases. The bones were
ground into fertilizer, and the tissue was used to make glue.*

*The whalemen realized that the sperm whale and, later on, the slow-
swimming humpbacks, could make them very rich quickly (whale products could bring in so much money that sea captains sometimes gave
whales to their daughters as dowries). Less than three years after Captain
Hussey's famous catch, the first deep-sea whalers were setting out from
Nantucket. The importance of the sperm whale to New England's economy is illustrated by the fact that it is Connecticut's official state animal.*

*The beautiful homes that sea captains and ship owners built and
that still stand in such seaports as Mystic, New Bedford, and Cape Cod
are testimony to the wealth that whales could bring. Many ship captains
(who often owned the vessels they sailed in) came from socially prominent
families, but the crew members were generally from the lower classes of
New England society and included newly arrived immigrants as well as*

farm boys looking for adventure. Many of the sailors on whaling ships, particularly in New Bedford, which had a substantial black population, were African Americans, for the whaling industry, with its high turnover rate, was one of the few industries that would hire them.

A deep-sea whaling voyage could last from two to four years, and conditions on the ships were often harsh. The ship would leave port with a good supply of fresh fruits and vegetables and a cargo of live chickens and pigs, but soon these sources of food would be depleted and the sailors would have to rely on such unsavory dishes as lobscouse, hard biscuits mixed with the greasy water left over after boiling salt pork or beef. With such poor food, nutritional disorders were common; on one ship, half the men died from scurvy, a disease caused by a lack of vitamin C in the diet. Men were often given a "taste o' the cat" (cat-of-nine-tails) for minor infractions, until Congress passed a law prohibiting flogging aboard merchant ships and whalers. Life was so miserable aboard the whaling ships that the captains were reluctant to stay too long in any one port, for fear that the men would desert.

To pass the time, the men told stories, sang songs, or carved whale teeth (a sperm whale's tooth can be nine inches long). The pieces that they made, including clothespins, boxes, and other objects, both decorative and useful, became known as scrimshaw (probably from the Dutch word skrimshander, meaning "to whittle the time away"). Some scrimshaw is so finely carved that it is still admired today.

Sometimes captains' wives accompanied their husbands on the voyages. Some seamen derisively referred to ships carrying women aboard as "hen frigates," but on other vessels, their presence was welcome. When the crew of the ship Powhatan came down with smallpox, a captain's wife, Caroline Mayhew, nursed them back to health. She even took over the navigation of the ship when her husband came down with the dreaded disease. Her husband later wrote, "to my utter astonishment, we all got through without losing a man." The grateful crew presented Mrs. Mahew with dozens of scrimshaw. Another whaling wife, Mrs. Charles Norton, was hanging out her wash on deck when she saw the spout of a whale in the distance. As it turned out, it was a large one that yielded many barrels of oil. Mrs. Norton was rewarded with a silver dollar, which the captain usually gave to the first man to sight a whale.

Ships could go for days before sighting a whale until one sailor, swaying high above the deck in the crow's nest, gave the much awaited cry, *"thar she blows!" Experienced sailors could often tell the species of whale from its spout. The right whale has a* **V***-shaped spout. The humpback's is shaped like an upside-down pear, whereas the blue whale's blow reaches about thirty feet and is shaped like a cone. The minke whale blows to a height of only three feet, but a medium-sized blow slanting forward and to the left meant that one of the coveted sperm whales was close by.*

Upon sighting the whale, several catcher boats, each loaded with about six men and more than 1,000 tons of gear, were lowered from the mother ship. Setting out after the whale, they tried to get near enough to harpoon it in the head, as close to the eye as possible. Such a huge animal is difficult to kill, however, and many a whale, enraged and in pain, would take the crewmen on a "Nantucket sleigh ride," towing the small boat for miles at such a fast pace that one man would be kept busy pouring water over the rope to keep it from burning! It could be hours or even days before the whale, weak and exhausted, finally bled to death.

The carcass was then towed back to the mother ship, where the dirty and dangerous job of flensing (cutting and removing the skin and blubber) began. The baleen was hacked away and, along with the precious oil, was stored in the holds of the ship. The rest of the carcass was abandoned at sea.

From 1825 to 1860, whaling was in its Golden Age. In 1846, more than 700 whaling ships left U.S. ports, most of them from New England. For many years, Nantucket was the region's most important seaport, but by 1846, another Quaker town, New Bedford, had succeeded it as the world's whaling center. Indeed, whaling was the lifeblood of the Massachusetts town. Ralph Waldo Emerson, who once taught in New Bedford, wryly remarked, "They have all the equipment for a whaler ready, and they hug an oil cask like a brother." In 1857, New Bedford's whaling fleet, worth more than $12 million and numbering 329 ships, employed 12,000 seamen and brought in $6 million worth of whaling products.

Sailors were not the only ones to earn their living from whales; others worked as suppliers to the trade. New Bedford's James Durbee, for example, manufactured and sold 58,517 harpoons between 1828 and 1868, and he was only one of New Bedford's ten manufacturers of whaling implements.

In 1849, however, when gold was discovered in California, many sailors left the New England ports to seek their fortune as "forty-niners." The whaling industry suffered another serious blow when petroleum was discovered in western Pennsylvania in 1859. Lubricants and lighting fuels made from the "black gold" replaced much of the whale oils that were used for lighting.

The Civil War dealt another death blow to the industry. Many whaleboats were refitted as battleships and pressed into service by the Union Army. Others were captured and destroyed by the Confederates. After the war, the whaling industry shifted to San Francisco, but it was never to regain the glory of its early years. Ships were left to rot on dilapidated wharves as Cape Cod, Martha's Vineyard, and other New England towns became fashionable summer resorts. In 1869, the last whaler left Nantucket, never to be seen or heard from again.

The Yankee whalers made more than an economic contribution to the nation's early history. In their never-ending search for new whaling grounds, they broadened the young nation's horizons, traveling to strange and exotic places and often gaining invaluable information about the world around them. It was a Nantucket sea captain, Timothy Folger, who first charted the Gulf Stream, that great ocean current that runs from the Caribbean to Europe. His cousin, a Philadelphia publisher named Benjamin Franklin, asked him to sketch a picture of it for him. Franklin was so impressed that he printed it, explaining that his relative was "extremely well acquainted with the Gulf Stream." Altogether, more than 400 Pacific islands were discovered and named by American whalemen.

Back From the Brink

Whalers knew for years that the giant cetaceans were becoming more and more scarce and that they had to go farther and farther out to sea to find them, but hunting still continued. In 1911, the British Museum undertook a study that found that the population of Antarctic whales was very low. Alarmed, the scientific community urged a ban on whaling activities, but their recommendations were ignored. The League of Nations produced a convention to regulate whaling, which was also disregarded. Whaling was big business, and many nations were unwilling to give up such a lucrative trade. By the 1930s, although some species such as the right whale were given protection under international treaties, many whales were on the verge of extinction. For example, the world population of blue whales had been reduced to one hundred. Finally, in 1946, the International Whaling Commission was formed. The IWC set quotas on the number of whales that could be caught. This quota limited the number of "blue whale units" each country could catch. A "blue whale unit" was calculated as 1 blue whale = 2 fin whales = 2.5 humpback whales = 6 sei whales.

Unfortunately, this system proved to be a failure, because the whalers hunted the largest whale (the blue whale) first. When the blue whale population had been decimated, they turned to the fin whales, and then to the humpbacks. This overhunting continued until only the minke whales were left in any significant numbers.

As environmental awareness increased throughout the 1970s and 1980s, more and more pressure was put on whaling nations to stop their whaling activities. Organizations such as Greenpeace engaged in dramatic confrontations with whalers, resulting in the sinking of one of the environmental group's ships, The Rainbow Warrior. More and more species were offered protection, and the last whaling station in the United States was closed in the early 1970s. Finally in 1986, an "indefinite moratorium" on whaling was put in effect.

In May 1993, the IWC renewed the whaling ban (native peoples such as the Inuit are allowed to kill twenty to thirty whales each year). Japan, however, still kills a small number of whales each year for "scientific purposes" (most of the whale meat, however, ends up in gourmet shops, where it sells for $55 a pound).

Other nations besides Japan continue to hunt whales. Iceland, which recently quit the IWC, has announced plans to continue whaling in the future. In June 1993, Norwegian whalers began to harvest minke whales, arguing that since minkes are so numerous (an estimated 86,700 live off the Norwegian coast alone), a controlled hunt would not harm the species. They were supported in this claim by the scientific committee of the IWC, which decided that this species of whale could tolerate a limited hunt. Nevertheless, Norway's action prompted some environmental groups to organize boycotts of the $1 billion dollars in Norwegian goods imported annually to the United States, and also of the 1994 Winter Olympics in Lillehammer.

Even if all whale hunting ended tomorrow, however, whales would still be in danger. Eight of the nine species of "great" whales found in North American waters (the gray, right, blue, fin, sei, humpback, bowhead, and sperm) are classified as endangered under the Endangered Species Act (the Bryde's whale is neither threatened or endangered). Today's whales face dangers that the whalemen of yesteryear could have never envisioned, including collisions with large ships, entanglement in fishing nets, and pollution.

Chapter Nine

LEAPIN' LAGOMORPHS: RABBITS, HARES, AND PIKAS

Rabbits, hares, and pikas belong to the order Lagomorpha. There are fifty-four species and they are found everywhere in the world except Antarctica. At one time, the members of the group were classified with the rodents, because both groups of animals have long front incisors that are continually growing. Lagomorphs, however, have four upper front teeth instead of the rodents' two.

Rabbits and hares look similar, but there are several important differences. Hares are generally larger, longer, and lankier than rabbits. Hares hop and leap, sometimes to great heights, whereas rabbits run and scamper.

Rabbits live in underground burrows, while hares live out in the open in shallow depressions called *forms*. A hare may have several forms: one for sunning and another located under a shady bush for keeping cool.

The most important difference between the two, however, has to do with the young of each species. Rabbit babies, called bunnies, are born blind, hairless, and helpless, while young hares, or leverets, come into the world with their eyes open and with a full coat of fur. Leverets are capable of hopping soon after they are born.

Pikas, small animals with round ears, look more like hamsters than rabbits. There are fourteen species, most of which live in colonies among rocks, usually at altitudes from 8,000 to 14,000 feet. Unlike rabbits and hares, pikas are quite noisy, often communicating to one another with whistling, high-pitched sounds. Pikas are diurnal, meaning they are active during daylight hours.

Rabbits and hares are *crepuscular*, meaning that they come out at twilight to forage for food and remain active until sunrise. They spend the daylight hours resting.

All lagomorphs digest most of their food twice, in a process called *coprophagy*. The undigested food passes through their bodies in the form of moist, soft pellets, which the animal immediately eats. As disgusting as this sounds, these pellets are rich in vitamin B and supply the animal with important nutrients.

We have all heard the phrase, "breeding like rabbits," and it is true that these animals have a very high rate of reproduction. Lagomorphs reproduce very rapidly. They can bear four to five litters per year. A single pair of cottontails and their offspring could produce 300,000 young in five years! Few of the young, however, survive to adulthood. Rabbits and hares are a popular food for many animals, including foxes, hawks and other large birds, and domestic dogs and cats. Their greatest enemy, though, is man, who poisons, hunts, and traps them. Many more are killed unintentionally by pesticides, farm machinery, and cars. It is no wonder, then, that scientists estimate 85 percent of all cottontails and 70 percent of all hares perish before their first birthdays. Those that make it have short lives: wild lagomorphs have a lifespan of about one year, although domestic rabbits can live up to ten years.

Because of their high rate of reproduction and voracious appetites, rabbits can become serious pests, as was the case in Australia in the last century. In 1859, an English settler imported a dozen pairs of wild European rabbits from Great Britain to an estate in Victoria province, intending to use them as game animals. The rabbits, however, soon escaped. Because there were no natural predators to control them, in just a few years, there were hundreds of thousands of rabbits hopping through the countryside, devouring acres of grass and destroying the grazing lands used by sheep.

There were numerous attempts to try to control the rabbits, including trapping, poisoning, shooting, even building a 2,000-mile fence, but nothing seemed to work. Finally, as a last resort, rabbits infected with a deadly disease called myxomatosis were deliberately released into the countryside (myxomatosis is fatal only to wild European rabbits; it does not affect cottontails or hares). The disease spread quickly from one rabbit to another and was also carried by mosquitoes. Soon the landscape was littered with heaps of tiny corpses, and Australia was finally free of its rabbit plague.

On a more pleasant note, rabbits make pleasant and easy-to-care-for companion animals. They can be taught to walk on a leash and even to use cat litter. Thousands of people raise rabbits as a hobby. All domestic rabbits are descended from European wild rabbit. Rabbit breeding probably began in the sixteenth century, when monks raised and selectively bred them. Here are some of the more interesting varieties:

- *Angora rabbit.* The Angora can be black, white, or other colors. It has a beautiful, silky coat that is called wool rather than fur. The rabbit's wool grows to about three inches and can produce four ounces of wool every three months. The animal is not killed for its wool; it is gently plucked from the rabbit by hand. Wool from the Angora rabbit is spun into a soft, fluffy yarn and made into sweaters, blankets, and other articles. Angora wool is expensive, selling for about $30 to $40 a pound (regular sheep's wool sells for approximately $3 to $10 per pound).

- *Belgian hare.* This lagomorph is not a hare at all, but a rabbit. Originally from Flanders in Belgium, this species made its American debut in the late 1800s and is the oldest species of domestic rabbit in the United States. It is called "the racehorse of the rabbit family" because of its long, lanky appearance and strong but slender legs.

- *Champagne D'Argent.* This rabbit comes from the French province of Champagne. It is an old breed, having been mentioned in French journals dating back to 1730. The bunnies of this breed are black when first born, but gradually turn silver as they mature—hence the name, "silver rabbit from Champagne."

- *Flemish Giant.* This is the largest domestic breed, weighing up to fifteen pounds. Another Belgian emigré, it is known for its pleasant disposition.

- *French Lop.* Lop rabbits have ears that "lop," or hang down. Lops are also an old breed, having originated in England in 1810. There are several varieties, including the English lop, whose ears can be twenty-five inches or longer.

- *New Zealand white.* This is the pink-eyed "Easter bunny" rabbit. It is also the number one meat rabbit in the country and is the species of rabbit most often used in laboratory experiments.

Chapter Ten

THE PRIMATES

T he primates constitute 195 species, including man. The members of this group have a number of features in common, including large, well-developed brains, grasping hands and feet with flat nails instead of claws, and complex social structures. Scientists who study primates are called *primatologists*.

THE PROSIMIANS

The most primitive primates belong to the suborder Prosimii. This group of small and medium-sized animals includes the mouse lemurs, true lemurs, indris, the aye-aye, lorises, bushbabies, and tarsiers. The first four species are found only on the island nation of Madagascar. The loris family inhabits southern and southeastern Asia and Africa; the three species of tarsiers are found in Sumatra, Borneo, the Celebes, and the Philippine island of Mindanao. Bushbabies are found in varous parts of sub-Saharan Africa. Most prosimians are nocturnal and arboreal.

Promsimians vary greatly in appearance, from the tiny mouse lemur, which, as its name implies, resembles a rodent, to the catlike black lemur. The smallest primates are the gray mouse lemur of Madagascar, which weighs less than three ounces and measures about five inches, and the pygmy marmoset, which is found along the upper reaches of the Amazon River in Ecuador,

Lemurs are among the most primitive of the primates. Courtesy of the Zoological Society of Philadelphia.

Columbia, northern Peru, and western Brazil. This tiny, chattering creature measures between five and six and a half inches (the marmoset's tail adds another six inches or so) and weighs less than three pounds. (On the other hand, the largest primates, gorillas, can grow to be six feet tall and weigh 600 pounds—and some hominids can weigh even more!)

Rare and beautiful, lemurs are fast disappearing from the jungles of Madagascar as these areas are being cleared for cultivation. The word *lemur* comes from the Latin *lemures*, meaning "ghost," referring to these animals' quick, agile movements. Since human beings arrived on the island of Madagascar one or two thousand years ago, fourteen lemur species have become extinct. Lemurs are sometimes called "sun children" because of their fondness for sunning themselves in the treetops.

The ringtailed lemur, as its Latin name, *Lemur catta*, implies, looks like a cross between a cat and a raccoon. The ring-tailed lemur has glands containing a strong-smelling substance on its forearms. During the mating season, males often have "stink fights," spraying each other with the odious fluid.

MONKEYS

Monkeys, apes, and man are classified as *anthropoids*. The monkeys are further divided into two groups. The New World monkeys of Central and South America (there are no primates in North America, although fossils of prosimians have been found) belong to the family Cebidae and includes squirrel monkeys, marmosets, howler monkeys, and others.

The Old World monkeys belong to the family Cercopithecidae. Including some seventy-six species, this group has a much broader range than the cebids and can be found in northwest to sub-Saharan Africa, southern and southeastern Asia, and the Philippines and Japan. The cercopithecids include such animals as baboons, mandrills, and languars.

There are several differences between the cebids and cercopithecids. New World monkeys can be distinguished by their prehensile tails, sometimes referred to as a "fifth hand" because of its usefulness in grasping objects. The cebids also have widely separate nostrils that flare to the side, whereas the nostrils of the cercopithecids are close together and open downwards. Old World monkeys often have tough, brightly colored callouses on their rumps, a characteristic lacking in their New World cousins. Both New and Old World monkeys are popular attractions in zoos because of their clever and amusing antics.

New World Monkeys

The capuchin monkey is named after the Capuchin monks, who wear cloaks that come down in a V over their foreheads, just like the brown hairs of this cebid. The capuchin was once used by organ grinders to beg for coins on city streets in the early part of this century (according to the *Philadelphia Inquirer*, there are only six authentic organ grinders left in the United States).

One of the most beautiful monkeys is the golden lion marmoset. The size of a squirrel, it is also called the golden lion tamarin. It has a leonine mane of silky golden hair surrounding its hairless face. This marmoset, of which there are three subspecies, can be found only in the coastal mountains of southwest Rio de Janeiro, where it lives in the tropical forests. Unlike other monkeys, marmosets often give birth to twins. In the nineteenth century, many golden lion marmosets were taken from the wild for the pet trade—as it was all the rage for fashionable ladies to travel about town with one of the tiny, chattering monkeys perched on her shoulder. Today, because of deforestation, the marmosets are in serious danger of extinction; it is estimated that there are only about 400 of them left. A breeding program has been implemented by the National Zoo in conjunction with other organizations, and some of the little monkeys have already been released into their native environment in the wilds of Brazil.

The howler monkeys, which live in the tropical forests of Central and South America, get their names from the loud "howls" they make, which can be heard up to two miles away. Troops of howler monkeys often give a collective "dawn roar" loud enough to rouse any animal in the jungle.

The red uakari of the upper Amazon has a bright red, hairless face that contrasts with its reddish-brown fur. When one of them is ill, however, the face turns pale pink. An angry uakari's face glows bright red, which is usually enough to frighten their enemies away. They are quiet animals, but sometimes emit sounds that sound like a human's hysterical laughter. Unlike other cebids, they lack a prehensile tail. Uakaris are very rare because they are hunted by the Indians of the region for their flesh. Unfortunately, they usually do not survive very long in captivity.

The owl monkey, also called the night monkey, is the only nocturnal cebid. It gets its name from its huge, round eyes and the owllike hoots it makes. The male monkeys, however, are the only ones that make this sound, and they seem to do it only on clear nights when the moon is full.

Old World Monkeys

The macaques (pronounced ma-*kaks*), a group of large ground-dwelling cercopithecids with doglike faces, belong to the genus *Macaca*. Ranging throughout Asia from Japan to the tropical equatorial regions, macaques are the most widely distributed primate group next to humans. Many species have cheek pouches in which they store food to eat at a later time. Perhaps the best-known example of this group is the rhesus macaque, commonly known as the rhesus monkey. The rhesus is the species most often used in scientific experiments. The establishment of the rhesus blood factor (Rh) and the Salk polio vaccine developed from experiments done with this animal.

Though most primates live in tropical climates and do not tolerate the cold well, the Japanese macaque is an exception. It makes its home in the mountains of northern Honshu, where the winter temperature often dips below freezing. Sometimes called snow monkeys, these macaques often keep warm by submerging themselves in the hot volcanic pools that are found in this area. The Japanese macaque is the largest of the macaques.

The Barbary ape is not an ape at all, but a cercopithecid, the only macaque found in Africa. It is also the only species of primate native to Europe. These large monkeys are found in North Africa and also on the tiny island of Gibraltar on the southern tip of Spain, where they mingle freely with humans and some-times raid gardens and orchards. Males of this species often groom, carry, and cradle infants, a behavior that scientists believe reduces tension between males in the group.

The pig-tailed macaques of Malaysia have been trained to pick coconuts in southern Thailand and Malaysia. Their skills are in such demand that there is a "Monkey Training College" in Thailand. The monkeys start training at six months. A well-trained coconut macaque can pick 500 coconuts a day, while a top performer can pick between 700 and 800! The monkeys are "paid" for their work with bananas!

The patas monkey of northwestern Africa is sometimes called the military monkey, because its reddish coat and white mustache make it look as if it were wearing a uniform. It is the fastest primate, reaching speeds of 35 miles per hour. Troops of patas monkeys can number up to one hundred.

The proboscis monkey of Borneo is distinguished by its huge, flabby nose, which may hang down over its mouth. The female has an upturned nose that is smaller than that of the male, but is still larger than that of most other mon-key species. The proboscis monkey uses its big nose to give loud resounding "honks" when in danger.

The black and white colobus monkey of central Africa was once widely hunted for its beautiful black and white pelts. It is estimated that 2 million of these animals were killed for their fur. The colobus monkeys are closely relat-ed to the langurs. One species of langur, the entellus, or Hanuman langur, is the sacred monkey of India. These langurs are allowed to roam freely through the streets of India and even live on the grounds of Hindu temples.

Many langurs are *folivorous*, meaning that they feed largely on leaves. The spectacled langur of southeast Asia often eats leaves that taste bad to other animals. Bacteria in these monkeys' stomachs neutralize the leaves' toxic chem-icals and ensure a food supply that is unappealing to other species.

Baboons, like macaques, spend most of their time on the ground. The best-known species is the hamadryas baboon. This baboon, found in dry, rocky areas in northeast Africa and southern Arabia, lives in groups that can number as many as 200 individuals, led by a large dominant male. Hamadryas baboons were once domesticated as pets in ancient Egypt. The baboons were also used to harvest fruit from fig trees (work that was also done by children and dwarfs) because they were lighter than grown men.

THE LESSER APES

The gibbons and siamangs, sometimes called the lesser apes, are found throughout southeast Asia to Sumatra and Borneo. These animals make up their own family, Hylobatidae. The lesser apes have a highly developed *brachiating ability*—that is, the ability to swing rapidly from branch to branch, using a hand-over-hand motion.

The gibbons are the smallest and most agile of the apes. In Java, some gibbons are called *wau-wau*, meaning "old woman," because of their humanlike facial expressions. With long arms that reach down to their ankles, they can jump as far as forty-five feet from one branch to another. They are so fast that they can capture a bird in flight.

Despite their small size (gibbons generally weigh from twelve to twenty pounds and are seldom taller than three feet), they are very strong. Gibbons in captivity have been known to seize adult humans and pull them up against the bars of their cages.

Siamangs live on the islands of Sumatra and Malaysia. They closely resemble gibbons but are larger and darker. The two species have not been known to interbreed in the wild, but in the summer of 1979, the mating of a female siamang and a male gibbon at Atlanta's Grant Park Zoo resulted in the birth of a hybrid called a siabon, which was named Shaun-Shaun.

THE GREAT APES

The orangutan, gorillas, chimpanzees, and bonobos belong to the family Pongidae. The pongids are the most advanced primates next to man. These apes are able to walk upright, but are usually *quadrupedal*, walking on all fours.

Chimpanzees

The chimpanzee is the smallest of the great apes and the one most closely related to man. There are two species: the common chimpanzee (*Pan troglodytes*) and the bonobo (*Pan paniscus*), sometimes called the pygmy chimpanzee. The common chimpanzee lives in west and central Africa and as far east as Tanzania. It is the species found most often in zoos.

Bonobos are found in the Congo basin and are smaller and much darker than the common chimpanzees. Many primatologists also consider them to be more intelligent than common chimpanzees. Common chimps are both terrestrial and arboreal. Bonobos spend most of their time in trees. Both species, however, build sleeping nests in trees about one hundred feet off the ground.

Both *P. troglodytes* and *P. paniscus* are in danger of extinction, but many live in captivity.

Chimps occasionally live alone, but usually can be found in groups that range in size from twenty to a hundred individuals. These groups are called *communities*. These communities may break up into smaller groups of six or eight when the chimps travel, groom, feed, and rest throughout the day. Chimp communities are led by a dominant, or alpha, male. The structure of these groups, however, is more fluid than those of other species, such as hamadryas baboons. As the females grow up, they migrate to other communities. The strongest bond in the chimp's world is between mother and child. Chimp babies can remain with their mother for up to ten years, but even when they are older and have left the group, they will sometimes come back to visit their moms.

Chimps spend from five to six hours a day feeding and foraging for food. They were once thought to be strict vegetarians, but they also eat meat, including baboons and other monkeys. Chimps are very strong and male chimps have been known to slam a small baboon against the ground to kill it. Chimps can be dangerous but will usually flee rather than fight if threatened.

Chimps are among the elite group of animals that use tools. They will place a stick in a termite mound, and as the insects come out the ground and crawl up the stick, they will lick them off. They also use a crumpled leaf to soak up water.

Like humans, a chimp's facial expression is often a clue to its emotional state. When frightened, a chimp draws back its upper lip and exposes its teeth. When happy, the face is relaxed, and the chimp sometimes makes an "oh-oh" sound that turns into a bark. A sad chimp will throw its head back, open its mouth wide, and shut its eyes. Chimps, however, like other nonhuman primates, do not shed tears.

Gorillas

Paul Du Chaillu, a nineteenth-century explorer, wrote that the (lowland) gorilla reminded him of "some hellish dream creature—a being of that hideous order, half-man, half-beast." For many years, gorillas were thought to be savage monsters that attacked humans unprovoked and tore them limb from limb, devouring their flesh with relish. Researchers such as Jane Goodall, George Schaller, and the late Dian Fossey discovered that these tales were entirely untrue, for despite their formidable appearance, gorillas are peaceful vegetarians and will attack only if threatened.

*Gorillas like the Philadelphia Zoo's "Snickers" are dangerously close to extinction.
Courtesy of the Zoological Society of Philadelphia.*

Grand Performance

When they feel threatened, mountain gorillas sometimes engage in something called a display. All gorillas do this, even the infants, but only the silverback puts on the full performance.

The display starts with a loud screaming and hooting, followed by symbolic feeding, such as placing a leaf in between the lips. The silverback then raises to his full height and slaps his hands to his chest, belly, or thigh, or sometimes even another gorilla, making a sound that can be heard a mile away. The silverback stands erect, pulling up vegetation from the ground and trees and hitting everything in his path, including the other members of the group. The display finally ends with the silverback beating the palm of his hand on the ground.

The species *Gorilla gorilla* includes two subspecies: the lowland gorilla of the Cameroon, Gabon, and Zaire, and the mountain gorilla of Uganda, Rwanda, and Tanzania. Gorillas spend most of their time on the ground. Adults venture into the trees only to build sleeping nests, though young gorillas often play in trees.

Gorillas are social animals, living in groups of two to thirty individuals, which are led by an older male called a "silverback" because of the saddle of gray hairs on his back (when a male gorilla is over ten years old, his fur starts to turn gray). They have many characteristics in common with humans. They form close family units, and, like human beings, they are left- or right-handed (left-handed gorillas will even pound their chests with their left hands!).

Both subspecies of gorilla are in serious danger of extinction, mainly due to habitat destruction and poaching. There are about 600 gorillas in captivity throughout the world, and the number is slowly increasing. Because gorillas raised together usually do not mate, zoos have started gorilla exchange programs with the hopes that the gorillas will form new social groups and reproduce.

Orangutans

The orangutan dwells in the forests of Borneo and Sumatra. It has orange red fur and can weigh up to 165 pounds. The word "orangutan" means "person of the forest" in Malay. There are two subspecies: the Sumatran orangutan and the Bornean orangutan. The females of the species look very much alike, but Sumatran males are taller and slimmer than their Bornean cousins and, when mature, have a long mustache and beard. The Bornean males are often darker than the Sumatran subspecies and have huge cheek flaps and a pouch under the skin.

Young orangutans stay with their mothers for as long as seven years.
Courtesy of the Zoological Society of Philadelphia.

In captivity, orangs adapt well to living in groups, but in the wild, adult males live alone, coming together with females on a temporary basis for mating. They are cautious and slow, rarely brachiating more than three to four yards a time with their long arms, which can reach eight feet. Orangs are called "imperfect brachiators" because they are too heavy to move swiftly through the trees. They sometimes fall out of trees—it is estimated that one-third of orangs have broken bones from such falls by the time they are grown.

Like other pongids, orangs are very strong. In their native lands, they are said to be able to kill crocodiles with their bare hands. But because of habitat destruction, orangutans are severely endangered. There are only about 4,000 of them left in the wild, and many primatologists believe that there will be few, if any, remaining in Sumatra and Borneo by the year 2000.

Chapter Eleven

ELEPHANT WALK: THE MIGHTY PROBISCIDEANS

Once upon a time, when the earth was still young, North Africa, now a desert, was a tropical paradise. Buzzing insects, some with wingspans of several feet, sailed through the humid air, and giant ferns and brilliant flowers filled the jungle with color. Strange beasts roamed through the forest, among them a peculiar little animal about two feet high. Called Moeritherium because its remains were first discovered on the shores of Egypt's Lake Mocris, this creature, which had a flexible snout and tiny tusks, was the distant ancestor of our modern elephants.

Over the course of the centuries, Moeritherium evolved into other animals of the order Probosicidea, including the first true elephant, Stegadon. Stegadon was nearly ten feet tall, had ridged teeth, and a long flexible trunk, the first probosicidean to have this true elephant feature.

From Stegadon developed the mammoths, including the famous woolly mammoths. Fossils of these massive animals, who were covered with coarse wool and long hair, have been found in Europe, Asia, and North America. In the Middle Ages, the remains of these animals were thought to be dragon bones.

Some of these mammoth remains have been remarkably well preserved. The flesh of the Beresouka mammoth, found in the frozen wastes of northeastern Siberia in 1900, was so unspoiled that the sled dogs of its discoverers greedily ate some of it.

The largest, however, was the imperial mammoth, which stood about fourteen feet tall and weighted up to twenty tons. The imperial mammoth lived on the grasslands of what is now the western and southwestern United States, as well as in Mexico.

Mammoths and another elephantlike creature, the mastodon, were an important food source for early man. Cave paintings from around the world show our ancestors hunting them. When archaeologists excavated a prehistoric hunter's camp in Predmost in Czechoslovakia, they found the bones of over 1,000 mammoths. Ancient men killed so many mammoths that in some places houses were constructed with mammoth bones instead of wood.

The last of the mammoths vanished at the end of the Ice Age, about 10,000 years ago. Scientists are unsure as to exactly what killed them. One theory is that the melting of the glaciers brought about a widespread change of climate, altering the character of the vegetation that the mammoths were accustomed to eating. With their food supply gone, of course, the mammoths starved.

About 350 species of proboscideans once roamed the earth, dwelling in every continent except Antarctica and Australia. Today, however, only two species are left: *Loxodonta africana*, the African elephant, and *Elephas maximus*, the Indian elephant. The two species never interbreed. Elephants are the largest land-living animals; only the great whales are larger.

The African elephant includes two subspecies: the bush elephant, which lives on the broad, grassy savannahs and the smaller, darker forest elephant. Elephants once lived throughout Africa, but are now found only in scattered populations in the sub-Saharan region. The total African elephant population, most of which is found in wildlife preserves, numbers about 600,000; the forest elephant accounts for about 35 percent of this total.

The Indian elephant is found in southeast Asia, from Sri Lanka and India to the islands of Sumatra and Borneo. Of the several subspecies of Indian elephant, there are about 35,000 left in the world today; about one third of them are domesticated. Indian elephants, usually females, are almost always the species found in circuses, because they are more docile and easier to train than the African variety.

African elephants are larger than the Indian species. There are several other differences between the two types, shown in the table on page 127.

AFRICAN ELEPHANT	ASIAN ELEPHANT
Color: Dark gray	Usually a lighter gray; may have light splotches over the body.
Size: Length of head and body, including trunk, up to 24.8 feet; shoulder height, up to 13 feet; weight may exceed 6 tons.	Length of head and body, including trunk, up to 21.3 feet,; shoulder height, 8.2–10.5 feet; weight up to 5.9 tons. As with the African elephant, females are somewhat smaller.
Tusks: Long tusks are found in both males and females. Average tusks measure 6 to 8 feet in the bull elephant, but are smaller in females.	Shorter than in the African elephant, measuring from 4 to 5 feet in bulls. In the female, the tusks are tiny or nonexistent. A subspecies in Sumatra is tuskless.
Ears: Large ears that can measure over a yard across. The forest elephant has smaller ears than the bush elephant.	Much smaller than in the African elephant.
Forehead: Flat forehead.	Two bumps on forehead.
Trunks: Ends in two fleshy lobes, sometimes called "fingers." The trunk has definite ridges.	Smoother trunk that ends in one "finger."
Other Differences: African elephant has three nails on hind leg, twenty-one pairs of ribs, and a concave, or sway, back.	Indian elephant has four nails on hind foot, nineteen pairs of ribs, and a convex back.

FAMILY STRUCTURE

Both African and Indian elephants have one thing in common: a complex social structure. Herds are led by an old cow, known as the matriarch. Her herd usually consists of her daughters and granddaughters, as well as her sisters and their offspring of both sexes. The young bulls, however, leave or are forced out of the herd when they reach maturity, between twelve and sixteen years of age.

Female elephants all take part in raising the young; an elephant mother will sometimes suckle one of her relative's calves. The herd will also take in young elephants who have been orphaned. The matriarch will not permit adult bulls to live within the herd on a daily basis. When one of the females comes into *oestrus* (meaning she is ready to mate), however, the bulls often hang around the fringes of the herd, vying for the fertile female's attention.

Mature bulls spend most of their time alone. Sometimes they form groups with other male elephants, but these bachelor herds are not based on strong, long-term social bonds, as the female-led groups are. When bull elephants are in their mid-twenties, they experience the onset of musth, a period devoted to mating and fighting with other males, sometimes to the death.

Elephants have the longest gestation period of any animal—twenty-two months, almost two years! A newborn elephant calf can be three feet tall and weigh 200 pounds. Like dolphins, elephant mothers are assisted in their deliveries by "aunties," usually older cows. Baby elephants are covered with hair, have tiny "milk tusks," and trunks that are all but useless. It will be about six months before they learn to use them. The mother elephant suckles the calf from two to seven years. Elephant calves often fall prey to lions, tigers, and even snakes; it has been estimated that only one out of three calves survive to adulthood.

ENORMOUS APPETITES

Elephants eat incredible amounts of food. They forage for food for about sixteen out of every twenty-four hours. A single bull elephant can drink 30 gallons of water and consume as much as 600 pounds of food a day. They are strict vegetarians who eat grasses, fruits, bark, and roots. They are also very wasteful eaters, pushing over trees with their huge foreheads, stripping off branches and bark, and strewing leftovers as they dine. Elephants will travel as much as twenty miles per day in their search for food.

Elephants digest only about half of the food they eat; 44 to 48 percent is excreted as waste. It has been estimated that one third of the tree species in West African forests depend on elephants to eat their fruit and disperse their seeds through their dung.

In areas where elephants live in close proximity with humans, the giant pachyderms occasionally raid crops, inflicting a great deal of damage—a few elephants can ruin a banana grove in an evening. For this reason, they are considered pests in some parts of Africa and Asia.

Elephants have huge teeth, each one weighing from eight to nine pounds. They have one set of four teeth at a time, one in each half of the upper and

My Achy Breaky Head

In ancient Asia, the awesome strength of elephants was sometimes used for a grisly purpose—the animals were used as executioners. The unfortunate victim was forced to place his head on a raised log or other platform, hands tied behind his back. Upon being given a special signal, the elephant would raise its massive foot and—well, you can guess the rest.

lower jaw. All their teeth are molars, used for grinding the vegetable matter the elephant eats. As one set of teeth wears down and falls out, new ones come in to replace them.

During its lifetime, the elephant gets six sets of teeth, one after another. When the last set of teeth is worn down, the elephant starves, because it cannot chew its food.

ELEPHANTS AT WORK

Today, African elephants are rarely domesticated, but their Indian cousins are still used for a variety of purposes in Asia. In Myanmar, elephants are used to harvest 50 percent of the teak trees from the country's forests. (Teak is a dark, durable wood that is very expensive.) Each elephant has a keeper called an *oozie*. The elephant is trained to respond only to his oozie's voice and can understand about thirty commands. A well-trained elephant can do the work of four bulldozers.

Asia's working elephants are generally well treated and have longer lifespans than their wild relatives. They are not truly domestic animals in the sense that horses and sheep are, however, for each new generation must be recaptured from the wild (working elephants rarely give birth in captivity). This practice threatens the survival of some wild herds. The Vietnam War also took a toll on southeast Asia's elephant population.

Like the primates and big cats, something about elephants intrigues us. The information collected about elephants could fill up several books. Here is a sampler.

FACTS OF LIFE

- One of the elephant's closest relatives is the hyrax, or dassie, an odd little mammal that resembles a rodent and is about the size of a rabbit, but is neither. The hyrax is found in Africa and the Arabian peninsula.

- A pygmy species of elephant, measuring about three feet at the shoulder, once lived in Sicily and was known to the ancient Greeks.

- An elephant's tusks are actually very elongated incisor teeth. The elephant's nose and upper lip have become fused to become its trunk. The

Swahili word for trunk, *mkono*, meaning "hand," describes its function as a kind of fifth limb for holding and manipulating objects. The trunk is also used to smell, bring food and water to the mouth, and explore unfamiliar objects. The trunk lacks bones, making it very flexible. It has about 100,000 tiny muscles that extend all the way to the tip.

Elephants that lose their trunks can sometimes survive for a while by learning to kneel and eat and drink with their mouths, but they eventually starve to death.

- Elephants can live as long as people. Some captive elephants have lived for more than sixty years.

- An elephant's heart can weigh thirty-five pounds.

- Elephants are generally peaceful animals, but occasionally, one of them, usually a bull, may become violent. These elephants are often bad-tempered because of injuries that cause them constant pain. Occasionally these rogue bulls are dangerous to other animals and have even been known to attack humans.

- For their size, elephants have small eyeballs, about the size of those of a human being. They cannot see very well, but their sense of hearing is very keen. Elephants can make sounds too low for the human ear to detect.

Elephant Soldiers

Both African and Indian elephants were once used in battle. The most famous fighting elephants in history were probably the pachyderms used by the Carthaginian general Hannibal during the Second Punic War (218–201 B.C.). Hannibal (when he was only nine his father had made him swear a sacred oath before the gods that he would always be an enemy of Rome) knew that if he entered Rome by sailing across the Mediterranean, the Romans would be waiting for him. In an ingenious move, Hannibal used the animals to enter northern Italy through the Alps. With 37 elephants and 50,000 foot soldiers, he made the treacherous journey across the mountains in the depths of a freezing winter.

Although Hannibal lost many men and a number of his elephants, his plan was at first successful—at the Battle of Terbia, the elephants so terrified the enemy that they helped the Carthaginians win a decisive victory. Hannibal went on to win a number of other important battles, but he never succeeded in conquering Rome. Eventually, Carthage was totally destroyed, and the defeated Africans were forced to surrender all their war elephants and pledge never again to train other elephants for military use.

The people of Carthage never forget their elephants, however. At the end of the Third Punic War, with the Roman army at the city's gate, some Carthaginians wandered through the streets, crying out the names of their elephants, perhaps hoping for a miracle that would bring the mighty beasts back to rescue them.

Fighting elephants were also used in other parts of the world. In 1398 the fierce Mongolian conqueror Tamerlane defeated an Indian prince and captured his 3,000 war elephants. When the huge beasts were delivered to the Mongolians, they were seen to be weeping salty tears at the outcome of the battle. Later, it was discovered that the defeated Indian warriors had sprinkled pepper into the eyes of the elephants to make it appear as if they were crying!

Hundreds of years later, the British successfully used elephants during World War II. In the steamy jungles of southeast Asia the members of No. 1 Elephant Company were used to pull transport vehicles over the mud, unload military supplies, and build bridges. In Myanmar alone they helped to build more than 200 bridges. They were also instrumental in the construction of the famous Burma Road into China.

No. 1 Elephant Company eventually came to number 1,000 animals. In the confusion following the Japanese surrender, many of them escaped, "retiring" to the jungles to join their wild companions.

Of Elephants and Ivory

For centuries, both Asian and African elephants have been coveted for their ivory tusks. Elephant ivory has been used to make piano keys, billiard balls, chopsticks, jewelry, and dozens of other items. Ancient sculptors covered the statues of their gods with it; one of the seven wonders of the ancient world was the statue of Zeus at Olympia, a fifty-eight-foot figure of wood covered by a thin layer of ivory. King Ahab of Israel had an ivory house, and the Roman emperor Caligula built an ivory stable for his horse.

The demand for ivory took an enormous toll on the elephant population, particularly in Africa. At one time, huge herds of elephants lived in North Africa, but by A.D. 400 these elephants were extinct, killed for their ivory. In ancient times, elephants were killed with spears and other primitive weapons. The invention of guns made killing the giant pachy-

African elephants have much larger ears than their Indian relatives. Photograph by Bob Bader. Courtesy of the Zoological Society of Philadelphia.

derms easier, and in the nineteenth century, ivory hunting became a big business. Between 1870 and 1881, 5,286 tons of ivory were shipped to England alone, and by 1900, the African elephant was almost extinct.

More recently, in the early 1980s poaching claimed from 3,000 to 4,000 elephants a year in Kenya. During this period, a pound of ivory could fetch as much as $150 on the black market. In many cases, the elephants were killed with powerful semiautomatic weapons. The tusks, even small ones from immature elephants, were hacked away from their faces and the bodies were left to rot.

Alarmed by the dwindling numbers of elephants, in 1989, the member nations of the Convention on International Trade in Endangered Species (CITES), including the United States, voted for a ban on commercial trade in ivory, which was renewed in 1992. "Save the Elephants" campaigns around the world have succeeded in reducing demand for ivory in many countries, including the United States; at the time of this writing, the black market price has plummeted to about $5 per pound, and fewer than fifty elephants are poached annually.

Ironically, the growing elephant population in African nations such as Zimbabwe and South Africa has meant the destruction of the habitat for other species, such as impala, giraffes, and monkeys. The increasing number of elephants has lead some to argue that in perhaps ten years, east Africa's herds may be large enough to allow a "sustainable harvest" of these animals for their ivory.

Chapter Twelve

THE RODENTS

Rodents are among the most abundant animals on earth. Two thirds of all mammals belong to this group. There are 1,600 species in 30 families, making them the largest group of mammals. Incidentally, shrews and moles resemble rodents, but they actually belong to the class Insectivora, meaning that they dine mainly on insects.

All rodents, from beavers to squirrels to mice, have one conspicuous characteristic: two pairs of long incisor teeth, one in the upper jaw and another in the lower. Since these teeth are constantly growing (a rat's tooth grows five inches a year), rodents are constantly gnawing on food, wood, or other objects. If a rat loses one of its upper teeth, the opposing lower incisor will continue growing, pushing into its brain and killing it.

The smallest rodent is the Eurasian harvest mouse, which weighs as little as 0.14 ounce. The largest rodent in the world is the South American capybara, which can weigh over 100 pounds.

Rodents are very adaptable creatures and can be found everywhere in the world except the frigid polar regions. When most of us think of rodents, mice and rats immediately come to mind, but this family includes many animals, such as woodchucks and squirrels.

FACTS OF LIFE

- Capybaras, sometimes called capys, are about six times larger and thirty times heavier than their nearest relative, the guinea pig. In South America, capys are sometimes kept as pets. They are also hunted for their flesh and hide.

- Guinea pigs are also natives of South America. They are docile, quiet creatures that are popular as pets. When alarmed or frightened, however, they make a high-pitched sound that sounds like a pig squealing. This characteristic, plus the fact that when they were first brought to England, they could be bought for a gold coin called a guinea, earned them their name.

- Yet another South American rodent, the agouti, looks like a giant guinea pig. Agoutis often follow troops of monkeys. The monkeys knock down fruit as they pass, which the agoutis eat or bury for later use. These rodents often cause serious damage to sugar cane plantations.

- Porcupine comes from two French words, *porc espin*, meaning "spiny pig." There are several varieties, including the American porcupine, which is found in parts of the United States and northern Mexico. The most distinguishing characteristic of these rodents are their long, sharp quills, which are found everywhere on their bodies except their soft bellies. One porcupine can have 30,000 quills. When "porkys" are angry, they shake their quills, making a noise like a rattle. If this is not enough warning, the would-be attacker might get a face full of quills (even baby porcupines have soft, short quills, which harden one hour after birth).

- Many people think of the golden hamster as an animal that lives in captivity, but there is also a substantial wild population living in Eastern Europe and the Middle East. Scientists speculate that all the domesticated golden hamsters in the world descend from a single female with twelve young which were dug from a burrow in Syria in 1930.

- Norway lemmings, found in the tundras and mountains of Scandinavia, do not "commit suicide," as some believe. Every two to three years, their population grows considerably, forcing these small rodents to travel to new areas in search of food. They migrate in huge numbers, not even pausing at large bodies of water. When the lemmings attempt to cross streams and even oceans, thousands, sometimes millions, drown.

● The name prairie dog comes from this animal's distinctive call, which sounds like the yapping of a dog. Black-tailed prairie dogs once lived on the plains of the American West in colonies that numbered in the millions. Because these gregarious animals graze on crops and pastures, farmers and ranchers set out to destroy them, reducing the prairie dog population by 90 percent in some areas by the mid 1890s. The destruction of the prairie dogs contributed to the decline of the black-footed ferrets, which prey on the prairie dogs. As a result, the black-footed ferret is one of the world's rarest mammals.

● The fat, or edible, dormouse, which lives in northern Spain and southern and eastern Europe, was highly prized as food by the ancient Romans. These dormice, which have busy tails like squirrels, were kept in special jars where they were fattened with fruits and grains. Dormice baked in honey was a special delicacy.

● The word *dormouse* comes from the French word *dormir*, meaning "to sleep." This refers to the fact that dormice hibernate in winter. The dormouse is not the only rodent to hibernate; others, such as the golden hamster, do too. During the summer, the hamsters store enormous quantities of food, including seeds and bulbs, in their burrows. A single hamster has been known to collect as much as 200 pounds of plant food! The hamsters eat constantly and get very fat; when winter comes, they curl up in their underground burrows and go into a very deep sleep. On warmer days, however, they do wake up and feed off their fat stores.

Busy as a Beaver

The beaver is North America's largest rodent, and the world's largest rodent after the capybara. It is also one of nature's best builders. Beavers, once called castors, construct dams and lodges and dig canals and tunnels in order to create living conditions that will keep them safe from predators. They are best known for the dams they build. The dams, made of mud, branches, and tree trunks, back up water to form shallow ponds, where the beavers build "lodges." These beaver lodges have two or more entrances below the water level and an internal chamber just above the water level. Beaver colonies are led by an alpha male who drives out young males approaching two years of age. The two-year-olds strike out on their own, searching for mates and forming new colonies.

Beavers work mostly at night and are rarely seen during the day.

With their powerful incisors, they can bring down four-inch-thick trees in less than fifteen minutes.

Because beavers have warm, thick fur, in the eighteenth and nineteenth centuries, millions were caught for the fur trade (the tall stovepipe hats of the Civil War period were made of beaver felt). In the early twentieth century, conservationists pushed for government protection of these industrious rodents, recognizing the important role they played in forest ecosystems (when beaver ponds dry up, they leave "beaver meadows" full of rich soil prized as farmland by early settlers). Today, beavers are abundant in many areas where they were once close to extinction.

THE MURIDS

Rats and mice are members of the family Muridae. These rodents have been uninvited guests in our homes for at least 10,000 years. Archaeologists have found their bones alongside those of humans in prehistoric caves.

Murids are *commensal,* meaning that they enjoy eating the same foods that humans do. Cheese, grains, peanut butter, chicken, and chocolate are their favorites. They are not too picky, though, for when nothing else is available, they can get along quite nicely on feces and urine. Each year rats and mice devour over 40 million tons of food. They also spoil tons more with their body wastes: In a single day, 100 rats can produce 5,000 droppings. As the droppings are only about an eighth of an inch, they easily pass undetected in foodstuffs. And in a single day, just one rat can produce three to six *quarts* of urine.

Rats are usually thought of as being an inner city problem; however, they are found in rural and suburban areas also. In fact, rats seem to thrive in the 'burbs, thanks to well-meaning homeowners who leave out bird feeders full of nice, juicy seeds and bowls full of fresh water and food for outdoor pets.

Curiously, the rats and mice that have become such pests in North American homes did not come from this continent at all. The common house mouse (*Mus musculus*) comes from central Asia. The black rat (*Rattus rattus*) was originally a wild rodent living in the deserts of southern Asia. These rats stowed away on the ships of knights returning from the Crusades (rats are good swimmers and can tread water for up to three minutes). From Europe, they spread to the New World.

Ironically, the most effective killer of the black rat (sometimes called roof rat, because it is a good climber) turned out to be a new rodent invader, the brown rat (*Rattus norvegicus*). This rat, which is bigger and stockier than its black cousin, was never seen in Europe before the eighteenth century; it orig-

Rat City

Rats are very prolific. If one pair of rats and their offspring were left totally undisturbed, they would produce 20 million rats in just three years.

Because of this high rate of reproduction and the fact that rats are very adaptable creatures, there is at least one rat for every person on earth. Some estimates put this figure as high as *three* rats per person. And according to the *Philadelphia Daily News*, the City of Brotherly Love has the dubious distinction of having more rats living in its sewers that any other town in the country!

inated in central Asia. In 1727, armies of brown rats were seen crossing Russia. In 1728, the rats reached England and from there spread to the rest of the world (this rat is sometimes called "the Norwegian rat," because it was believed at one time that it had come to England on a Norwegian timber ship). Ironically, the white laboratory rat that has helped save many lives is a relative of this destructive little beast.

The brown rat is very aggressive and soon killed off most of the black rats. Today *Rattus rattus* thrives only in tropical climates, because it cannot tolerate cold weather.

Today, rats are serious pests throughout the world. They have been known to attack invalids, the elderly, and children—in Philadelphia in the 1970s, a child died after receiving dozens of rat bites. Besides eating millions of tons of food every year, rats can carry over thirty different diseases, including murine typhus and rabies.

One of the most mysterious diseases carried by rodents is hantavirus, which is caused by contact with rodent droppings. In spring of 1993, twenty people, most of them from the Four Corners region of the southwest (where New Mexico, Arizona, Colorado, and Utah meet) were killed by this disease. Hantavirus had been diagnosed in Asia, where it causes kidney disease, but the U.S. version acts on the lungs. Scientists believe that this strain of hantavirus is carried by deer mice, which are found throughout the United States.

The rodent-borne disease that has killed more people than any other is bubonic plague, The Black Death.

You Dirty Rat: How A Rodent Helped Change the Course of History

In the year 1347, a merchant ship from the East entered the Sicilian port of Messina, carrying with it fine silks, aromatic spices, intricately woven rugs, and scores of rats. Rats were a common sight in medieval towns, especially since sanitation practices were generally poor. But these rats, proba-

bly of the species Rattus rattus, *were different, for they carried on their slick black backs a flea with a gut full of the deadly bacillus* Yersinia pestis.

The residents of the sunny Italian port soon began to come down with a strange and terrible disease. At first, the symptoms were relatively mild—headache and a general feeling of weakness. Soon, however, the victim would experience aches and chills in the upper leg and groin. Then the pulse quickened, the speech became slurred, and a white coating appeared on the tongue. By the third day, a tender swelling, about as large as an egg, appeared on the groin as the lymph nodes began to swell. Unsightly purplish blotches appeared on the skin, and the heart fluttered wildly as it struggled to pump blood through swollen tissues. The victim's nervous system began to collapse, causing terrible pain. By the fourth or fifth day, the skin began to blacken, and a horrible stench came from the victim's body. Finally, he or she died in agony.

The panic-stricken populace, realizing that the horrible disease had come from the sick and dying crews of the ship at the dock, drove the unfortunate sailors back out to sea. But it was too late—the Black Plague had come to Europe.

Actually, there are three different forms of the plague. The first is transmitted from rat to person by the bite of the rat flea, a creature no bigger than the o on this page (the term bubonic plague comes from the Greek boubon, *meaning "groin," because it is the lymph nodes of the groin that commonly swell*). When the rats died, the fleas quickly left the corpses (a rat flea can jump 150 times its own height and has been known to leap four inches straight in the air) and searched for a warm body to live on. Once it landed on human skin, the flea began to feed almost immediately, transmitting the bacillus to its host.

Pneumonic plague occurs when the bacillus invades the lungs. After two or three days, anyone with pneumonic plague would develop a bloody cough, and the foul-smelling sputum spewed into the air would be full of Yersinia pestis. *Pneumonic plague is fatal almost 100 percent of the time, and historians believe that this was the most common form of the plague in the Middle Ages. The third form, septicemic plague, occurs when the bacillus enters the bloodstream and it is* always *fatal.*

For centuries, there has been a reservoir of Yersinia pestis *living in wild rodent colonies in China, India, southern Russia, and the western United States. Historians believe that the plague, having devastated the populations of India, China, and parts of the Middle East, eventually reached the Crimea on the northern coast of the Black Sea, where Italian* merchants had prosperous trading colonies. From that area, the plague was spread by returning merchants to a number of Italian ports, including Messina.

From the Sicilian town, the plague spread like the proverbial wildfire to the port cities of Venice, Genoa, and Pisa, as well as London, Bristol, and Marseilles, leaving devastation in its path. The Italian author Boccaccio, wrote: "Brother was forsaken by brother, nephew by uncle, brother by sister, and oftentimes, husband by wife; nay what is more and scarcely to be believed, fathers and mothers were found to abandon their own children, untended, unvisited, to their fate, as if they had been strangers. . . ."

The measures taken to control the plague were often harsh. In Milan, all the occupants of a victim's house, whether sick or not, were walled up inside together and left to perish. Because such a drastic measure proved to be somewhat effective; however, Milan had a lower mortality rate than other cities.

Today, bubonic plague can be successfully treated with antibiotics, but in the fourteenth century, a number of bizarre cures were offered by the physicians of the day. Rhubarb, onions, leeks, and saffron were recommended, as well as medicines containing powdered emeralds and pearls. In the heat of the Avignon summer, Pope Clement VI sat for hours between two roaring fires (the pope survived the plague, probably because the heat of the flames discouraged the fleas). Others bathed in urine or swallowed the stinking pus of plague victims. Some doctors recommended bland diets or mild exercises; others suggested inhaling the aromas of certain flowers. Some scholars even speculate that the nursery rhyme, "ring around the rosy, pockets full of posy" refers to this practice. The line "ashes, ashes, we all fall down," of course, refers to the death and cremation of the plague's numerous victims.

Although many speculated that the Black Death was God's punishment on a wicked and sinful world, others came up with strange theories to explain the cause of the horrible disease. Scandinavians believed that a "Pest Maiden" came from the breath of the dying in the form a blue flame and flew through the air to infect the next victim. Astronomers claimed that the disease was a result of a misalignment of the planets. Others suspected that animals were the cause of it and killed dogs and cats. Others accused gypsies, lepers, strangers from other countries—and the Jews. Rats, which were a common fixture of medieval life, were curiously not suspect.

Persecution of the Jewish people was a sad and shameful fact of life in the Middle Ages and was often condoned, if not encouraged, by the church. Even the early church fathers were not immune to anti-Semitism. Centuries before, St. Augustine had written that the Jews were "outcasts" for failing to accept Christianity. St. John Chrysostom, whose very name means "golden-mouthed" because of his brilliant oratory, proclaimed to the Jews, "God hates you."

Throughout Europe, the Jewish people were despised and scorned. Writes the late Barbara Tuchman in A Distant Mirror: The Calamitous 14th Century, "What man victimizes he fears, thus the Jews were pictured as fiends filled with hatred of the human race, which they secretly intended to destroy."

One of the means of this destruction, of course, was the Black Death. Jews were accused of causing the plague by poisoning the wells, and thousands were slaughtered as a result of this ludicrous charge. The pogroms began in southern France, where a number of Jews had confessed to poisoning the wells with the help of the local rabbinate only after being hideously tortured. From France, the persecution spread throughout Europe. In Basel, all the Jews were locked inside wooden buildings and burned alive, and a decree was passed that they were not to settle in that Swiss city for 200 years. In Narbonne and Carcassone, Jews were dragged from their houses and thrown screaming into bonfires. In Munich, Frankfurt-am-Main, and dozens of other towns, pogroms took place in which Jewish men, women, and children were brutally murdered. In Strasbourg alone, 16,000 were killed. At Worms in 1349, the Jewish community, like their ancestors at Masada centuries before, took their own lives rather than face the murderous crowds.

In an effort to check the madness, Pope Clement issued a bull proclaiming that those who blamed the plague on the Jews had been "seduced by that liar, the Devil," and pointed out the obvious fact that Jews were being killed by the plague just as Christians were. He instructed local clergy to take the Jews under their protection, but his pleas were largely ignored. By the time the plague had run its course, Europe's Jewish population had been decimated.

The plague subsided in the fall of 1348, only to break out again in spring and summer of 1349. After a decade's respite, it struck again in 1361 and 1369, and periodically to the end of the fourteenth century.

The Black Death took an enormous toll on Europe's population. Agents for Pope Clement estimated that as many as 24 million people *had died in the first onslaught of the plague, and perhaps another 20 million by the turn of the century. Altogether, about one third of the continent's population had perished.*

The plague had a great impact on European society. Because of the deaths of so many people, wages rose dramatically, giving workers a chance to improve their lot in life and helping to foster the growth of the middle class. The feudal system, with its rigid three-class system—clergy, nobility, and peasantry—was in shambles. Agricultural prices dropped, weakening the power of the aristocracy, whose wealth and prestige was largely based on land ownership.

But perhaps the most important and long-lasting effect of the plague was not a change of living conditions, but a change of mind. For centuries, the Catholic church had been the central authority in medieval life. Now that the church had seemingly failed to rescue even the most devout from the plague, that authority was questioned, paving the way for dissidents such as Jan Hus of Bohemia, England's John Wycliffe, and, ultimately, the Protestant Reformation. Secular concerns became increasingly important as man began to question the relationship of man to God, intensifying the struggle between faith and reason. As Barbara Tuchman writes: "Once people envisioned the possibility of change in a fixed order, the end of an age of submission came in sight; the turn to individual conscience lay ahead. To that extent the Black Death may have been the unrecognized beginning of modern man."

Chapter Thirteen

GRAZERS, BROWSERS, AND TROTTERS: THE UNGULATES

U ngulates are animals with hooves. They can be divided into two orders: Artiodactyla and Perissodactyla. The artiodactyls, or even-toed ungulates, consists of 181 living species native to all continents except Australia and Antarctica. Bovids (cattle, sheep, goats, and bison), camels, cervids (deer and antelopes), hippos, and pigs belong to this group.

Bovids, cervids, and camels belong to the suborder Ruminantia. Ruminants have a stomach consisting of several compartments and chew a cud that is made of regurgitated, partially digested food.

The perissodactyls, or odd-toed animals, are a much smaller group, encompassing only sixteen living species. The equids (horses and their relatives), tapirs, and rhinoceroses make up this group. In equids, the toe has developed into a single digit.

THE ARTIODACTYLS

Ships of the Desert

Camels have been used as beasts of burden since antiquity. Centuries ago, caravans of up to 20,000 animals would traverse the burning sands of the world's deserts, loaded with human riders and all sorts of goods. Although motor

143

vehicles have replaced these caravans in many places, camels are still used in some remote parts of the world.

There are two species of camel: the two-humped Bactrian camel (named after an ancient nation in western Asia) and the one-humped dromedary. The dromedary is almost entirely domesticated, but a small population of wild Bactrian camels lives in the Gobi desert.

Camels walk by bringing the two legs on the right side forward as a pair, then bringing forward the two legs on their left side. Cats, elephants, giraffes, and young colts also walk in this matter. This motion is called *pacing*. Camels walk with a rolling gait and were sometimes called "the ships of the desert." Individuals who have ridden camels sometimes report that they feel seasick!

The camel's ability to live with minimal amounts of water is legendary. Camels can survive for up to ten days and sometimes even longer without water. While a 12 percent water loss in humans causes death, camels can survive a 33 percent loss of water with no negative effects.

Contrary to popular belief, however, camels do not store *water* in their hump(s). When food is plentiful, they store food there as fat. During times of famine, the hump becomes a loose bag of flesh drooping from the camel's back.

Camels are stubborn animals, known for their bad tempers. When they are loaded with a burden that they feel is too heavy, they will refuse to move, despite prodding. When particularly annoyed, they will spew a mouthful of foul-smelling cud at their unfortunate victim.

FACTS OF LIFE

● In the nineteenth century, European settlers brought dromedaries to the barren Australian desert to use as pack animals. Many of the camels escaped, and today there is a large population of wild dromedaries living in this desert.

The Lamoids

Llamas, guanacos, alpacas, and vicunas are known as lamoids. These animals live at high altitudes in parts of South America and are close relatives of the camel. All except llamas are wild.

Llamas have been domesticated for about 2,000 years. Their coarse, shaggy coats are well adapted for the harsh climate of the *altiplano* (the upland plateaus of the Andes), where South American peasants use them as pack animals much as their ancestors did centuries ago. Only the males work; the females are used for breeding. Young llamas are sometimes kept as pets.

The coarse hair of the llama is also used for clothing, and their meat is eaten. Llama flesh is sometimes sundried and used to make *charqui*, or jerky.

Like their camel cousins, llamas are temperamental. Not only do they spit, when they are extremely angry, they *vomit*!

The Bovids

Iceland has more cattle than any other nation. In some states and provinces, including Alberta, Montana, and Wyoming, there are more cattle than people.

Cervids such as deer, moose, and elk have branched appendages of dead bone called antlers; bovids, including antelope, sheep, and cows have horns, which are unbranched hollow sheaths covering small bony cores. Horns are permanent, but antlers are shed and regrown every year.

Many female bovids have small horns, but the only female cervid with antlers is the caribou, or reindeer. Reindeer, found on the Arctic tundras of Scandinavia, Asia, and northern North America, have been domesticated by the Lapps, who travel with them across the cold northern regions of Norway.

Cows were first brought to the Americas in the early 1000s by the Vikings. These cows were descendants of wild European cattle, *Bos taurus*. Christopher Columbus brought long-horned cattle from Spain to Santo Domingo on his second voyage to the New World in 1493. The famous Texas longhorns are descendants of these cows.

Cows have four stomach chambers. Partially chewed vegetation is swallowed and then goes into two connecting chambers, the rumen and reticulum, where it is broken down into pulp and later regurgitated as cud. After the cud is rechewed, it passes into two other chambers, the abomasum and the omasum. In the abomasum, the cud is worked on by the cow's gastric juices before entering the intestine, through which the nutrients are absorbed. Grass passes through a cow in this manner in about twenty-four hours, but coarser food, such as hay, may take up to seven days to digest.

Some countries have more sheep than people. Australia has ten sheep for every person; New Zealand, twenty sheep. Today, there are 800 breeds and varieties of sheep. Perhaps the best-known breed is the merino. Merinos are a type that originated in fifteenth-century Spain. They are known for their fine, soft wool. There are more sheep with merino blood than any other variety.

Bambi and Company: The Cervids

The graceful, sloe-eyed white-tailed deer of *Bambi* fame is a familiar sight throughout many areas of the United States. When European settlers first came to North America, there were 24 to 34 million white-tailed deer living in the United States. The population began to decline with heavy deerskin trading between whites and Native Americans. In the late 1800s, habitat destruction and hunting combined to reduce the deer population to only about 400,000 by the early 1900s. A combination of legislation and decreased hunting has caused the white-tailed deer population to rebound to about 14 million today.

During rutting (mating) season, bucks often engage in fierce battles over does, using their sharp, pointed antlers as weapons. Occasionally, their antlers will lock together, and the bucks will slowly starve to death.

Pére David's deer once ranged throughout central and northern China. They were thought extinct until the French Jesuit missionary and naturalist whose name they bear discovered a small herd living in the Imperial Park in Peking. Today, there are only about 200 of these deer left in game parks and zoos.

The tiny key deer, which is found only in the lush, beautiful Florida Keys, are the smallest deer in North America. While the white-tailed deer bucks that live on the Florida mainland weigh from 110 to 155 pounds, key deer males weigh from 80 to 110 pounds and are about the height of a large dog. Some full-grown key deer does weigh only about 35 pounds.

These graceful, elusive deer were once close to extinction until the National Key Deer Refuge was established in 1957. Now there are several hundred of these tiny ungulates living on a 7,000-acre refuge that includes all or part of eighteen keys.

The Giraffe Family

Giraffelike creatures could once be found throughout the world, including southern Europe and southeast Asia, but today, there are only two members of the family Giraffa, the giraffe and the okapi. The okapi, one of the world's rarest animals, is found only in the Ituri forest of northeastern Zaire.

In ancient times, the giraffe was called a *camelopard*, because it was thought to be a cross between a camel and a leopard. The ancient pharaohs would present giraffes to their allies as gifts.

The reticulated, or Nubian giraffe, is the type most often seen in zoos.
Courtesy of the Zoological Society of Philadelphia.

The giraffe is the tallest animal on earth. They can grow up to twenty feet tall and weigh more than one ton. Even newborn giraffes are tall, standing about six feet, and weigh over one hundred pounds. Giraffes give birth standing up.

Despite their long necks, giraffes have the same number of vertebrae in them as most mammals do—seven. Their vertebrae are much larger, though— one measures eight inches!

Giraffes are *browsers*, meaning that they feed on the leaves, seeds, flowers, and fruits of trees. Their tongues can measure up to twenty-nine inches, making it easy for them to reach the tallest branches. Their favorite food is the leaves of the acacia tree, which is avoided by most other animals because of its sharp, thorny spines. Acacia leaves contain 74 percent water, so giraffes seldom drink except in very dry weather. A giraffe can drink up to ten gallons of water at one time.

Scientists generally recognize nine subspecies of giraffe, some of them nearly extinct. Each subspecies has a different coat pattern. There are two types of markings: reticulated and blotched.

The Nubian, or reticulated, giraffe is the most common variety. *Reticulated* means "marked like network," and these giraffes look as if they were covered by a white net. Giraffes with a *blotched* pattern have irregularly shaped spots spread by broad bands of a lighter color. The very rare Thornicroft's giraffe of northern Zimbabwe has a beautiful pattern of starlike splotches. The subspecies of giraffe occasionally interbreed, producing an even greater variety of patterns.

You Pig

Domestic hogs, also called pigs, are descended from the European wild hog, *Sus scrufa*. The wild boar was known for its ferocity and to kill one was considered the mark of a skillful hunter. Today, about one fourth of the meat consumed in the United States comes from hogs.

There are about 840 million hogs in the world. China has the most hogs of any nation, about 40 percent of the world's total. Since hogs consume about 20 percent of the corn grown annually in the United States, most hog farms are in the cornbelt states such as Iowa and Nebraska.

Many people believe that hogs are dirty. In fact, they are actually cleaner than most other farm animals. When pigs wallow in mud, they do so in an effort to keep cool.

The River Horse

There are two species of hippopotamus: the river hippo, which can weigh as much as 5,800 pounds, and the much smaller pygmy hippo, which weighs from 400 to 600 pounds. The pygmy hippo lives in forests and spends much of its time on land.

Hippos once ranged throughout Africa. Ancient Egyptian paintings show pharaohs hunting them on the Nile River. They have disappeared from northern Africa, however, and are becoming increasingly rare in their central and southern African homelands. The hippo's decreasing population can be traced in part to the demand for their flesh, which is said to be low in fat and delicious. Hippo hide soup is a great delicacy in some parts of Africa. In addition, hippos are voracious eaters, devouring fifty-five to eighty pounds of food a day (like elephants, they are strict vegetarians). They sometimes feed on grain and other food crops and are shot by farmers as nuisance animals.

Hippopotamos is Greek for "river horse," and true to its name, the river hippo spends much of its time in the water. They are so heavy that they cannot float, sinking instead to the bottom of rivers and other bodies of water, where they stay underwater for as long as six minutes, feeding on aquatic vegetation. They then stick their massive faces out of the water for a quick breath of air.

Hippo or Rhino?

Many people seem to get hippos and rhinos confused. After all, they're both big, ugly, and can be found in Africa.

There are important differences between the two, however. For one thing, rhinos are covered with plates of hardened skin resembling armor; hippos are smooth skinned. Rhinos also have horns that can reach up to four feet in length; hippos are hornless.

Both hippos and rhinos can be dangerous. Rhinos can run thirty-five miles an hour, and are fiercely protective of their young. And hippos have killed more people in Africa than all the lions, elephants, and water buffalo combined, usually by trampling.

Sadly, these two ungulates have something else in common: They are both in danger of extinction. Neither species may survive in the wild into the twenty-first century.

THE PERISSODACTYLS

The Equids

Horses belong to the family Equidae. Domestic horses are classified as *E. caballus*.

There are more than 150 breeds of horses. China has nearly 11 million horses, more than any other nation in the world.

The smallest horse is the Falabella, which were originally bred in Argentina as pets. They stand only thirty inches high at the withers (the ridge between the shoulder bones). The largest horse is the Shire, which can stand more than five and a half feet. This breed was developed in England after King Henry VII had all horses less than five feet tall destroyed as useless.

The earliest ancestor of the horse was Eohippus, the "dawn horse," which lived about 55 million years ago in what is now North America and Europe. Eohippus, which stood only about fifteen inches high, looked more like a greyhound than today's horse.

Horses were first used as a source of meat. Discoveries at the city of Susa in southwestern Asia show that they were probably tamed and ridden about 5,000 years ago.

Horses were first brought to the New World by the Vikings in the 1000s. Five hundred years later, Spanish explorers brought horses with them to Mexico in 1519. Some of these horses escaped and became wild. These wild horses were tamed by the Native Americans about 1600. The descendants of these feral horses, sometimes called mustangs, once roamed the Western plains in herds that numbered about 2 million. Many of them were killed, however, often for use in pet food. Today, the 20,000 or so mustangs that remain are protected by federal law.

Prezewalski's horse, which once could be found in great numbers on the steppes of Mongolia, is the only true wild horse left. Because it interbreeds readily with domestic horses, it is likely that the only pure examples of this sturdy, fierce horse may be left in zoos.

Zebras are unique among the equids because of their stripes. The ancient Greeks believed that the horse was a cross between a tiger and a horse and called it a "*hippotigris*, or "horse tiger." Early Romans who tamed these

Beating the Odds

Mules are the offspring of donkeys and horses. They are almost always sterile; the chances of a mule reproducing have been estimated at about one in 5 *billion*.

A mule named Krause, however, who lives on a farm in Champion, Nebraska, beat the odds not once, but twice. Her first colt, born in 1984, was named Blue Moon (as in "once in a . . ."). Four years later, she produced her second foal, White Lightning (as in "lightning doesn't strike twice"). Krause's offspring, who were fathered by a mule, are called "donkules."

All zebras don't look the same; each has a pattern of stripes as unique as a human's fingerprints. Courtesy of the Zoological Society of Philadelphia.

animals for their circuses called them "the horses of the sun that resemble tigers."

A zebra's stripes serve a very important purpose by creating an optical illusion that helps camouflage it. This effect, called *disruptive coloration*, makes the animal's body very difficult to distinguish from its surroundings.

There are three subspecies of zebra. Each one has a different pattern of stripes, and the patterns may vary from individual to individual.

Zebras can congregate in herds as large as 150,000 individuals. They can run about sixty miles per hour for a few hundred yards and can maintain a speeds of thirty to forty miles per hour for up to fifteen miles.

Zebras sometimes associate with other animals, such as gnus and giraffes. They can be seen running with them from predators and also drinking water near them. Their attitude towards these beasts can be characterized as "benign indifference." Antelopes and zebras, however, have a special affinity for each other and actually seem to enjoy each others' company.

Through the centuries, many people have tried to use zebras as pack animals. Although zebras are sometimes seen in circus acts, they do not enjoy being ridden and tend to be unpredictable in their behavior. For these reasons, most attempts to domesticate them have failed.

FACTS OF LIFE:

- Donkeys were the first equids to be domesticated. Like the horse, they were first introduced to the New World by Spanish explorers, who called them *burros*.

The Vanishing Rhino

The largest land mammal that ever lived was the giant hornless rhinoceros, Indriocotherium, which roamed throughout Asia 30 to 40 million years ago. Indricotherium weighed about thirty-three tons and was so tall that a modern giraffe would not reach its shoulder.

In prehistoric times, one- and two-horned rhinos could be found on every continent, but today there are only five subspecies of rhinoceros remaining, all of which are in danger of extinction. In the Indian subcontinent, there are only about 1,500 of the greater one-horned rhinoceroses left. In 1968, there were 65,000 black rhinos living in the African bush, but today there are only about 2,400. The white rhinoceros, found in southern Sudan and South Africa, numbers approximately 4,000.

Rhinoceros horns are not made of bone, but of keratin. The tightly compacted keratin that forms the rhino's horn is part of the animal's skin, not its bone structure. Despite this fact, rhinoceros horn has been thought to have magical powers for centuries. In India, powdered rhino horn was used as a male aphrodisiac, and it was thought that anyone who drank from a rhino horn beaker would be immune to poison, smallpox, and even stomachache!

Unfortunately, rhino horn is still highly valued today, particularly in Taiwan, South Korea, and China, where it is used in folk medicine to treat snakebite, typhoid, and even insanity. Although rhino horn has absolutely no medicinal value at all, it can fetch very high prices—a fairly large horn in good condition can bring in anywhere from $5,000 to $15,000 on the black market.

Despite the fact that the killing of rhinos is illegal, poachers are willing to risk stiff penalties, since the demand for rhino horn is so high. In desperation, some wildlife biologists in African game reserves have started anesthetizing rhinos and removing their horns to discourage poachers.

FACTS OF LIFE

● The Malayan tapir, which lives in the forests of Thailand, Myanmar, Malaysia, and Indonesia, has changed little in 20 million years. This perissodactyl is in danger of extinction, largely because of habitat destruction.

How the West Was Lost: The Twilight of the Bison

The first European ever to set eyes on a bison was probably the Spanish conquistador Hernando Cortez, who came upon the animal in the zoo of the emperor Montezuma in 1521 in what is now Mexico. Cortez was intrigued when he learned that the huge, shaggy creature had come from a country "many leagues to the north" and ordered the historian and artist of the expedition to draw the great beast. Although Cortez recognized that the animal was a member of the cattle family, he assumed that it was a freak, the only one of its kind.

Several centuries later, the first Europeans to reach the western United States were amazed at the vast herds of huge, shaggy beasts roaming the dusty plains. The enormous herds stretched as far as the eye could see, the strong odor of their bodies filling the air.

Bison bison is the scientific name for these large bovids (males can weigh more than 2,000 pounds and stand five to six feet at the shoulder; females are smaller). The French explorers, recognizing their relation to domestic cattle, called them le boeuf, *which English speakers mispronounced as "buffalo."*

White settlers often referred to bison as "Indian cattle," a fitting title, for as many as 300,000 Plains-dwelling Native Americans depended on these bovids for their very survival. Tribes such as the Blackfoot, Sioux, and Cheyenne ate the meat of the buffalo (what could not be eaten fresh was sun-dried or salted for later use). Dried buffalo dung, called bois de vache, *or "wood of the cow," by the French, was a valuable source of fuel on the treeless Great Plains, which stretched westward from the Mississippi to the Rockies and northwards into Canada and southward into Texas. The Plains people used buffalo horns for making cups and spoons and the bones for making knives and tools. The bison's shaggy winter coat was used to make warm clothing, and the untanned hide, or rawhide, formed waterproof bags for storage. The brains were employed in tanning, and the gallbladders, to make yellow paint. A poor buffalo hunt meant hardship and even starvation for the people of the Plains.*

The bison were always on the move, migrating south during the winter months in search of food, and the Plains tribes moved with them. Indeed the whole lifestyle of these Native Americans depended on the bison. Tribes such as the Mandan, who once lived in what is now North Dakota, performed a "buffalo dance" before each hunt, praying to the Great Spirit, "Great bull of the prairie, be here with your cow."

For centuries, the bison were hunted on foot. The Blackfoot, who originally lived in Montana, Alberta, and Saskatchewan, chose their swiftest runner to wear a buffalo head mask and robe as a disguise. When he found the herd, he started a stampede, driving them into a canyon or over a cliff. Stampeding herds could be as long as thirty miles wide and sixty miles long. Then the animals would be killed with bows and arrows or large stone hammers. Bison can be startled easily, from which we get the term "to buffalo," meaning to intimidate or bewilder someone. When the Native Americans learned to ride the wild horses that the Spanish had left behind, they were able to kill many more bison.

The first Europeans to settle in the West were trappers, and in the beginning, they were more interested in the plush, thick pelts of the beaver than in buffalo hides or meat. But the "castors" became scarcer and scarcer, and around 1830, the high stovepipe hats that were made of out of beaver felt went out of fashion. Fur trading concerns such as John Jacob Astor's American Fur Company discovered there was money to be made from buffalo robes, and by 1844, Astor and his competitors were buying 95,000 buffalo hides a year.

Most of the buffalo robes shipped to the East were ordinary tan "buckskin robes," which could be bought by a trader for $1.50 worth of trade goods. "Blues," soft, long-haired robes with a distinctly bluish cast, could be had for $16, and "beaver" robes, which were especially processed to look like the silky fur of the castor, were sold for a retail price of about $75. But the most valuable buffalo robes were made from the creamy white pelts of albino bison and could fetch a whopping $200. These "albinos" were very rare, and, to the Plains people, the white buffalo was sacred. Any Native American lucky enough to have such a robe was usually unwilling to part with it, no matter what the price.

At first, the Plains peoples and the European settlers coexisted peacefully, but as time went on, the Native Americans grew increasingly hostile. Everywhere they looked, they could see white men shooting buffalo, usually taking only the hides and leaving the carcasses to rot in the sun.

As the market for buffalo robes grew, camps of white buffalo hunters sprouted up all over the prairie. Armed with weapons like the long range .50 caliber Sharps buffalo rifle, they approached the herds on foot. Bison are matriarchal, and the hunters knew that if they killed the old cow that led the herd, the huge bovids, who are not bright, would become confused and would not stampede. At least fifty head a day could be killed in this manner. Some settlers made money by picking up the bison bones and horns, which could be sold for $8 a ton and were used for everything from bone china to fertilizer. Often the piles of bones were ten feet high.

The white hunters spread across the Great Plains, shooting and skinning with ruthless efficiency. Dodge City of Wyatt Earp and Bat Masterson fame was originally the camp of white buffalo hunters operating on the Santa Fe Trail. Some of these men became known for their hunting prowess. One of them, William F. Cody, who provided meat for crews working on the Kansas Pacific Railroad, could shoot more than fifteen bison in three days and became famous as "Buffalo Bill." Cody bragged that he had killed 4,280 bison in a period of 18 months!

Not only were buffalo slaughtered for their flesh and hides, they were often killed for sport, something that was incomprehensible to the Native Americans. "Excursion trains" leaving from cities like Cincinnati, Chicago, and St. Louis promised travelers that "Buffalos are so numerous along the road that they are shot from the cars nearly every day." The number of bison killed was enormous. One scientific study published in 1876 found that 2.5 million bison per year were killed between 1870 and 1875!

Angered not only by the slaughter of the buffalo, but also by the destruction of their way of life, the Plains tribes took to the warpath. Skirmishes broke out between Native Americans and whites that eventually developed into full-fledged warfare. Led by men such as Crazy Horse, Rain-in-the-Face, Yellow Knife, and Sitting Bull, war parties roamed the Plains, battling Army forces and sometimes killing innocent men, women, and children.

One of the most famous battles in U.S. history took place on a hot day in June 1876, when an Army commander, Lieutenant-Colonel George Armstrong Custer, was greeted by 3,500 Sioux, Cherokee, Gros Ventres, and Arapaho warriors in the valley of the Little Bighorn. After a bloody and fierce fight, the lone survivor among the Army forces was a horse, ironically named Comanche. The tribes' victory, however, was short-lived, and within a few years, most of the tribes had been subdued and "resettled" into reservations. Removed from their ancestral lands, with the once-vast herds of buffalo all but gone, the Native Americans had to depend on the government for food.

In 1890 the ghost dance swept the Great Plains. Originating with a vision of a Paiute prophet named Wovoka, and heralded by such signs as a terrifying eclipse of the sun, the ghost dance, or wanagi-wachipi, was a religion of despair. The ghost dancers performed in a circle, holding hands and chanting mournful ghost dance songs. Their clothing, brightly painted with images of stars, the moon and sun, and magpies, were supposed to make them bulletproof. The dancers swooned and collapsed in a trance. When they regained consciousness, they reported that they had been in a beautiful, green land full of buffalo, where they had been welcomed by their long-dead relatives. The ghost dance, so the prophet Wovoka said, would magically transform the world back into what it had been before the white man came. And so Wovoka and his followers danced, in their clothing figured with suns and stars, stretching their arms to the heavens in a desperate plea.

But the buffalo never came back. In December 1890, an Indian agent at the Pine Ridge Reservation in South Dakota, under the impression that the ghost dance was the signal for an uprising, called in the army. Among the soldiers summoned that day were many who had served under Custer and were anxious to avenge his death. At Wounded Knee Creek, eighteen miles northeast of Pine Ridge, the army open fired with deadly, quick-firing Hotchkiss cannon, killing 250 people, mostly women and children. The mass grave in which they were buried remains there today.

In 1889, only 541 buffalo were left in the whole United States, and those few were rapidly being killed by hunters. In 1905, an alarmed group of citizens, including Theodore Roosevelt, formed The American Bison Society in an attempt to save the vanishing animal. Herds were established in Yellowstone State Park, Theodore Roosevelt National Park, and other national state parks and reserves.

Today, there are about 100,000 bison in the United States; about 35,000 are on public lands. Many of the bison on private lands are being raised for their meat. Buffalo meat not only is said to be sweeter and more tender than beef, it is lower in calories (93 per ounce as opposed to beef's 183) and has less fat and cholesterol than even chicken or turkey. Ironically, bison may be getting a new lease on life because of something that nearly drove them to extinction in the first place—the demand for their meat.

Chapter Fourteen

OTHER MAMMALS

Besides monkeys, cows, mice, and other familiar mammals, there are many unusual and unfamiliar members of this group, including the following.

The seven species of pangolin, or scaly anteaters, constitute the order Pholidota. These animals live in the tropical and subtropical regions of southern Asia and Africa. These strange animals have bodies covered with overlapping scales, which are actually modified hairs, making them resemble giant pinecones. When threatened, they roll themselves into a tight ball, which makes them virtually invincible. Their scales are razor-sharp and the pangolin can inflict a nasty wound by lashing out with its tail.

The sirenians include four living species, one dugong and three manatees. These gentle mammals are entirely aquatic and can grow up to ten feet long and weigh 450 pounds. Despite their aquatic nature and appearance, along with the hyrax, they are the closest living relatives of the elephant.

The xenarthrans are New World animals that include the sloths, anteaters, and armadillos (*armadillo* comes from a Spanish word meaning "little armored one"). The ancestors of today's xenarthrans were huge. The glyptodont, which once roamed from Arizona and Florida to Central and South America, had a twelve-foot body covered with bony, iron-hard armor and a massive tail with sharp spikes.

Gentle Giant of the Sea

The West Indian manatee, which feeds on sea grasses, is found in parts of the Caribbean and off the southern coast of Florida. Many manatees are killed each year by boat propellers, and these shy creatures are in danger of extinction.

Anteaters have long, narrow noses that are specially adapted to dig up the ants and termites that they feed upon. They scoop up the insects with their long, sticky tongues. A few species, such as the collared anteater of South America, can climb trees.

Sloths spend almost all their time in trees, rarely coming to the ground. The three-toed sloth of Central and South America is a specialized eater, feeding only on the fruit and leaves of a species of trumpetwood leaves, which it finds by smell, as its sight is very poor. Both two- and three-toed sloths sometimes have a greenish appearance because of algae growing on their long, thick hair.

Chapter Fifteen

THE REPTILES

Snakes, lizards, turtles, and alligators all belong to the class Reptilia, which includes 6,000 species. The largest and most famous reptiles, of course, were the dinosaurs, meaning "terrible lizards." The first dinosaurs appeared on earth almost 200 million years ago and died out about 66 million years ago, leaving no descendants. But one group of ancient reptiles, the sphenodons, do have a surviving relative, the tuatara, which is found only on the islands around New Zealand.

Because they are ectothermic animals, which thrive in warm climates, only a few are able to survive in cooler environments. In cool climates, many of them hibernate for the winter. They cannot stand too much heat either, however, and when it is very hot, they hide in the shade. Some desert-dwelling reptiles bury themselves deep in the cool sand to avoid the burning midday sun.

Reptiles also have a number of other features in common, including dry, scaly skin, and a lack of external ears (though in some species the eardrums are visible). Most reptiles lay eggs, although others, including some species of lizards and snakes, give birth to live young.

The rarest reptiles are the crocodilians. This group includes only twenty-five species, many of which are endangered. There are more types of lizards and snakes than of all the other kinds reptiles put together.

159

THE CROCODILIANS

Alligators, crocodiles, caimans, and gavials belong to the genus *Crocodilia*. Crocodilians cannot tolerate cold weather, thriving in climates where the temperature stays between 80°F and 90°F. Most crocodilians are found only in fresh water, but a few live in saltwater environments, including the American crocodile, the only crocodile in the eastern hemisphere. The American crocodile is found in the extreme southern tip of Florida and some parts of the Caribbean. The marine crocodile, also called the saltwater crocodile, lives in salt or brackish water in parts of India, southeast Asia, and Australia.

Crocodilians date back to the Mesozoic era of 245 to 65 million years, and look much the same as their ancient relatives did. Prehistoric crocodilians, however, were much larger, growing up to sixty feet! Today, the largest crocodilian is the marine crocodile, which can reach about twenty-three feet, and the smallest is the rare Chinese alligator, which grows to approximately five feet and is confined to a small area in the lower Yangtze River valley. Besides the Chinese variety, there is only one other species of alligator—*Alligator mississipiensis*, the American alligator. The gavials, of which there are two species, one in India and one in Malaysia, have long, narrow, tooth-filled snouts that look very different from those of other crocodilians.

How can alligators and crocodiles be told apart? Alligators are darker than crocodiles and their noses are broader and blunter. When their mouths are closed, crocodiles expose the fourth tooth on either side of the lower jaw. This tooth fits into a notch on the outside of the jaw. In alligators and caimans, all the teeth are concealed. Individuals who have worked with crocodiles and alligators also report that crocs are faster and more aggressive than gators, and meaner, too.

FACTS OF LIFE

● Alligator comes from the term "*el largato*," (Spanish for "lizard"), which was the name given to the alligators the early Spanish explorers found basking in the Florida sun. Before the days of human interference, American alligators could reach nineteen feet, but now range from about nine to twelve feet (females are smaller than males). Crocodilians keep growing all their lives, so a very large gator or croc is also a very old gator or croc.

● Crocodilians can live to be about fifty years old. Biggy, a saltwater croc in the National Zoo, lived to be fifty-seven.

- Crocodilians are good, swift swimmers and can stay submerged for up to an hour. On land, they usually move slowly, but when frightened or threatened, some species can run about eighteen miles per hour!

- An alligator's jaws have very powerful muscles that can easily crush large turtle shells. They gulp their food whole. Large prey, however, are usually torn into chunks to be eaten.

- A strong, quick human being can easily close an alligator's jaws. In Florida and other parts of the country, alligator wrestlers immobilize the animal by flipping him over on his back. Blood flowing to the gator's small brain causes it to black out. Alligators have been known to attack and kill humans, but this is very rare.

- Alligators make good mothers. They build a large nest of leaves and rotting vegetation up to three feet high, packing it down by crawling over it. The mother guards the eggs until they hatch and will viciously attack any intruder who tries to tamper with her nest. When the young are about to

A crocodile. Note the exposed teeth. Courtesy of the Zoological Society of Philadelphia.

hatch, they give high-pitched yelps. The mother then digs out the eggs, and the young alligators hatch looking like miniature versions of adult gators. The babies will stay with their mother for up to two years.

● Alligators are beneficial animals that play a crucial role in the ecology of wetland areas such as the Florida Everglades. In periods of drought, alligators dig deep holes with their powerful claws, not stopping until they find water. These artificial ponds can be big enough for several alligators and are often the only source of water for all other animals in the area. When the rains return, the wetlands are repopulated with the fish, insects, and other animals that drew sustenance from these "gator holes."

● Alligators were once a common sight on the coastal plain stretching from North Carolina to Florida and west to Texas. Habitat destruction, however, plus the slaughter of gators for their handsome hides, took such an enormous toll on the population that in 1967, the U.S. Fish and Wildlife Service classified the American alligator as an endangered species. Hunting alligators was strictly forbidden. By 1977, the gator population had increased to the point where they were reclassified as threatened, and limited hunting was allowed. Today, American alligators can be found throughout much of their former range. In Florida, they sometimes wander into backyards, where they have been known to devour family pets.

LIZARDS

There are about 3,750 species of lizard. The majority live in warm climates, but a few, such as the common lizard, live as far north as Finland. The smallest species is a gecko that measures about one and a half inches, while the Komodo dragon of Indonesia can grow up to ten feet and weigh more than 300 pounds. The Komodo dragon often feeds on animals larger than itself, and it can kill and eat a hundred-pound wild boar in one sitting. They also have been known to devour humans, although this is rare.

FACTS OF LIFE

● Geckos get their name from the sounds they make: *geck-ooh, geck-ooh!* Some geckos also chirp and bark. In some parts of the world, geckos are kept in homes, because they eat all kinds of harmful insects. After eating a meal, geckos will clean themselves with their long tongues, even licking their eyeballs.

- Geckos have special climbing pads on the undersides of their feet. These friction pads work so well that they can run upside down across a ceiling.

- Like all lizards, if a gecko loses its tail, it will grow a new one. But the new tail is smaller and never looks quite the same as the old one. Some lizards will even sprout a double or triple tail. The glass snake, found in the southern United States, is not a snake at all, but a legless lizard. When threatened, it has the ability to detach its tail at will.

- The gila monster is found in the deserts of the southwestern United States. Along with the beaded lizard of Mexico, they are the only venomous lizards. The gila monster's poison glands are located in its lower jaw. This lizard transmits the poison to its victim by gripping it in its strong jaws and chewing the flesh. While painful, the gila monster's bite is seldom fatal to man.

- There are 120 species of iguana. These lizards are found in Central and South America. Most large iguanas can be recognized by the ridge of scales on their backs. In some areas, iguana meat is highly prized as food. In countries like Panama, it is even possible to buy iguana burgers at snack bars!

- Some species of chameleon, a group found in Africa and India, have the ability to change color in response to temperature, light, or their emotional state. They become darker in sunlight and can change their skin to blend in with the colors of a tree's leaves and bark. If a chameleon has lost a fight, it will hang its head and turn dark green. If you annoy a chameleon, it may get so angry that it turns black!

- Basilisks are a variety of lizard found in the tropical Americas. One basilisk, which lives by rivers and streams in Central America, is called the "Jesus Christ lizard" by local people because it can walk on water for short distances. The lizard's large feet and great speed prevent it from sinking. Many basilisks can rear up and run on their hind legs.

SNAKES

Carolus Linneaus, never at a loss for colorful language, wrote in 1797 that "reptiles are abhorrent because of their cold body, pale color, cartilaginous skeleton, filthy skin, fierce aspect, calculating eye, offensive smell, harsh voice, squalid habitation, and terrible venom; wherefore their Creator has not exerted his powers to make many of them." No doubt the famous biologist's strong words describe the feelings that many people hold toward snakes, the most maligned and feared of the reptiles.

Actually, most of the 2,500 species of snake are quite harmless, and some are beneficial, devouring rodents and other pests (all snakes are flesh-eaters). Those of you, however, who still fear and dislike these sinuous reptiles might consider moving to Hawaii or Iceland, where there are no snakes at all.

FACTS OF LIFE

- Most snakes cannot see very well, and they are also deaf. They track their prey with their long, forked tongues, which are flicked out to "taste" for a trail, then are pulled back into their mouths, where there is a very sensitive taste-smell organ.

- Snakes have sharp, pointed teeth that are good for holding their prey but are useless for cutting or grinding food. For this reason, they eat only fairly small creatures, because they must swallow their food whole. The prey is swallowed headfirst to prevent its legs from sticking in the snake's throat.

Cobras and Cottonmouths: A Poisonous Primer

Of the 2,500 species of snakes, only 250, or 10 percent, are poisonous and only slightly more than half of these are really dangerous to human beings. These poisonous snakes are divided into four groups, including the cobras and close relatives, such as the mambas and coral snakes. A second group is made of poisonous sea snakes. The third group consists of the true vipers. The fourth includes the pit vipers, most of which live in North and South America, although some are found in Asia.

The cobras of Africa and Asia, the coral snakes of America, the mambas of Africa, and all the poisonous snakes of Australia (the only place where poisonous snakes outnumber nonpoisonous ones) are known as elapids. Elapids have poisonous fangs that are rigidly fixed in their upper front jaws and are always erect and ready for use. The poison of the elapids attacks the nervous system.

The fangs of most poisonous snakes, including the elapids, have a hollow channel inside them. This channel has a tiny opening in the upper end to receive the venom from the snake's poison glands. At the lower end, there is an even smaller hole just above the pointed tip through which the poison is injected into the snake's prey. The hypodermic needle was modeled after the fang of a poisonous snake.

The elapid family includes some of the largest and most lethal snakes in the world, including the king cobra. Often growing to lengths of fourteen feet (one was measured at eighteen feet), the king cobra is the largest poisonous snake in the world. Aggressive and quick—it can rear up six feet from the ground to strike—its poison is powerful enough to kill an elephant, and there have been reports of this actually happening.

Another dangerous elapid is the black mamba of Africa. A fast, slender snake, it often stays hidden from view among rocks or tall vegetation, striking without warning.

The coral snakes of North and South America are beautifully colored, most with alternating bands of red, yellow, and black. They rarely bite humans, and when they do, their venom is usually not fatal.

The death adder lives in Australia, home to about eighty-five different kinds of poisonous snakes. It is one of the most poisonous of the elapids. About 50 percent of people who are bitten by the death adder will die. The taipan is another deadly Australian snake. It injects an enormous amount of highly poisonous nerve venom into its victim. A person bitten by a taipan will die within a few minutes. Fortunately, the taipan lives in very lightly populated areas of northeast Australia, and, if threatened, it will usually try to escape rather than attack.

Sea snakes are found in the warm coastal waters of the western Pacific and Indian oceans. They are very dangerous—one variety has poison that is fifty times more venomous than that of the king cobra. Although they rarely bite humans, they are nonetheless dangerous. The U.S. Navy, on a scale of 1+ (minimum danger) to 4+ (maximum danger) rates sea snakes as 3+ and advises divers to leave the water when they are around.

The fangs of the true vipers, unlike those of snakes in the cobra family, are not fixed in the jaw, but lie folded back along a depression in the upper jaw. The long, curved fangs spring forward when the viper is ready to bite. One of the most lethal of the true vipers is the puff adder, which is found everywhere in Africa except the rain forests. This snake gets its name from the way it puffs itself up and hisses a warning when alarmed. The puff adder strikes very quickly, and although its poison is slow acting, it often causes death. Another deadly snake is Russell's viper. This aggressive snake is probably responsible for more deaths than cobras (when Arthur Conan Doyle wrote the story *The Speckled Band*, he was referring to this snake).

The pit viper earned its name from the depression, or pit, located between the eyes and the nostrils. Although the pits look like a second pair of nostrils, they are really special organs that are sensitive to warmth. The snake uses the pits to detect homoiothermic prey with amazing accuracy. A person's hand, for example, can be sensed by a pit viper from only a foot away. Pit vipers can sense the location of anything that differs in temperature from its surroundings by as little as 4°F.

The bushmaster of Central and South America is the largest viper in the world, sometimes growing to over twelve feet. It is also one of the most dangerous and has been known to attack people for no apparent reason. Even more poisonous than the bushmaster is the fer-de-lance. This viper gives birth to fifty or more living young, at a time, each of which is able to inflict a poisonous bite soon after it is born.

In the southeastern United States, the water moccasin is a well-known and dangerous snake. When excited, it opens its mouth wide. The white inside of its mouth stands out against the dark brown or green of its body, and for this reason, it is sometimes called the cottonmouth.

The most famous pit vipers are the rattlesnakes, which are found in every state except Alaska, Hawaii, Maine, and Delaware. More rattlesnakes live in the southwestern United States and northwest Mexico than in any other section of the Americas. The rattlesnake is unique in that it has a rattle made of interlocking scales at the end of its tail. When excited, it shakes its tail—sometimes as quickly as sixty times a second—and the rattles hit against one another, making a noise that can be heard one hundred feet away and that sounds more like hissing steam than a rattle. One of the more unusual rattlesnakes is the sidewinder. Unlike most snakes, which move forward, the sidewinder moves sideways. Wildlife experts advise visitors to areas where rattlers are known to live to wear long pants and heavy-soled shoes, and to avoid sticking their hands under rocks, inside hollow logs, under stones, or other places where the snakes might be sleeping.

In the United States, there are about 45,000 reported cases of snakebite annually, but only an average of ten people die every year from these. Fortunately, there are antivenoms available to counteract the poisons of rattlers and other venomous serpents. Snakes are kept on snake farms and "milked" of their venom every few days by a specially trained worker. The venom is collected in a jar and then treated and weakened. The toxin is injected into a horse or other large animal, which over a period of time develops substances in its blood that counteract the venom. These antivenoms are then removed from the animal's blood and stored for use.

Antivenoms have been responsible for saving thousands of human lives. Despite their availability, however, about 30,000 people throughout the world are still killed every year by snakes. More than half of all snakebite deaths are in India, where health care is poor and there are about eighty different kinds of poisonous snakes, including at least a dozen that are very dangerous. It is believed that each year, anywhere from 15,000 to 20,000 Indians die of snakebite.

Deadly Hugs

Constrictors, including pythons, boas, and the water-loving anacondas, are nonpoisonous but nonetheless very dangerous snakes. Constrictors can grow to be huge. The giant anaconda of South America, for example, can reach 37 ½ feet and weigh 400 pounds.

Contrary to popular belief, these snakes do not crush the bones of their victims. Instead, they coil their bodies around them, exerting pressure on the diaphragm until the animal loses consciousness. Once the constrictor senses no heartbeat, it starts to swallow its victim whole. After feeding, it takes a long time for the snake to digest its food. The giant anaconda takes about a week to digest a six-foot caiman, and it may not eat again for months.

Constrictors are able to open their mouths very wide, for like all snakes, their jaws are only loosely connected to their skulls. The jaws also separate into left and right sections joined by a flexible ligament. The throat walls are also very stretchy, and the snake's brain is protected by a casing of bone, which prevents it from being damaged during the stretch. Constrictors can also breathe when their mouths are full (don't try doing this at home)!

There have been many tales of constrictors devouring cattle, horses, and other large animals. They can, however, swallow only animals weighing one hundred pounds or less. Constrictors have been known to seize and devour people.

TURTLES

There are 250 species of turtle, the only reptiles with shells. Tortoises spend their lives on land. Turtles and terrapins spend most of their lives in water. Their shells are usually flatter and lighter than those of their land-living cousins. Terrapins are often small and brightly colored.

A turtle's shell consists of a *carapace* covering the back and a *plastron* on the bottom. The carapace and plastron are joined together by a bony structure called the *bridge*. In most species, the outer layer of shell consists of hard, horny structures called *scutes*, which are formed from skin tissue. In soft-shelled and leatherback turtles, the outer layer is of tough skin instead of scutes.

When turtles feel threatened, they pull their arms and legs completely underneath the carapace. The box turtle of the eastern United States has the tightest-fitting shell of all turtles. This turtle, which is only about five or six inches long, can close its shell so securely that it is impossible to slip even a blade of grass between the upper and lower shells.

FACTS OF LIFE

- Another common resident of the eastern United States is the musk turtle, also called the "stinking jenny." If handled roughly, this turtle will let go with a foul odor that come from glands just in front of its hind legs.

- Turtles do not have any teeth. They tear up their food with sharp beaks. They are the only reptiles, besides the Komodo dragons, to do this.

- There are seven varieties of sea turtle, some of which can be quite large. The leatherback turtle may weigh almost 2,000 pounds. Like all sea turtles, its front legs have become stiff paddles, which it uses to glide through the water.

- One sea turtle, the hawksbill, has been used for centuries to make tortoiseshell jewelry. The Roman emperor Nero had a bathtub made of tortoiseshell. In ancient times, it was believed that the shell from a living turtle was more beautiful than that from a dead one, and boiling water was sometimes poured on the turtle in order to loosen its shell. Live fires were even built on the hawksbills' backs to remove the valuable shell. These cruel methods did not immediately kill the turtles, but without their tough shells for protection, they soon perished.

  Today in most western countries, the sale of tortoiseshell jewelry is prohibited. Curiously, even though hawksbills are still killed for their shells, their flesh is rarely eaten. This is because this turtle feeds in coral reefs and also on the bottoms of shallow waters, where poisonous medusas, sponges, and other animals live. These toxins don't kill the turtle, but sometimes poison its flesh, making it dangerous to eat.

*Giant tortoises such as this pair can outlive human beings. Note the powerful claws,
which the females use to dig holes in the sand to lay their eggs.*
Courtesy of the Zoological Society of Philadelphia.

- Small freshwater turtles, including the colorful red-eared turtle, were once popular additions to home aquariums. It has been estimated that 13 million were sold as pets. It was discovered, however, that these turtles can carry deadly salmonella bacteria, and in 1975, the U.S. Food and Drug Administration prohibited their sale.

- There are about fifty species of tortoise. They range from tiny specimens to animals weighing 500 pounds. The largest shell from a giant tortoise measured 49½ inches.

Giant tortoises can still be found on the Galapagos Islands, where they are legally protected by the government of Ecuador, which owns these islands. These huge reptiles were also once common on many islands near Madagascar. In the nineteenth century, however, many were killed, often by sailors on whaling voyages seeking fresh meat. It is estimated that in the eighteenth and nineteenth centuries, 200,000 to 300,000 giant tortoises were slaughtered. Pigs and rats introduced to the islands by sailors also ate tortoise hatchlings and eggs.

As a result, giant tortoises are now extinct in the region, except on the Aldabra atoll, home of the Aldabra tortoise. A colony of these tortoises were transferred to the Seychelles in 1978.

Giant tortoises can be destructive, but generally, they are placid creatures. Craig and Jan McFarland, a husband and wife naturalist team who studied the Galapagos tortoises, found these giant reptiles so docile that they used their huge shells as a changing table for their infant daughter!

● Giant tortoises are among the most long-lived of all animals. The oldest authentic record is 152 years for an Aldabra tortoise.

Chapter Sixteen

THE HALL OF SHAME: EXTINCT, ENDANGERED, AND THREATENED SPECIES

All the animals languish, filling the air with lamentations.
—*Leonardo da Vinci*

Since life began, species of animals have come and gone. One million years ago, elephantlike mastodons, giant Irish elks, and enormous stabbing cats (commonly called sabre-toothed tigers) roamed the earth. Today, all that is left of these animals are their fossil remains.

Animal and plant species are disappearing at an alarming rate. According to the Washington-based World Wildlife Fund (WWF), in 1970, an average of one plant or animal species per *day* disappeared forever; by 1990, the rate had increased to one per *hour*. In the past 400 years, 40 species of mammals have vanished forever.

How does a species become extinct? Scientists speculate that some pre-historic animals, such as the stabbing cats, may have failed to adapt to the changing weather conditions that ushered in the Ice Age and died off. The Irish elk, with antlers that sometimes stretched eleven feet from tip to tip and weighed one hundred pounds, may have been a victim of its own size; evidence of many skeletons culled from ancient bogs suggest that the weight of the antlers mired the animals there and made them easy prey for both wolves and early man.

Today, destruction and degradation of habitat are the major threats facing many species. Woodlands, forests, and grasslands are disappearing at an alarming rate. It has been estimated that the tropical rain forest, the home of at least 5 million species of plants and animals, is vanishing at the rate of 42 *million* acres per year. This is an area almost the size of Oklahoma. If the present rate of destruction continues, the jungles will be almost all gone by the year 2030.

Rain forests are not the only habitats that are in danger. It has been estimated that only 5 percent of the U.S. virgin native forests remain. The world's coral reefs, home to thousands of species of plants and animals, are also threatened due to pollution and the destructive practice of dynamiting the waters in order to catch fish.

Hunting is also a major factor contributing to the extinction of animals. The elephant population in Africa has dropped by 75 percent since 1970, due largely to the demand for these majestic animals' ivory tusks. Although it is illegal to import elephant ivory into many countries, it is still sold in some parts of the world.

Many rare plant and animal species are under pressure from illegal wildlife smugglers. It has been estimated that trafficking in protected species may be the world's third largest illegal trade after drugs and arms, with an annual turnover of $5 to $10 *billion*. For example, about one third of the world's 335 parrot species are threatened by extinction, due, in part, to the illegal traffic in these exotic birds for the pet trade. For every one hundred birds taken from the jungle for this purpose, only ten will survive long enough to be sold. With a rare species such as the hyacinth macaw going for as much as $10,000 in the United States, it is difficult to halt this lucrative commerce. Law enforcement officials have even found that some drug traffickers are now entering the illicit bird trade, tempted by the large amounts of money that can be made in the "bird biz." Wildlife authorities advise that anyone wishing to purchase an exotic bird should check to see if it was raised in captivity, rather than culled from the wild.

Although most fur coats today come from the skins of animals raised specifically for that purpose, the hunting of animals for their skins has been a major contributor to the demise of many species. The South Chinese tiger, ruthlessly hunted for its magnificent coat, once inhabited fourteen provinces. In 1949, there were 4,000 of these animals; today, the population is down to less than half that amount. The giant beaver (which measured six feet from the tip of its nose to its tail), the sea mink, the North American jaguar, and Dawson's caribou are just a few of the animals that have been slaughtered out of existence for their hides. Today, the snow leopard and the Bengal tiger, although protected, are still killed for their skins. In some parts of Asia, the skin of a giant panda, which is commercially worthless except for use as a wall trophy, can fetch $100,000 on the black market.

The chinchilla, a small rodent that once was abundant in the Chilean Andes, was nearly exterminated because of the demand for its silky silver-gray pelt. This animal is virtually extinct in the wild. Ironically, most of the captive chinchilla population lives on fur farms.

Some animals, such as Pére David's deer, exist only in captivity. Others, including the European bison, which once grazed throughout central and northern Europe, have been bred in zoos and then reintroduced to the wild.

One of the strangest stories in the sad annals of extinction concerns the auroch, or European ox, a large bovine with spiral horns. The auroch stood a majestic six and a half feet and was known to our early ancestors; drawings of this animal have been found in prehistoric caves. Charlemagne and other medieval rulers considered it a fine game animal, and it was hunted to extinction by 1627. In 1907, however, scientists at the Berlin Zoo began crossbreeding several species of cows genetically similar to the auroch, including such domestic species of cattle as the Holstein. The descendants of these hybrids were introduced into the wild, where they became aggressive and developed a distrust of man. By 1932, a new race very similar to the ancient aurochs had been developed by this process of *reverse crossbreeding*. These ersatz aurochs can be seen today in some zoos.

THE ENDANGERED SPECIES ACT

To protect animals in danger of extinction, in 1973 Congress passed the U.S. Endangered Species Act, which defines an endangered species as "any species which is in danger of extinction throughout all or a significant portion of its range." At the time of this writing the list of endangered species native to North America has grown to include more than 700 plants and animals. A threatened species is one that is likely to become endangered within the foreseeable future throughout all or a significant portion of its range; there are about 138 plants and animals native to the United States on the threatened list.

Although it is credited with bringing such animals as the brown pelican, the bald eagle, and the American alligator back from the brink of extinction, the Endangered Species Act, as well as the U.S. Fish and Wildlife Service, the federal agency that is in charge of determining whether or not animals are "endangered" or "threatened," has not been without its critics. The best-known controversy involving the U.S. Endangered Species Act is the conflict over the spotted owl.

In the late 1980s, it was discovered that this creature was in danger of extinction. This small, elusive bird inhabits sections of the "old growth" forests of Washington, northern California, and Oregon, woodlands full of trees about 200 years old that timber companies also find attractive. Lumber companies are allowed to log in national forests, a policy that environmentalists vehemently oppose. Groups such as the Sierra Club took their case to court, and in 1991, after a long, bitter battle, logging was banned on millions of acres in seventeen national forests and five Bureau of Land Management parcels where the spotted owl was known to dwell.

The court's decision caused a great deal of anger among those who depended on logging for a living. Bumper stickers saying "Save a Logger, Shoot an Owl" sprouted like mushrooms after a rainstorm throughout the Pacific Northwest, and the lumber industry blamed environmentalists for the loss of at least 30,000 jobs. The Sierra Club countered with an accusation that "timber exports and robotization of the timber industry, not environmental regulations, are the principal causes for a poor northwestern economy." Although both sides in the controversy have made steps toward a compromise, including a "timber summit," which was held in April 1993 in Portland, it is certain that the spotted owl will continue to be the center of controversy for some time to come.

INTERNATIONAL CONSERVATION

On an international level, the Convention on International Trade in Endangered Species (CITES) was implemented in 1975. CITES is designed to protect wildlife against overexploitation by trade and to prevent international trade from contributing to the extinction of a species. To accomplish its aim, the Convention has implemented a worldwide system designed to control the traffic in wildlife and wildlife products by stipulating that government permits be required for such trade. Security paper and stamps are often used for these permits to prevent such abuses as forgery. By 1990, one hundred nations had signed CITES.

An organization called TRAFFIC International (The Trade Records Analysis of Flora and Fauna in Commerce) helps determine whether or not a species is endangered by trade. TRAFFIC is under the auspices of the World Wildlife Fund (WWF). The International Union for the Conservation of Nature, based in Geneva, also publishes the *Red Data Book*, listing endangered species around the world.

Despite these efforts, the march toward destruction continues for many species. Some scientists feel that it may already be too late to save the giant panda, the blue whale, and the black rhinoceros from becoming extinct during the next twenty-five years. At the present rate, the WWF estimates that 20 to 50 percent of all species existing today will be lost by the year 2000.

The main problem with the CITES treaty is a lack of cooperation, because adherence to the agreement is purely voluntary. We have seen how the use of tiger body parts in traditional Asian medicine is driving this magnificent big cat to extinction. Not only are the bones used, every part of this animal's body is valuable: a tiger skin can fetch as much as $15,000 on the black market, and a bowl of tiger penis soup, said to enhance sexual prowess, sells for more than $300.00. Taiwan (which is not party to the CITES treaty, as it is not recognized by the United Nations), for many years has carried on a thriving trade not only in tiger body parts, but rhinoceros horns, spotted cat skins, and other wildlife products.

In May 1994, the Clinton administration invoked the Pelly Amendment against Taiwan. This federal legislation authorizes the use of trade sanctions against nations whose activities harm endangered species. This is the first time that the Pelly Amendment has been used in the continuing war against illicit wildlife traffickers. Effective in June 1994, a trade embargo was imposed on wildlife products coming out of Taiwan, including reptile-skin handbags and shoes, edible frog legs, coral jewelry, and other items. As the United States imports an estimated $25 billion in products from Taiwan annually, these sanctions will have little effect on the average Taiwanese (or American, for that matter). But the Clinton administration hopes that it will send a message to Taiwan that the United States government is serious about curbing the illicit trafficking in international wildlife.

But even when a nation is party to the CITES treaty, this is no guarantee that trade in illicit wildlife will not continue. Singapore has signed the CITES treaty, but there is still a thriving trade in endangered wildlife in this island nation. Of major concern to environmentalists are rare and endangered parrot species, which are smuggled from the jungles of Laos, Cambodia, and other countries in southeast Asia into Singapore. Says Dorene Bowze of New York's Wildlife Conservation Society, "a major problem with Singapore and many other nations is that compared to such issues as drug abuse and crime, protection of wildlife is just not considered a top priority."

Cheetahs are among the world's most endangered species. In a five-year period during the 1960s, almost 29,000 were killed for their coats. Today, there are less than 29,000 left in the world.

Humans are not always the culprits when it comes to extinction, however. The record for the fastest destruction of a species belongs to a cat, which was owned by a lighthouse keeper on Stephen's Island in New Zealand. The

Endangered Species: *In a five-year period in the 1960s, 25,000 cheetahs were killed for their beautiful coats. Today there are fewer than 25,000 cheetahs left in the entire world. Courtesy of the Zoological Society of Philadelphia.*

ferocious feline singlehandedly (or single *paw*edly) wiped out all sixteen specimens of the species *Xenicus lyalli*, the Stephen's Island's wren, in the space of
a few months. Fortunately, the cat did not devour the little birds after killing
them, enabling scientists to at least have specimens of it.

Here are just a few of the animals that have disappeared during the last
300 years:

Barbary Lion. This animal, which once roamed through much of North
Africa, was the largest of the lions. The males measured ten feet from nose
to tail, and could weigh up to 550 pounds. This beast was known
throughout the ancient world and is probably the species of lion mentioned in the Bible. Julius Caesar owned one hundred of them, and they
were often used in the games in the Roman Colosseum. These were also
the lions that Nero and other emperors used to terrorize Christians. The
lions preyed on sheep and other animals and were killed in great numbers
for this reason. They were often hunted as a trophy—as it was a mark of
valor to be able to slay this ferocious animal. By the twentieth century,
they were scarce. A pocket of these animals remained in the Central Atlas
mountains, where they were still hunted. The widespread use of firearms
hastened their demise, and by 1922, they had been wiped out. A close relative of the Barbary lion, the Cape lion of South Africa, was described as
having "the head of a bulldog, black mane, and tuft of black hair under
the belly." The Cape lion met the same fate as its northern cousin; the last
one was killed by the Boers in 1865.

Carolina parakeet. This bird, with its bright green body and orange-yel-
low head, was the only parrot native to North America. It was a familiar
sight throughout the southeastern states up to the early twentieth century. The Carolina parakeet had the unfortunate habit of twisting green
fruit from trees and was considered a pest. It was also hunted for sport.
Thousands of these birds were tamed and kept as cage birds, but they
never bred successfully in captivity. The last Carolina parakeet in captivity
died in the Cincinnati Zoo in 1914 (ironically, a passenger pigeon, also
the last of its kind, perished in the same zoo the same year). A flock of
thirty Carolina parakeets spotted in Florida in 1920 was the last ever seen
of this bird. Although these birds were exterminated in large numbers by
man, disease may have also played a part in their extinction.

Dodo. Perhaps the most famous of extinct animals, the dodo was the first
bird to disappear during modern times. It lived on the islands of Mauritius, Reunion, and Rodriguez in the Indian Ocean. A visitor to Mauritius

in the 1700s wrote: "It is a thoroughly stupid animal. . . . Its head is long, broad and deformed. Its flesh is covered with fat but is also so nourishing that three or four of these birds suffice to fill the stomachs of a hundred persons." Although the flesh of this clumsy, flightless bird was prized for human consumption and as food for livestock, pigs and rats brought to the island by sailors also killed many dodos. The defenseless dodo was easy prey, and by the end of the seventeenth century, it had been wiped out.

Falkland Islands fox. This fox was a native of the islands that lie in the South Atlantic about 300 miles from the southeastern coast of Argentina. It was much larger than the European fox, being about the size of an English mastiff. Charles Darwin wrote of this animal, "I think, be doubted, that as the islands are now being colonized, before the paper is decayed on which this animal has been figured, it will be ranked among these species that have perished from the Earth." The Falkland Islands fox was known for its ferocity. Its tendency to attack human beings, as well as domestic animals, caused it to be killed in great numbers. Some of the Falkland Islands settlers also believed it was a vampire, which did nothing to improve its reputation. The fox's pelts were also used in the fur trade. In 1876, the last Falkland Islands fox was killed. Seventeen years after the publication of *The Origin of Species*, Darwin's sad prediction had come true.

Great auk. This goose-sized bird dwelt in the North Atlantic, and, like the ill-fated dodo, it was unable to fly but was an excellent swimmer. It was killed for its meat, feathers, and fat and was often used as fish bait. The last known specimens, a breeding pair, were killed in Iceland in 1844.

Ivory-billed woodpecker. One of the largest of the woodpeckers, it measured twenty inches from beak to tail. It was highly prized by the Native Americans for its beautiful cream-colored beak, which was used to make crowns for their chiefs and bravest warriors. This attractive bird was very common in the United States until 1930. The ivory-billed woodpecker's story is a classic example of how destruction of the environment hastens a species' extinction. This bird required a certain habitat in order to survive. It lived in vast, undisturbed tracts of dense forests located close to waterways. Hunting and draining of the wet areas it frequented severely depleted the bird's numbers. The woodpecker also nested in dead trees in riverside forests, so logging also took a toll on its population. The last five birds were sighted in 1962.

Passenger pigeon. Incredibly, this bird, which resembled the common mourning dove, was once the most numerous animal in North America. In the early nineteenth century, it is estimated that there were 3 to 5 *billion* of these pigeons in the United States. In 1910, one flock was estimated at 2,230,272,000 birds. Eyewitness accounts tell of the sky being darkened by the passage of the passenger pigeons. They were much in demand for their delicious flesh and were often hunted for sport. Their crowded nesting grounds and communal flights made them easy prey for wholesale shooting and netting; often whole trees were felled in order to get the roosting birds. Passenger pigeons were popular with plantation owners in the antebellum South as a cheap and seemingly endless source of food for their slaves. By 1880, the once vast flocks had been reduced to the point of no return. The last wild passenger pigeon was killed in 1900. Martha, an inhabitant of the Cincinnati Zoo and last of her kind, died in 1914. Her stuffed body is on display at the National Museum in Washington, D.C.

Pennsylvania bison. It is hard to imagine bison grazing where the city of Philadelphia now stands, but *Bison bison pennsylvanicus,* one of four American subspecies of this huge bovine (two are now extinct), once roamed through much of the northeastern United States. Hunting severely depleted the herd, however, and by 1790, there were only about 400 of these animals left. The harsh winter of 1799–1800 took a severe toll on the increasingly small numbers. The last male was killed in 1802, and the remaining two Pennsylvania bisons, a cow and her calf, were killed in West Virginia in 1825.

Quagga. This relative of the zebra once roamed the grasslands of South Africa in large numbers. Wrote naturalist William Burchell of the quagga in 1811: "The whole plains seemed alive and appeared chequered black and white with their congregated masses. . . . [Their hoofbeats sounded like] the din of a charge of calvary." Thousands of these animals traversed the plains in single file, giving the shrill, barking cry that gave them their name, *kwa-ha! kwa-ha!* Quaggas could be domesticated with relative ease and were used as pack animals. They were also trained to guard sheep and other livestock from wild dogs and hyenas. A pair of quaggas imported to England in the early nineteenth century were even taught to pull a coach. These animals were killed by the thousands for their meat. The quagga also had the misfortune of having a handsome reddish brown coat with white and brown stripes on its neck and was hunted for its hide. The skins were tanned and used for leather, and dried hides were used as grain sacks. When striped harnesses became all the rage in Europe, the quagga was doomed. Sadly, no one realized that the quagga was in danger of extinction until it was too late. In 1878, the last wild quagga was shot. Five years later, a European zookeeper wired his African game supplier to send a quagga to replace one that had died. The sad reply came back: "But there aren't any more."

Stellar's sea cow. This placid, defenseless sea mammal, a thirty-foot cousin of the dugong and manatee, was killed for its hide and flesh in such numbers that it had vanished by 1768, only twenty-seven years after its discovery.

Tasmanian wolf. Also called the thylacine, this nocturnal predator had powerful jaws that it used to kill kangaroos, wallabies, and, often, sheep and other herd animals. Although it resembled a wolf, it was actually a marsupial, like the kangaroo and koala. The Tasmanian wolf often preyed on livestock, which prompted the government to offer a bounty for any thylacine killed, and 2,268 of these animals were destroyed from 1888 to 1914. Alarmed by its dwindling numbers, the Australian government offered legal protection to the Tasmanian wolf in 1938, but, by then, it was too late. The last thylacine, a young male, was shot in 1961.

How the Whooping Crane Was Saved . . .

Sometimes a species can be brought back from the edge of extinction. One encouraging story is that of the whooping crane.

Standing five feet, and with a wingspan of seven feet, these majestic birds—called "whoopers" by their admirers—are the tallest birds in North America and one of the rarest. They once had a wide breeding range, from New Jersey to South Carolina to midwestern states such as Iowa and into Canada.

Long before the arrival of humans, however, natural forces had begun drying up the northern marshes that the birds called home. Though their populations was never large, the cranes' numbers gradually decreased so that by 1870, there were only between 1,300 and 1,400 of these birds in the United States and Canada. As farmers began to drain their wetland habitats (Minnesota alone has lost 42 percent of its wetlands since the 1780s), the cranes' nesting grounds and habitat continued to shrink. The last whoopers disappeared from Iowa in 1894, and by 1926, not a single whooping crane nest was found in the original breeding range.

Although the birds appeared in Texas every autumn to spend the winters in the warm coastal waters, no one knew exactly where they nested. As the years went by, the birds' plight worsened, and in the fall of 1941, only sixteen whoopers showed up in the Texas wintering grounds. Scientists, realizing that when the population of a species falls below fifty individuals its chances for survival are limited, braced themselves for the stately bird's extinction.

In 1954, however, a whooper nest was discovered in Canada's frigid Northwest Territories, 2,500 miles north of the Texas coast. The birds' Texas wintering areas (now called Arsanas National Wildlife Refuge) were protected in 1937, but the whooper population did not grow rapidly. In 1966, with the flock numbering only forty-three birds, Canadian and American wildlife authorities, along with the National Audubon Society, decided to take an active role in assuring the bird's future. Because whoopers usually lay two eggs but rear only one chick (the abandoned bird almost always dies, usually of starvation), scientists found that they could take the surplus eggs, place them in the nests of sandhill cranes, or incubate them artificially.

The program has proven to be successful. In 1990, the flock numbered 148, an 824 percent increase over the 1941 low. Even though the whooping crane will never regain the numbers it did before the coming of the Europeans, its future looks secure.

. . . And the Giant Grebe Was Lost

Unfortunately, despite the best efforts of conservationists, it is just too late to save some species. The giant grebe, a plump bird with a short neck and pointed bill, lived only in Guatemala's highlands, on the shores of mile-high Lake Atitlán. In 1960, there were 200 of these flightless birds, which were called pocs by the local Mayan Indians.

Four years later, scientists were alarmed to see that the population had dropped to only eighty. One reason for this plunge were largemouth bass, which had been introduced into the lake to help encourage tourism. The fish not only competed with the grebes for the small fish, crabs, and frogs that formed the birds' diets, they also dined on the young chicks (bass are notorious carnivores), pulling the little birds under as they swam on the lake. But with the cooperation of the Guatemalan government, a wildlife refuge was formed to protect the birds, and by the early 1970s the population of grebes had climbed to 232.

In 1976, however, an earthquake devastated Guatemala, killing 23,000 people and opening fissures in Lake Atitlán. The water level *rapidly decreased, causing the reed beds where the birds nested to dry up. In 1980, there were only 130 giant grebes left.*

The development of the Atitlán area as a tourist attraction and the continued lowering of the water level took a severe toll on the birds. Guatemala, a very poor country often engaged in internal conflicts, had little money to spend on conservation, and by June 1987, the giant grebe was extinct.

Chapter Seventeen

EVOLUTION OF THE ZOO

Zoos have existed for thousand of years. When Hannibal's elephants were not occupied with fighting, they were kept in a public park, where the people of Carthage came to admire them.

Most early zoos, however, were private menageries kept by monarchs for their personal enjoyment, as well as for religious ceremonies. These zoos consisted not only of local animals, but also of species collected from all the known world. The first recorded animal-collecting expedition was sent out by the Egyptian queen Hatshepsut fifteen centuries before Christ. The expedition brought back dozens of animals from Africa, including lions, monkeys, and even a giraffe.

In ancient Greece, collections of animals were kept by wealthy citizens. The Greeks, however, did more than use their zoos as a source of entertainment. In the fourth century B.C., the Greek philosopher Aristotle owned what he called an "experimental zoo." Aristotle observed and recorded the behavior of 300 species in his book, *History of the Animals.*

The Romans were also fond of zoos and sent expeditions across the known world to collect animals for them. Many of these creatures, however, including lions, tigers, crocodilians and elephants, were destined for the cruel spectacles held in the Circus Maximus (later called the Colosseum). Maddened by intoxicants, the animals were forced to fight each other, or were pitted against gladiators. In many cases, though, these human combatants were not professional warriors, but slaves and prisoners of war who were often unarmed. These bloody and bizarre spectacles cost thousands of lives, both human and animal. While human victors were sometimes allowed to go free, archers stood ready in the stands to kill any animals who managed to survive.

Later on, the Byzantine Empire maintained zoos visited by thousands of people in the great cities of Antioch and Constantinople. Charlemagne, emperor of the Holy Roman Empire, established three zoos and in A.D. 800 ordered bishops and abbots to convert portions of their lands into wildlife parks. Some of these areas were later used for private hunting preserves.

One of the most fabulous zoos of all times, according to the narratives of early Spanish explorers, was the menagerie of the ill-fated Aztec high priest and emperor, Montezuma. The zoo, located in what is now Mexico City, had bronze cages holding powerful jaguars, tiny monkeys with wrinkled little faces, and other exotic creatures. Giant sunken basins teemed with fish and snakes, and ten giant ponds held native waterfowl. Brilliantly colored birds, from noisy parrots to tiny hummingbirds, flew overhead in huge aviaries that seemed to stretch to the very heavens. The birds' feathers were collected and used to make splendid ceremonial robes and headdresses worn by Aztec priests and royalty. Sadly, the zoo also displayed humans with various deformities: dwarfs, giants, and "bearded ladies" who were forced to live in cages alongside the animals.

Montezuma's zoo was destroyed by the Spanish and the animals eaten by the starving Aztecs in 1521. But tales of the marvelous menagerie piqued European interest in strange and exotic species. It became a status symbol for the jaded aristocracy to have unusual animals in their private collections. Christopher Columbus supplied Ferdinand and Isabella of Spain with animals captured on his voyages to the Americas.

Later in the sixteenth century, the zoo of Joachim I, the elector of Brandenberg, became the first zoo to be supported by donations from private citizens. Most zoos, however, such as the Jardin du Roi of Louis XIV of France, remained under royal control (after the French Revolution, the Jardin du Roi was renamed the Jardin des Plantes and was opened to the public).

One factor in the growth of public zoos was the traveling menageries that traversed Europe and the United States in the mid-1800s. One of these, the "Senegalese Show," featured not only elephants and other animals, but also human beings, including the deformed and "savages" such as Inuits, Lapps, Pygmies, and other indigenous peoples from distant lands.

These traveling shows were so popular that many cities and towns around the world decided that they wanted to have permanent animal exhibitions, and zoos sprang up all over the country. Many of them, such as the Central Park

Zoo, were located in the middle of city parks so that they would be accessible to the greatest number of people. Well-known architects and designers were often called upon to create the new facilities, which offered a much-needed respite from nineteenth-century urban life. With their wrought iron cages, elegant pavilions and gazebos, and spacious landscaped walkways, these new zoos were showplaces of Victorian design.

In 1859, the Philadelphia Zoo became the first in the country to obtain a charter. The Civil War, the difficulty of transporting animals from faraway places, and a lack of funds, however, delayed the zoo's opening until July 1, 1874. Among the animals to be exhibited were five female black bears received from Mormon leader Brigham Young in Utah.

In March 1889, president Grover Cleveland signed a bill creating the National Zoological Park, which was funded with monies from the national treasury and the District of Columbia. The purpose of the National Zoo was "for the advancement of science and the instruction and recreation of the people." Frederick Law Olmsted, a renowned landscape architect who had designed New York's famous Central Park, was recruited to design the zoo, located in Washington's hilly Rock Creek valley. In 1891, the zoo opened, including among its exhibits two circus elephants, Dunk and Gold Dust. The Asian elephants had been donated by showman Adam Forepaugh, a rival of P. T. Barnum.

With funds from private organizations, the New York Zoological Society, and the City of New York, the Bronx Zoo opened in 1899. In September 1906, alongside the zoo's exhibits of orangutans and chimpanzees in the Monkey House, was a Congolese Pygmy named Ota Benga (Ota Benga had also been displayed at the 1904 St. Louis World Fair, along with Geronimo and representatives from fifty other Native American tribes). Crowds flocked to see the young "savage," while in scientific circles, debate raged as to whether Ota Benga was really human or a highly advanced type of ape. The *New York Times* proclaimed in an article dated September 9, 1906, "Bushman Shares a Cage With Bronx Park Apes—Some Laugh Over His Antics, but Others Are Not Pleased." Protests by clergy and other outraged citizens, plus the fact that the young Pygmy had become "unmanageable," finally put an end to this inhumane and racist display on September 27, 1906, and Ota Benga was removed to a home for "colored" orphans. After spending time at a Virginia seminary and with the African American poet Ann Spencer, Ota Benga, realizing he would never go back to his African home, committed suicide on March 20, 1916.

These early public zoos usually featured animals behind bars in concrete-floored cages. In 1907, however, the "open zoo" concept was introduced

Holy Cow!

The Jerusalem Biblical Zoo, established more than forty-five years ago, is one of the world's most unique menageries. Six hundred animals, most of which are mentioned in the Bible, live at the Zoo in a new $18 million home in the southwest part of the city. Signs and plaques indicate the appropriate biblical passages where the animal is mentioned. The zoo is very popular with ultra-religious Jews, for whom attending movies, watching television, and participating in other secular amusements is off limits.

by Carl Hagenbeck, a German animal dealer. At his zoo, the Tiergarten, located in suburban Hamburg, Hagenbeck removed the iron bars and added artificial mountains and greenery in an attempt to simulate the animals' natural environments. Moats separated the animals from the zoo visitors. The Tiergarten caused a sensation, but like many European zoos, it was bombed and most of the animals destroyed during World War II.

Modern zoos have come a long way from the days of Queen Hatshepsut and have taken the open zoo concept to levels Herr Hagenbeck never dreamt of. Today's zoo visitors not only see animals from all over the globe in environments that simulate their native habitats, they also can step into recreations of entire ecosystems.

At the National Zoo, for example, the visitor can get a sense of life in the Amazon rain forest by visiting its "Amazonia" exhibit. After walking through the lower level of the building, which contains displays of tropical flora and fauna, as well as a replica of a field station where scientists live and work, the visitor climbs to the second level, a slice of the rain forest in one of the world's busiest cities.

The hot, humid air is the first thing that strikes the visitor upon entering the exhibit. A 200-foot kapok tree rises to the glass-enclosed ceiling, and parrots screech in palm trees. Tiny, bright-eyed titi monkeys chatter among the leaves of a cashew tree, and a huge iguana, the color of unripe bananas, crawls lazily on a branch.

Another interesting exhibit is the Metropolitan Toronto Zoo's ten-acre Marco Polo Trail, which is designed to give visitors an idea of the sights that the famed Venetian explorer encountered on his overland journey to China 700 years ago. Set in the Eurasian section of the zoo (the Toronto Zoo, like many others, is divided into "zoogeographic areas" where animals are grouped according to where they live in the world), the Marco Polo Trail includes exhibitions of falconry, silkworms feeding on mulberry bushes, Tibetan yaks, Mongolian wild ponies, and other animals.

Chapter Eighteen

QUIZ ANSWERS

BIRD QUIZ, PAGE 22

1. f. Albatross   2. b. Cormorant. In Asia, flocks of these large birds are kept on leashes, and rings are placed around their necks to prevent them from swallowing the fish they catch. When the cormorant catches a fish, the bird is hauled in by the leash and the fish is removed from its beak. Once it has made several catches, the ring is removed so it can feed itself.   3. j. Owl   4. c. Raptors   5. h. Swallows   6. c. Brown pelicans   7. d. Cardinal   8. g. Murres   9. i. Golden plover   10. a. Flyways. Some authorities recognize as many as seven major flyways in the United States alone.

FISH QUIZ, PAGE 29

1. b: Pilchard   2. c: Carp   3. d: Dogfish   4. a: Lamprey   5. d: Gar   6. a: Hatchetfish   7. b: Tarpon   8. a: Shad   9. c: Morays   10. b: Sturgeon   11. c: Bass   12. a: Bluefish   13. a: Red snapper   14. c: Haddock   15. b: Bass

WILD DOG QUIZ, PAGE 74

1. h. Coyote. The coyote, which was called the "brush wolf" by early settlers, originally ranged from Central America to Alaska but was extermi-

nated throughout much of its range. It is now making a comeback in many areas, where it is filling the ecological niche once occupied by the wolf.

2. j. Dingo. Resembling a large yellow dog, it preys on rabbits and sometimes even kangaroos, which it hunts in packs.

3. d. Jackal. Some species, such as the simian jackal, sometimes prey on livestock and are therefore ruthlessly hunted in some areas of the world, making them an endangered species.

4. i. Arctic fox. This fox first turns cream colored in the summer, and then enters the "blue" phase, taking on a beautiful, grayish blue hue.

5. b. Dhole, or red dog. This species lives in India, Malaysia, Thailand, and Java. Unlike some other canids, it will not mate with domestic dogs.

6. a. Hyena. There are several species of hyena, all of which belong to the family Hyaenidae. Hyenas can attack and kill prey the size of a gnu, but like jackals, also feed on carrion.

7. e. Bush dog. This dog lives in Central and South America.

8. f. African, or Cape, hunting dog. This species is a very efficient predator, playing the ecological role of the wolf in Africa. This dog is social, living in packs that number from five to twenty individuals and can include as many as fifty.

9. c. Paraguayan fox.

10. g. Red fox. Silver and "cross" foxes, which are marked with darker hairs on their backs in the rough shape of a cross, are the two color phases.

WHAT AM I? QUIZ, PAGE 84.

1. Puma. This graceful cat, known for its unearthly caterwauling, is also called a cougar. Like bobcats and lynxes, pumas are classified with the small cats (even though they can weigh more than 200 pounds) because their body structures are more similar to those of the small animals than those of the big cats. Cougars are making a comeback in many areas, putting them in conflict with local communities. In suburban San Francisco recently, a cougar attacked and killed a forty-year-old jogger.

2. Jaguarundi.

3. Caracul. The caracul is a powerful hunter; it has been known to kill eagles roosting in trees.

4. Ocelot. Ocelots have sometimes been kept as companion animals. They can be friendly and affectionate, but are also unpredictable; ocelots have been known to suddenly attack people that they have known for years.

5. Serval. In east Africa, this small cat, which weighs about forty pounds, is also hunted for its flesh and fur.

Part II

A TALES OF THE DREAMTIME: ANIMALS IN MYTHS, FOLKLORE, AND SUPERSTITION

Z

ANIMALS OF THE IMAGINATION

Animals figure prominently in the myths, legends, and folklore of world cultures. The Koori of Australia tell of a period in their history before the coming of the white man known as the Dreamtime. During the Dreamtime, the great god of creation, Julunggul, in the form of a giant rainbow serpent, dug out many rivers as he crawled through the desert sand; this is why these bodies of water have serpentine shapes. During the Dreamtime, giant kangaroos hopped across the desert sands, and mighty heroes, often with the help of animal companions, performed feats of superhuman strength and skill.

Every culture has its own version of the Dreamtime, when anything and everything was possible and animals could converse with humans. In this section, we will explore the animal legends of various cultures.

Chapter Nineteen

MARVELOUS MYTHICAL BEASTS

Mythical beasts have been a staple of human imagination for thousands of years. One of the most enduring animals of the imagination, of course, is the unicorn, which William Butler Yeats referred to as "a noble beast, a most religious beast [which] dances in the sun."

The unicorn was well-known in the ancient world. The Persian writer Ctesias, who lived in the fifth century B.C., gave this description: "There are in India certain wild asses which are as large as horses, and larger. Their bodies are white, their heads dark red, and their eyes dark blue. They have a horn on the forehead which is about a foot-and-a-half in length. The base of the horn is pure white, the upper part is sharp and a vivid crimson; and the remainder, or middle portion, is black." Ctesias ended this remarkable description by writing, "The animal is exceedingly swift and powerful, so that no creature, neither the horse nor any other, can overtake it."

Other ancient writers disputed Ctesias's description. Pliny the Elder (A.D. 23–79) wrote: "The Indians hunt many wild beasts, the fiercest of which is monoceros ["one-horned" in Greek]. The monoceros has a body like a horse, a head like a stag, feet like an elephant, and a tail like a boar. It makes a deep bellow, and one black horn about three feet long projects from the middle of its forehead. This animal cannot be taken alive."

Another Roman, Julius Caesar (100–44 B.C.), in his book *The Conquest of Gaul*, told of a unicorn that lived in the vast Hercynian Forest of Germany, a huge, densely wooded area that once extended from the Danube River in southwestern Germany all the way to what is now Czechoslovakia. Wrote the Roman statesman: "There is an ox shaped like a stag, with a single horn in the middle of its forehead between the ears. This horn sticks up taller and straighter than those of the animals we know, and at the top it branches out widely like a man's hand or a tree."

When most of us think of a unicorn, however, we envision a beautiful white horse with a long flowing mane and tail, and a single horn growing from its head. Tradition says that this gentle creature could be caught only by a virgin seated alone under a tree. Upon seeing the chaste maiden, the unicorn would became tame and lay at her feet. Then it could be killed easily, singing a sad and beautiful song as it died.

Why destroy such a wonderful and gentle creature? Apart from man, the unicorn's only other enemy was believed to be the lion. Although ancient authorities disagreed about the unicorn's appearance, they were all sure that the animal's horns had magical properties. Hildegarde of Bingen (1098–1179), a German nun, naturalist, and mystic, believed that shoes made of unicorn hide would ensure healthy feet and legs. Belts crafted of unicorn leather, claimed Hildegarde, would keep away fevers and plague, and unicorn liver, ground up and combined with egg yolk, was a surefire cure for leprosy.

Unicorn horn was also believed to act as a poison detector. Beakers and other vessels made of the precious stuff would "sweat" when filled with poisonous substances. For this reason, the eating utensils of monarchs were often made of "unicorn horn." The horn was also used to heal wounds.

Where did these "unicorn horns" come from? The white, spiraled horns of the narwhal were often sold as the genuine article in London, Brussels, and Paris, where they fetched very high prices. A complete horn could be worth twice its weight in gold. The flamboyant King Frederick III, who ruled Denmark from 1548 to 1670, had a throne whose legs, arms, and supporting pieces were all carved from horns. Rhinoceros horns, dinosaur fossils, and even the bones of dogs, pigs, or other animals were often passed off by unscrupulous dealers as genuine unicorn horn.

Centuries ago, a book called the *Physiologus*, a collection of legends and factual information about forty different animals, was so popular that it was translated from the original Greek into a dozen languages. Each chapter began with the words, "The physiologus [the scientist] says . . ." hence the book's name.

"The Unicorn in Captivity"—The unicorn is perhaps the most beloved of all imaginary creatures. Here is a scene from the famous "Unicorn Tapestries," (French or Flemish, fifteenth century.). Courtesy of The Metropolitan Museum of Art, The Cloisters Collection, Gift of John D. Rockefeller, Jr., 1937.

By the twelfth century, enlarged versions of the *Physiologus* became known as *bestiaries*. Along with descriptions of such real life animals as lions, giraffes, and weasels, these books included creatures such as the bonnacon, a beast with a bull's head and a horse's body. The bonnacon had horns so cumbersome that it could not use them in battle, but instead excreted a foul and fiery substance that was harmful to everything in its path.

Another incredible creature was the amphisbaena, a snake with two heads: one in the proper place and one at the tail. The amphisbaena moved by holding one head with the teeth of the other, rolling around like a hoop. These animals were said to be aggressive and poisonous, and supposedly fed on corpses. Despite its gruesome diet, prophetesses and other prominent women in ancient Greece wore gold bracelets carved in the image of the amphisbaena to signify their power.

The manticore was a fearsome creature with a face of a man, bloodshot eyes, the body of a lion, and a tail like a scorpion's stinger. If all this was not scary-looking enough, the manticore had a triple set of teeth he would not hesitate to use on human beings. The manticore was so powerful and was able to leap so high that no wall was ever built that could confine him. With his sharp, terrible teeth, he was able to devour the flesh, bones, and clothing of his hapless victim, which explained to the ancients why some individuals would occasionally disappear without a trace.

One of the more unusual mythical creatures was the bicorn, which had the head of a cow and the body of a panther. The bicorn dined exclusively on the bodies of hen-pecked husbands, and its sleek and well-fed appearance was said to be due to the fact that its prey was so plentiful!

Obviously unicorns, manticores, bonnacons, and their kin are creatures of the imagination, but it is thought that some mythical animals did have their basis in fact. The mermaid is said to be based on sightings of the manatee. It is not difficult to see how this homely creature may look vaguely human if viewed from the side of an ancient ship by a homesick and superstitious sailor on a cold and misty night.

We have come a long way from the days of the medieval bestiaries, accomplishing things that our ancestors never dreamed of. We can travel around the world in a few hours, build tunnels along the ocean floor, and fly to the outermost corners of the galaxy. But with all of our sophistication, these beasts of wonder still have a grip on our imaginations: Witness the continuing fascination with such creatures as the Loch Ness monster (known affectionately as "Nessie" to monster-watchers) and Sasquatch (a.k.a. "Bigfoot") hold, even for those of us who would never be caught dead reading a copy of *The National Enquirer*.

QUIZ: ANIMALS IN CLASSICAL MYTHOLOGY:
A MAGICAL BESTIARY

Below are descriptions of twenty mythical creatures from Greek, Roman, and Norse mythology. Match them with the names at the right. Answers can be found on pages 233–235.

a. Python　b. Centaur　c. Sleipnir　d. Fenrir　e. Basilisk　f. Chimera
g. Satyr　h. Minotaur　i. Epona　j. Griffin　k. Jomungandar　l. Hydra
m. Catoplebas　n. Harpy　o. The Erymanthian Boar　p. Cerberus
q. Pegasus　r. Hippogriff　s. Siren　t. Sphinx

1. Ugly creature with the head of a woman and the body of an eagle.

2. Vicious wolf, the evil spawn of an ogress and the Norse trickster-god Loki, that was so huge it could block out the light of the sun.

3. Originally a Celtic nature goddess, adopted by the Romans as the goddess of horses and mules.

4. Half-goat, half-human mischief makers.

5. Black as night, with blood red eyes, an evil creature that terrorized the Greek countryside.

6. Fierce serpent of Greek mythology who dwelt within a cave, at Mount Parnassus.

7. Winged being, with the upper body of a woman and the lower body of a lion, who dwelt near Thebes.

8. Symbol of love in ancient Greece.

9. Odin's eight-legged horse, who could travel by land or sea.

10. Lethal sea creature that took the form of a beautiful woman with the legs and talons of a bird.

11. Beast with the upper body of a bull, the lower torso of a man, and a taste for human flesh.

12. White winged horse, offspring of the sea god Poseidon and the snake-haired Medusa.

13. Fire-breathing female monster with an upper body like a lion, middle part of a goat, and a tail end like a serpent.

14. Half-man, half-horse creatures.

15. Lizardlike monster whose looks could literally kill.

16. Huge reptile with nine heads, one of which was immortal.

17. Giant sea serpent, one of Loki's children by the sister of Fenrir.

18. Beast with the legs and body of a lion and the wings of an eagle.

19. Ferocious three-headed dog that guards the entrance to the underworld (Hades).

20. Huge, buffalolike creature, thought by the Greeks to dwell in Ethiopia, that could kill with a mere glance.

QUIZ: GODS AND GODDESSES OF ANCIENT EGYPT

Today, Egypt is predominantly Muslim, but thousands of years ago, the people of this arid nation worshipped a multitude of gods and goddesses. Many of these deities were associated with particular animals and, in some cases, even took on the physical attributes of these beasts, something anthropologists call *zoomorphism*. Match each description with the correct animal-like god or goddess. Answers can be found on pages 235–236.

1. The goddess of truth and justice and the daughter of the great sun god Ra, she wore a single ostrich feather in the center of her forehead.

    a. Mab   b. Maat   c. Lakshmi   d. Fatima

2. A daughter of Isis, the Egyptian goddess of the earth and moon, she is the goddess of childbirth and fertility and was portrayed with the head of a cat.

    a. Hathor   b. Basht   c. Nefertiti   d. Hatshepsut

3. Thought to be the ancestor of the pharaohs, his emblems included the falcon and the scarab, or dung beetle.

    a. Tutankhamen   b. Rakin   c. En-lil   d. Ra

4. God of the dead, he is depicted with the head of a jackal.

    a. Thoth   b. Set   c. Anubis   d. Ramses

5. This fierce deity, the goddess of warfare and battles, was depicted with the head of a lioness.

    a. Sesha   b. Sekhmet   c. Inanna   d. Isis

6. The Egyptian sky goddess, this giantess was called The Sow Who Eats All Her Piglets.

   a. Oannes   b. Nut   c. Keres   d. Ariadne

7. Crocodiles were sacred to this god of evil and death.

   a. Hastor   b. Mithras   c. Seth   d. Fuath

8. The god of sunlight and daybreak and another child of Isis, he was known by his devotees as He Who Is Above. In hieroglyphics, he is usually depicted by his sacred animal, the sparrow-hawk.

   a. Osiris   b. Seth   c. Nike   d. Horus

9. The chief of the Egyptian gods, he was known as Lord of the World Order and is usually depicted with a ram's head.

   a. Ptah   b. Nun   c. Ares   d. Lamas

10. The first ruler of Egypt, he taught the people how to sow grain and make beer, and patronized the development of music, art, and perfume-making.

   a. Gilgamesh   b. Baal   c. Osiris   d. Orfeo

QUIZ: WHO SLEW WHOM?

Centuries before Superman or Batman, heroes with fantastic abilities rescued fair maidens, and performed feats of incredible valor, and conquered dragons and other terrifying creatures. Try to guess the names of these beast-conquering heroes of ancient legend. Answers can be found on pages 236–237.

1. He killed the evil giant Fafnir, who had turned himself into a wicked dragon in order to guard his horde of gold.

2. The chimera was slain by this Greek hero with the help of Pegasus.

3. The Minotaur was finally conquered by this Greek hero.

4. He defeated the hideous snake-haired Medusa by tricking her into looking at her own reflection.

5. This Greek superhero not only killed the fierce Erymanthian boar, but also slew the Hydra, the man-eating Nemean lion, and the Stymphalian birds, who devoured sailors unfortunate enough to be marooned in the swamplands near Lake Stymphalis.

Chapter Twenty

ANIMALS IN FOLKLORE

THE ENCHANTED ISLES

Besides having had an impact on world history disproportionate to their small size, Scotland, Wales, Ireland, and England are rich in the lore of the supernatural and for this reason are sometimes called "the enchanted isles."

Cats play an important role in the folklore of these nations. Perhaps the most famous are those fighting felines from Ireland, the Kilkenny cats:

> *There once were two cats of Kilkenny,*
> *Each thought there was one cat too many;*
> *So they fought and they fit,*
> *And they scratched and they bit,*
> *'Till excepting their nails,*
> *And the tips of their tails,*
> *Instead of two cats there weren't any.*

Today, the expression "fighting like Kilkenny cats" is sometimes used to describe individuals involved in a skirmish, verbal or otherwise.

Other felines take on more frightening dimensions, such as the Scottish demon-cat known as Big Ears, sometimes called the King of the Cats. Those who wished to ask favors of this demon cat (the most common requests were for wealth, heirs, or the gift of second sight) would perform a gruesome and sadistic ceremony called the *Taghairn*, or *Taigheirm*, which can be translated as "armory," or more tellingly, "cry of the cats."

First, black cats, symbolic of darkness and evil, were collected. Then, over a period of four days, beginning at midnight between Friday and Saturday, the participants, who ate no food during the time, would skewer and slowly roast the live cats on a spit. Only those with the strongest stomachs could complete the ritual, for during the entire period there could be no pause in the proceedings, despite the appalling screams of the burning cats.

Supposedly, the continuous torture of the poor animals would cause numerous devils to converge on the area in the form of black cats. Finally, Big Ears, the chief devil cat, would appear. The giant, green-eyed creature would grudgingly grant all requests in order to stop his friends from being tortured.

The *Taghairn* was said to have been performed on the island of Mull, located in the Hebrides of western Scotland, by two brothers, Lachlain and Allan Maclean, in 1750. At the end of the fourth day, a monstrous black cat with fiery eyes and huge pointed ears supposedly appeared. Big Ears was said to have let out a terrible howl that could be heard clear across the Strait of Mull. Allan, completely exhausted from the ordeal and frightened by the demon, could only gasp out "prosperity," but his older brother, Lachlain, asked for heirs and wealth. Both of the brothers were granted their requests.

Many years later, at Allan's funeral, those at the graveside who possessed the "second sight" claimed they could see Lachlain, who had died earlier, standing in the distance watching the proceedings, fully armed, and behind him a host of black cats. Today, visitors to the island of Mull can see the claw marks on the stone where Big Ears is supposed to have last appeared.

Other magical cats were more benevolent. Caith Sith, a black fairy cat found in the Scottish Highlands, could be recognized by the large round white patch on his chest and was known to mind children and guard houses against intruders.

Fairy dogs with some nasty characteristics are also found throughout the British Isles. One of them, Ce Sith, has a dark green coat. If you see him, he will do you no harm; but if you speak to him or touch him, you will fall senseless to the ground, and there is a very good chance that you may also be torn to pieces.

The Gabriel Hounds, also known as the Sky Yelpers, were once thought to be ghostly wolves with human heads who roamed the skies during storms. English country folk believed that they were the souls of unbaptized babies or unrepentant sinners, and that their unearthly howls were an omen of death to all who heard them. Today, it is thought that these dreadful animals are in fact night-flying geese. To superstitious peasants who did not understand bird migration, the flapping of the geese's wings and strange cries must have sounded frightening indeed.

For centuries, the Black Dogs, headless beasts about the size of ponies, have been said to roam the roads of Devonshire in southwest England at dusk, searching for the newly dead. They make no sound as they run, but anyone hearing their eerie howls will die within a year. These evil dogs can be laid to rest only by ringing a bell that has been blessed in a church near where they are sighted. The bell must then be tossed in one stretch of water and the clapper in another. The Black Dogs will be able to resume their hauntings only if someone is foolish enough to reunite the two items.

Other legendary canines come closer to the age-old image of the dog as man's best friend. From Wales comes the tragic tale of a deerhound named Gerlert. One of Gerlert's duties was to watch the infant son of his master, the brave and noble Prince Llewellyn, while the handsome young nobleman was away. One day, a ferocious wolf entered the baby's nursery, and after a terrible fight, Gerlert managed to kill the intruder. Prince Llewellyn, upon returning to the castle, saw the baby's crib overturned and the dog covered with blood. In a rage, he unscathed his sword and mortally wounded Gerlert, who managed to lick his hand before he died. Only then did Llewellyn find the huge body of the wolf and the baby, stunned and frightened but safe, huddled in a corner. Today, the Welsh town of Beddgelert is named after the faithful dog. Versions of this Welsh legend can be found throughout the world.

The Mimicke Dog, a playful pooch with curly ringlets instead of fur, first made its appearance in England in the late 1500s. This creature, described as having "an ape's wit and a hedgehog's face," could imitate human voices and behavior, often causing mischief in a household. This animal was thought to be raised by apes in Africa, and Queen Elizabeth I was supposed to have owned one.

The British Isles are full of tales of "bogey beasts" that can change their shapes at will. One of the most malicious is the *each-uisge* of Scotland, which most often appears as a handsome horse. The foolish person who mounts this beast, however, soon finds that he cannot get off, for the horse has sticky skin that glues the rider to its back. The evil creature then plunges into the water to devour its victim. The *each-uisge* sometimes appears as a handsome young man, but can always be recognized by the fact that the roots of its hair are tangled with seaweed and sand.

The Irish *aughisky* is similar to the *each-usige*, usually taking the form of a long-haired horse that is found near salt water. The *aughisky* likes to prey on cattle, herding them to the water and then eating them. If a man is crafty and strong enough to capture an *aughisky*, saddle and bridle him, and turn inland, he will have a fine, strong horse. If the creature is ever allowed the scent or sight of sea water, however, it will gallop with the rider beneath the waves and devour him, leaving only the liver to float to shore.

Perhaps the most horrible water creature of all, however, was the Scottish *nuckalavee*. The *nuckalavee* has the torso of a man and the legs of a horse, fearsome staring eyes, and horrible poisonous breath. Worst of all, the *nuckalavee* is skinless, so that its muscles and sinews are exposed, and shreds of rotting, stinking flesh drip from its body.

Years ago the *nuckalavee* was greatly feared, because it was thought to spread disease among cattle and other livestock, kill crops with its poisonous breath, and slaughter any human it came across. Curiously, even though the *nuckalavee* comes from the water, it is said to be terrified of fresh running water, so that one could escape it by crossing over a mountain stream or river.

THE FABULOUS BEASTS OF ANCIENT ASIA

When many of us think of Asian countries such as Japan and South Korea, the images that come to mind are of high-tech affluence: ultra-modern factories producing goods sold all over the world, and bustling, crowded cities. What is often forgotten is the other side of the Orient—a land of lush green countryside, ancient traditions, and a rich and enduring folklore in which animals are respected and sometimes feared.

Perhaps the best-known creature in Asian legend is the dragon. In the West, these huge, scaly reptiles were depicted as frightening and evil, spreading death and destruction wherever they went. The Greek poet Hesiod, who lived in the eighth century B.C., illustrates this attitude in *The Shield of Hercules*:

> *The scaly monster of a dragon, coil'd full in the central field—*
> *unspeakable, with eyes oblique retorted that aslant shot gleaming*
> *fire. . . .*

During the Christian era, the dragon become symbolic of Satan himself.

The dragons of the East, however, were often kindly and wise, and they played an important role in Chinese legend. In fact, the dragon was considered one of the four superior creatures (the others included the tortoise, the phoenix, and the *ki-lin*, the Chinese unicorn). To see a dragon in the sky was a good omen. They came in a variety of colors, including bright red, and had sheer, gold-tipped wings. They were also associated with royalty—in ancient China, the emperor's throne was referred to as the Dragon's Throne and his face, the Dragon's Face. At the emperor's death, it was said that he ascended to heaven like the dragon.

Instead of fire, Asian dragons breathed mist, and for this reason they were thought to be responsible for making clouds and controlling the weather. Legend has it that the glorious colors of autumn leaves are a result of a near-by dragon yawning and tingeing them with its warm breath before settling down to its winter sleep.

The dragon king, Lung Wang, was in charge of making rain. The six-teenth-century Chinese medical almanac, *Pan Ts'ao Kang Mu*, gives the fol-lowing description of the dragon god:

> *Its head is like a camel's, its horns like a deer's, it's eyes like a hare's,*
> *its ears like a bull's, its neck like a snake's, its belly like a clam's, its*
> *scales like a carp's, its claws like an eagle's, and its paws like a tiger's.*

In order to please Lung Wang and petition him for good weather, the Chinese offered the emerald-scaled dragon god roasted swallows' hearts and red lotus blossoms.

Another creature of Asian mythology with a western counterpart is the phoenix. The ancient Greeks believed that the phoenix lived in ancient Arabia and Egypt and had a golden head and beautiful iridescent feathers that reflect-ed all the brilliant colors seen in fire—crimson, gold, orange, lavender, and bright turquoise. This beautiful bird has appeared only five times in the histo-ry of the world, the last time being at the coronation of the Emperor Constantine in A.D. 334.

The phoenix was thought to live anywhere from 300 to 1,000 years. Near the end of its allotted time it would construct a pyre made of fragrant spices, such as myrrh, cinnamon, and frankincense, in a palm tree, which became known as a "a phoenix tree". The nest was then ignited by the sun and the bird went up in flames, singing gloriously as it died.

The Chinese called their phoenix *fung*, or *fun*, and believed it was sacred to the element of fire. It is described as having:

> *. . . the forepart of a goose, the hindquarters of a stag, the neck of a*
> *snake, the tail of a fish, the forehead of a fowl, the down of a duck,*
> *the marks of a dragon, the back of a tortoise, the face of a swallow,*
> *the beak of a cock, is about six cubits high and perches only in the*
> *Woo Tung tree.*

The phoenix's image was often embroidered on the cloaks of mandarins and emperors.

The Chinese unicorn, or *ki-lin* (pronounced *chee-lin*), was a solitary animal that dwelt in deep forests and high mountains. Like its occidental counterpart, it had a single horn in the middle of its head, but its smooth skin included patches of black, white, red, yellow, and blue—the five sacred Chinese colors. The *ki-lin* is said to have brought the gift of writing to the Chinese people.

Cats figure prominently in Asian folklore. From Japan comes the tale of the *nekomata*, a demon cat in the guise of an orange-red tabby that has the power to transform itself into an ugly old woman. The only way this evil creature can be destroyed is by a dog.

In ancient Thailand, when a member of the royal family died, a live cat was buried with the body. Small holes were strategically placed around the burial site so the cat could eventually find its way out. When the cat finally escaped, the temple priests explained to the people that the soul of the dead person had passed into the animal.

The beautiful and graceful Siamese, which originated in Thailand, is one of the world's most popular breeds of cat. The Thai say that one day, a god picked up the cat by the scruff of its neck, and ever since that time the shadow of the deity's hand has appeared on its descendants.

The striped cousin of the cat, the tiger, often appears in the lore of Asia, where it is considered the king of the jungle. This beautiful but dangerous animal is said to be a shape-changer and can often appear in human form. In Asian folklore, tigers and dragons are mortal enemies.

The graceful white crane, or *tsuru*, holds a special place in Japanese culture. It is said that these birds live 1,000 years, and those wishing for good luck often string a thousand origami cranes into a long wreath or lei. Even luckier than 1,000 cranes, however, is the *tsuru-kame*, the combination of a crane and tortoise; this reptile is said to live for *10,000* years. Even today, the *tsuru-kame* is used on cakes, cards, banners, medallions, and other objects in Japan as a powerful symbol of good luck.

Another animal found in Japanese folklore is the *kitsune* (fox). Foxes are fond of playing tricks on people and are shape-changers, often turning into beautiful young women. These fox-women are usually benevolent and sometimes marry mortal men, and even bear human children with thin, vixenish faces. They can often be recognized, however, by a spurt of flame flickering over their human heads. If a fox-woman looks into the water, only her fox features will be reflected. The appearance of a dog, however, forces the fox-woman to reveal her human shape, because these two creatures are bitter enemies.

The Japanese fox spirits known as *koki-teno* were malicious. These spirits wandered about cemeteries until they found a human skull, which they put on their heads. After turning to the North Star, they would take on the appearance of a human being, most often a young woman in a long white gown. The *koki-teno* were known for their ravishing beauty and their powers of seduction were legendary. The victims of the *koki-teno* would eventually become subject to "fox possession," growling and running about on all fours. They were also easily frightened by dogs.

In old Japan, the hare was held in great esteem and was said to live a thousand years. In fact, instead of a man in the moon, Japanese children see a hare in the moon.

According to legend, the Japanese islands rest on the back of a giant carp, and it is the thrashings of this fish that have caused this nation's numerous volcanoes, earthquakes, and hurricanes throughout the centuries. Despite its moodiness, the carp is a symbol of courage in Japan, and one of the nation's most popular professional baseball teams is called the Hiroshima Carp. Another water creature, the frog, is associated with rain; to the Vietnamese, the croaking of a frog means that wet weather is on the way. One story from Vietnam concerns Kim Qui, a golden idol in the shape of a turtle, who often steps down from his temple perch to help the less fortunate.

Rats also appear in Asian folklore. These rodents are generally feared and disliked in the West, but in Japan, the rat is a messenger of the god of wealth. If a rat gnaws on the New Year cakes, there will be a good harvest.

The Chinese take a more ambivalent view of rats. While they are a symbol of prosperity, they also symbolize meanness, and in Chinese astrology, the "Year of the Rat," which occurs every twelve years, is an unlucky time to be born.

THUNDERBIRDS AND TRICKSTER GODS: MAGICAL ANIMALS OF THE NATIVE AMERICANS

Living so closely to natural world, Native Americans developed a unique relationship with animals. In their book *American Indian Myths and Legends*, Richard Erdoes and Alfonso Ortiz write: "In the Indian imagination there is no division between the animal and human spheres; each takes the other's clothing, shifting appearances at will."

Animals figure prominently in the creation myths of various Native American cultures. According to the Iroquois, Toad dives for mud and makes the earth on the back of a giant turtle. The Arapaho, in a variation of the story, say that a tortoise or turtle swam to the bottom of a vast lake and brought back pieces of clay, from which it made the dry earth.

Some Native Americans believed that they were actually descended from animals. The colorful and beautifully carved totem poles of Northwest Coast tribes such as the Kwakiutl, who now live on Vancouver Island and along the coast of British Columbia, served as family crests, depicting the clan's legendary descent from such animals as the salmon, raven, bear, or killer whale. When visiting a strange village, a traveler would look for a house with the totem pole of his own clan animal, where he was sure to be received warmly.

Marriages between humans and animals are also common in Native American tales. Often the animal would look human, but underneath his or her skin was actually a bison (in the southwest and Plains), a whale (in the northeast), a dog, or bear by night.

In the folklore of many nations, there is a character, either human or animal, who is a mischief-maker and rebel against authority, a creature who breaks all the rules. In Europe, he is Reynard the Fox (in Germany, he is called *Reinecke Fuchs*). Among the Native Americans, Coyote was the great trickster, who, as Erdoes and Ortiz say, was "at the same time, imp and hero, the great culture bringer who can also make mischief beyond belief, turning quickly from clown to creator and back again." Other animals known for their cleverness were the raven, bluejay, mink, and beaver.

Most of us know the rabbit as a shy and timid creature, but among the Algonquin, the deity known as Michabo was known as the Great Hare. His gifts to the Algonquin were many. Not only did he steal fire from heaven to give to man, he also devised the art of knitting fishnets by watching spiders spin their webs. In the autumn, when he takes his winter sleep, Michabo fills his great pipe with holy tobacco and smokes, and the smoke that arises is seen in the air as the haze of Indian summer.

Birds appear throughout Native American mythology. The eagle in particular was highly regarded. Its feathers composed the war flag of the Creeks, and the Zuñi of New Mexico used four of its feathers to represent the four winds when invoking their rain god.

In western culture, owls are often a symbol of wisdom, but to many tribes, the owl was associated with death. The Algonquin, for example, believed that the owl was an attendant of the Lord of the Dead. Native Americans of the Northwest believe that the owl calls out the names of men and women who will soon die. Among the Sioux, a huge owl named Hin-Han guards the entrance to the Milky Way, which the souls of the dead must pass over to reach the spirit land. Those individuals who do not pass the owl's inspection because they do not have the right tattoo on their wrists or other part of their body are thrown into a dark, bottomless pit. Among the Pima Indians of the Southwest, the owl was one of the symbols of the souls of the dead, and a dying person was always given its feather to help him or her into the next world.

Camazotz was the ancient Mayan god of hunting and fate, and as Lord of the Wind, also controlled thunder, rain, and lightning. Camazotz was usually portrayed as a bat with two curled fangs. He often played dice with warriors, gambling for the gift of immortality. If they lost at the game, the bat-god swiftly beheaded them, and their spirits appeared as stars in the eastern sky. If Camazotz was in a good mood, however, he would instead turn the unlucky losers into fruit bats, who would then serve Camazotz and his court for eternity.

Among the most fantastic creatures of Native American lore are the thunderbirds. The voice of the thunderbird is the mighty clap of thunder, and the smaller rolling thunders that are sometimes heard in the sky are the cries of his children, the little thunderbirds. Lightning occurs when the thunderbird blinks his eyes.

According to the Brule Sioux, there are four major thunderbirds called Wakinyan. The chief thunderbird of the West, Wakinyan Tanka, is clothed in clouds. Wakinyan Tanka is black in color and has no head, feet, or body, but does possess enormous claws, a huge sharp beak, and giant, four-jointed wings. Wakinyan Tanka lives in a giant tepee in a nest of dry bones. Inside this nest is a giant egg, which is bigger than the entire state of South Dakota. It is from this egg that the little thunderbirds hatch.

Dogs were important in many Native American cultures, but their primary purpose was not that of a companion animal. They were employed as beasts of burden and at times were also eaten. Dogs were used in religious rites by some tribes; a red dog was sacrificed by the Aztecs to carry the soul of a dead ruler across a deep stream or to announce the king's arrival into the other world.

The introduction of the horse by the Spanish in the mid-1500s changed Native American society forever. There was no word for this amazing new animal in the Native American vocabulary, however, so these creatures were called Elk Dog (because they carried burdens like a dog), Spirit Dog, Sacred Dog, or Moose Dog.

In a beautiful story told by the Blackfoot, a young man named Long Arrow travels to the bottom of the Great Mystery Lake, where he finds a mysterious land ruled by an ancient chief with flowing white hair and the black robes of a medicine man. There he sees a herd of magnificent animals with glossy coats, long flowing manes and tails, and gentle brown eyes—Elk Dogs. The spirit chief gives Long Arrow a robe made from the hair of the sacred white buffalo to capture the wonderful animals. When Long Arrow reaches the village astride one of the horses, he is at first mistaken for a monster, half animal and half human. Some of the terrified villagers raise their weapons to strike him, but he cries, "Grandfather Good Running, it is your grandson Long Arrow! No longer will we have to travel by foot, for I have been brought back a wonderful gift from the Spirit Chief of the Great Mystery Lake—creatures called Elk Dogs." With the Elk Dogs, the Blackfoot were able to become great riders of the Plains.

The serpent holds a central place in North American mythology. Legends in many tribes tell of a horrible, snakelike monster called Uncegila, who had scales of glittering mica and was as long as one hundred horses placed head to tail. This terrible monster, however, had an ice-cold heart of flashing red crystal, and whoever possessed it would be more powerful than anyone in the world.

Quetzlcoatl was the plumed serpent god of Central America, a magnificent creature with brilliant, multicolored scales and bright feathers reaching from head to tail. His rival was Tezcatlipoca, (meaning "smoking mirror," referring to the shiny black obsidian used by the high priests of the Aztecs to divine the future). Tezcatlipoca was the Aztec god of war and was described as having a bear's face and a man's body. A cruel and temperamental god who enjoyed playing malicious tricks on mortals, Tezcatlipoca's most evil act was to introduce the Spanish conquistadors to South America. At first, the conquistadors were welcomed as the reincarnation of Quetzlcoatl, but in a relatively short period of time, they brought about the downfall of Aztec civilization.

In the beginning, Quetzlcoatl and Tezcatlipoca created earth by dragging the goddess called "the hungry woman" out of the sky and spreading her body over the ocean. They did this by changing into two large snakes and stretching the goddess into four equal parts. The hungry woman was infuriated by such rough treatment. The two gods sought to appease her by descending to her surface and making forests, flowers, valleys, and other pleasant features. The earth, however, was not satisfied, for she craved the beating hearts of humans and desired to be watered with their red blood—hence the bloody, gruesome sacrifices of the Aztecs.

According to the Aztecs, Quetzlcoatl was defeated by the evil Tezcatlipoca, whereupon the serpent god immolated himself upon a funeral pyre. Rare and beautiful birds were said to have risen from his ashes, and his heart was placed in the heavens, where it still shines down upon the earth as the morning star.

Like all cultures, Native Americans have stories of how the end of the world will come about. According to the Cheyenne, somewhere there is a great pole made of an enormous tree trunk. This pole is what holds up the world. The Great White Grandfather Beaver of the North sits at the base of the pole, gnawing away. He has been nibbling at the pole with his great, sharp teeth for centuries, and more than half of it is already eaten through. When the Great White Grandfather Beaver of the North is angry, he grinds away at the pole even faster. Once it has been gnawed through, the pole will collapse, and everyone on earth will crash into a bottomless pit. For this reason, the Cheyenne never ate the castor's flesh, or even touched a beaver skin, for fear of angering Great White Grandfather Beaver of the North.

OUT OF AFRICA: ANIMAL TALES OF A CONTINENT

The African continent has long been known as the home of some of the world's most fascinating animals. Although the seemingly endless herds of wildlife have been seriously depleted by hunting and habitat destruction, this vast continent has much to teach both the naturalist and the student of folklore. Indeed, the variety of legends surrounding African animals mirrors the richness and diversity of the wildlife.

In most native African cultures, the image of a Creator God was essential. Humans were created not to dominate the earth, but to live in harmony with the world around them. For example, according to the Bushmen of southern Africa, the Creator first made the earth and all the plants upon it. Then, tired of being alone, he decided to create some companions. Striking the baobab tree, he caused the animals to walk through a great rent in the mighty tree's roots. The Creator, along with his helper Mantis, gave each creature a role in the scheme of things. Last of all came Man, to whom the Creator and Mantis gave the role of Hunter-Gatherer. The Bushman fulfilled his role faithfully, living in close harmony with the animals and other living things on earth.

Many African peoples believe that humans originated from animals. According to the Shangaan of South Africa, humans were created when N'wari, the great bird god, flew down from his home high in the mountains to the edge of a river. There, N'wari bored a hole in a river reed and laid a huge egg in it. After some time, the egg hatched and the first man was born.

The Venda, another tribe of South Africa, believe that in the beginning, a giant snake called Tharu (Python) lived in the rugged mountain slopes that are now the home of the Vendas. During a time of great drought in the land, Tharu divided himself into two parts: Thoho, the Head, and Tshamutshila, the Tail. Both Tail and Head went searching for food and water. Tshamutshila went westward, into the land that is now the country of the Vendas. There he became a human being, gathered herds of cattle, and became the ancestor of the Venda people. Thoho went east to the country that is now called Mozambique and founded the Ronga people.

Animal tricksters appear frequently in African folklore. Ijapa the tortoise appears in many stories, songs, and proverbs of the Yoruba, a people that live in what is now called Nigeria. This giant tortoise is described as being "shrewd, conniving, greedy, indolent, unreliable, ambitious, exhibitionist, unpredictable, aggressive, generally preposterous, and sometimes stupid. . . . He is used as a kind of yardstick against which human behavior, human foibles, and moral strength are measured."*

Thousands of Yoruba were enslaved and transplanted to Brazil (particularly the Bahia region), Cuba, and other islands in the Caribbean, where some of their customs still persist. Yoruba were also brought to the United States, where Ijapa has survived in African-American folklore as "Brother Terrapin."

Indeed, many of the animals found in African stories were transplanted to American soil via the slave ships of the eighteenth and nineteenth centuries, where they underwent changes in their new surroundings. The African jackal became the American fox and the African hare, the American rabbit. The "Uncle Remus" stories, popularized by the nineteenth-century-writer Joel Chandler Harris, tell of the exploits of Brer ("Brother") Rabbit, the Tar Baby, and other characters, all of whom can be traced directly to African sources thousands of years old.

"Aunt Nancy," or "Sis Nancy," a mischievous spider found in the folklore of the American South, Jamaica, and other areas of the West Indies, is based on "Anansi" (sometimes called Kwaku, or Uncle Anansi), a trickster-spider that is featured prominently in the tales of the Ashanti and related Akan-speaking peoples of Ghana. In fact, it is said that Anansi owns all the stories and tales (called *anansesem*) that were ever told.

*Harold Courlander, *A Treasury of African Folklore*, p. 221.

Anansi plays an important and sometimes contradictory role in the folk-lore of these peoples. While he has frequent encounters with the supreme sky god himself, Onyame, and has a number of great achievements to his credit—including the creation of the moon and the human tongue, and the gift of the hoe to mankind—the *anansesem* also relate that he is responsible for all the greed in the world and the fact that a man has debts.

Why Cheetah's Face Is Stained With Tears

One day in Zululand, a lazy and evil-minded hunter was sitting under a tree, watching as a female cheetah went hunting. The man was amazed at the speed and accuracy with which the big cat stalked and finally caught her prey, a fine, fat springbok, and was also surprised at the three young cheetah cubs who sat in the distance under the shade of a tree, watching as their mother caught their dinner. Knowing that chee-tahs are shy and timid creatures that never attack man, and being the slothful sort that he was, the man decided that he would take one of the cubs and train it to hunt for him. He waited until the sun set and the mother cheetah went hunting again. Quickly he went to where the young cheetahs were sleeping peacefully in the grass. Because he could not decide which one to take and was greedy as well as lazy, he stole them all.

When the mother came back some time later with another springbok, she called to her children with that strange cry that cheetahs make, a sound more like that of a bird chirping than of the roar of a big cat. She called and called until she realized that her babies were gone. Brokenhearted, she started to cry. She cried and cried, and the tears ran down her cheeks and made dark stains. Her weeping was so loud that an old man heard the noise and came to her lair to see what was going on.

When the old man heard what had happened, he became very angry. Not only had the evil man stolen the cheetah's children, he had also behaved dishonorably, for the rules of the hunt stated that a man must use only his own skill and strength and not take advantage of others. The wise old man went and told the elders of the village, and they, too, became angry—so angry that they banished the wicked, lazy man from the village forever.

When the old man returned the cheetah's cubs to her, she was over-joyed, but her long period of weeping had left dark stains on her face, stains that are there to this day.

The Dog and the Jackal

According to the Mbundu of Zaire, the dog and jackal used to live together in the bush. One day Jackal sent Dog to the human village to steal some fire. "When you come back," said Jackal, "we will burn the grass and catch locusts for our dinner." Dog nodded and made his way to the village. He looked into a window, where he saw a woman serving her child mush. Noticing Dog, she motioned for him to come over and gave him the scrapings from the pot. "Hmm," said Dog, as he gratefully licked the mush, "why should I scrounge around and eat scrawny locusts and other nasty things when there is good eating right here?" He forgot all about Jackal waiting for him and the fire, and decided to stay in the village.

Jackal waited and waited, until he realized that Dog would not come back. When Jackal howls, he is asking for his friend Dog to come back with the fire, so that they may once again live as kinsmen.

Why the Hippo Is So Ugly

The Ndebele of Zimbabwe say that many, many years ago, hippos did not live in pools and rivers as they do now; they dwelt in the bush in great herds, like antelopes or zebra. Hippo looked completely different from the way he does today, with a coat of glossy chestnut brown hair, soft round ears, and a beautiful bushy tail. Hippo would spend many hours at the watering hole, admiring his handsome reflection. One day, while preening by the riverside, he said to himself, "Oh, what a gorgeous and lovely creature I am! Surely I'm the most elegant beast on the planet. Look at this hair, these cute little ears, these elegant, dainty hooves! Why, I'm nothing like that ridiculous elephant, with that long, wrinkled nose, or that ugly hare, with those absurd, long ears, that stupid twitching nose, and that ludicrous stump of a tail!"

Hare just happened to be hopping by and was enraged by the Hippo's words. Crafty creature that he was, he decided to get even with the vain animal. Quickly, he built a nest of soft, sweet-smelling grass under a large umbrella tree. Hopping over to Hippo, he said, "Oh, most excellent and beautiful creature of the bush, I have prepared a bed for you under that umbrella tree. Winter is coming and the nights are growing cold, and you will need a warm place to sleep."

Hippo sniffed around the pile of grass for a few minutes and plopped his chunky body in the middle of it. "I guess it will do," he sighed. "And I am glad you realize your responsibilities to a creature such as myself."

Hare could barely contain his rage, but nodded humbly and hopped stealthily away to a nearby village. When nobody was looking, he crept up to the cooking fire and stole some glowing embers, which he placed in a shard of broken clay pot.

Hare returned to find Hippo snoring away happily in his grass bed. Hare crept up and threw in the burning embers, puffing on them until he had a brisk blaze going. Hippo awoke to find his bed on fire and Hare hopping away, chuckling nastily to himself.

Hippo's haughty attitude disappeared rapidly as the red hot flames roared about him. Confused and frightened, he thrashed about wildly, trying to put out the fire, but as it reached his skin, he howled in pain and rushed toward the water hole. He gave a mighty sigh of relief as the cool water rushed over his body, soothing his agony.

The bushfire the vengeful hare had set burned for many hours, but finally died out. Hippo stayed in the water all during the time, planning to give the evil Hare a thrashing he would never forget. As he climbed out of the water, he caught a glimpse of his reflection. He could not believe his eyes! Instead of the handsome creature with the glorious coat of silky hair, a pinkish grey, bald one stared out at him. His beautiful plumelike tail was gone, and his silky ears had been burned down to ugly, round stubs. He had once thought of himself as "pleasingly plump," but without his elegant pelage, he was just plain fat.

Horrified at his appearance, Hippo hurried back in the water on his short, stumpy legs, weeping loudly. So ashamed was he of his appearance that he sank below the surface of the water so that only his great nostrils and tiny eyes showed. And this is the way he can be found most of the time today, his body submerged under the water. Only under the cover of night, when no one can see and ridicule him, does he come out, to walk and remember the time, many moons ago, when he was handsome.

How Death Came Into the World

To the Hottentots, the Moon was a great deity. One day, in the beginning of the world, she sent an Insect with a message for humankind. "Tell them," she said, that as I die, and in dying live, so shall you also die, and *dying live." The Insect was puzzled by the strange message, but nevertheless went to do the Moon's bidding. On his way to earth, he met the Hare. "Where are you going?" the nosy creature asked.*

"I'm heading toward Earth with a message from the Moon, to tell them that as she dies, and dying lives, so they also shall die, and dying live."

The Hare, who thought that he was much smarter than he actually was, shook his head. "You're such a slow and awkward runner, you'll never make it. Let me go with the message instead." Before the Insect could open his mouth to answer, the Hare was off.

Soon he came to the village of Men. "I come to you with a message from the Moon," said the hare pompously. "She said, 'As I die, and in dying perish, so shall you also die and come to an end.'" The Men looked at one another in shock and dismay at the dire proclamation, but the Hare, quite satisfied with himself, hopped away, returning to the Moon.

When the Hare told the goddess what he had said, she became furious. "How dare you tell the people something that I did not say?" she cried. She was so angry that she picked up a nearby piece of wood and hit him hard on the nose with it. This is why the Hare's nose is slit, and Men do not live forever, but perish.

The Zulu tell a variation of this tale. One day the great god Unkulunku, known as The Irresistible and He Who Bends Down Even Majesties, sent a lizard and a chameleon to earth with messages for humankind. The chameleon was to tell the people that "eternal life was possible," but the lizard's message was that "all mankind must die." The lizard reached earth before the lazy chameleon, who loitered on the way. When the chameleon did finally reach earth, the people were not prepared to believe him.

Chapter Twenty-One

ANIMAL SUPERSTITIONS: AN INTERNATIONAL SAMPLER

AMPHIBIANS AND REPTILES

- In some parts of Asia, geckos are considered good luck. As long as there is a gecko in the house, the family will be blessed with good fortune. If a gecko barks while a child is being born, the baby will grow up to be successful.

- In Sri Lanka, it was once believed that a lizard had wisdom in its tongue. Parents would feed their children banana-and-lizard-tongue sandwiches so that they would grow up to be clever and well-spoken.

- It was once thought that if an turtle lost its shell, it would grow another one. This, of course, is not true; if a turtle loses its shell, it will die within a short period of time.

- The Kooris of Australia thought that if anyone killed a lizard, the sky would fall.

- The crocodile was an object of fear in many cultures. In some West African societies, crocodiles are believed to be the reincarnation of murder victims, and in Hindu legend they are the reincarnation of murdered Brahmins.

- In the Middle Ages, Arabs would throw accused criminals in a lake of crocodiles. If the crocodile ate the man, he was guilty; if not, he was blameless. More people were found guilty than innocent, indeed!

- Because of their association with water, toads and frogs were often thought to have the power to bring rain. The Thompson River Indians of British Columbia believe that if you kill a frog it will rain.

- In medieval times, it was believed that the toad had a precious stone in its head. These "toadstones were thought to possess magical powers, including the ability to detect and neutralize poisons.

APES AND MONKEYS

- In ancient Egypt, apes were considered sacred and were embalmed upon their deaths. The Hebrews, however, thought just the opposite. In the Talmud, if one sees a monkey, it is a sign of bad luck.

BATS

- The bat, because of its ugly appearance and nocturnal habits, has been an object of fear and revulsion for centuries. In Europe, it was said that the devil took the form of a bat, and the animal was therefore regarded as a symbol of death. Some Sicilian peasants also believe that the bat is the devil incarnate, and upon catching one of the winged mammals, they either crucify it or burn it over a candle.

- Bats' blood was thought to have magical powers. Many recipes for "flying ointments" in the Middle Ages mentioned this as a central ingredient.

- In many Asian countries, bats are a symbol of good luck. The Chinese Five Bats, a design with a quintet of these animals arranged in a circle, indicates wealth, love, virtue, old age, and natural death. This symbol is called the *wu-fu* and is often used as a good luck charm. To insure the blessings of the *wu-fu*, the Chinese eat bats, as do some residents of African nations.

BEARS

- In the Middle Ages, bear cubs were thought to be shapeless lumps at birth, no larger than mice, without fur, eyes, hair, or limbs. The mother bear would lick this mass into shape, eventually forming a bear cub.

- The body parts of bears were often used in medicines. To prevent fits, it was once advised to take fur from a live bear's belly, boil it in alcohol, and put it on the soles of your feet. "Bear grease," a salve made from the fat of a bear, was said to cure baldness.

BIRDS

- Ravens and crows have been associated with the world of the supernatural for centuries. The Irish use the phrase "raven's knowledge" to describe a person's ability to see the future. In ancient Rome, if you wanted to ward off evil spirits, all you had to do was kick a crow. A Cornish legend says that the great King Arthur still lives in the form of a huge raven, and since any one of these birds might be the legendary king, none of them should be killed.

- In many cultures, the raven is an omen of impending death. Some Englishmen still believe that when the ravens at the Tower of London desert their home, the tower will come tumbling down.

- Ravens, because of their inky plumage and noisy cawings, were sometimes referred to as "Satan's messengers." Because the birds moult in midsummer and are usually absent from their usual haunts, some English countryfolk say that they visit hell during this time of year and make payment in the form of their dark, glossy feathers to the devil.

- Did you ever notice that blue jays and other jaybirds seem to be in scarce supply on weekends? That's because on Fridays most of them fly down to hell to help the devil by reporting all the miserable things humans have done during that week. They also bring him twigs to keep the hell fires burning. An old song from the Ozarks goes:

> *Don't you hear that blue jay call?*
> *Don't you hear them dead sticks fall?*
> *He's a throwin' down the firewood for we-all*
> *All on a Friday morning.*

The few jaybirds you do see hanging around on weekends are there to check on you and your neighbors—*so watch out!*

● In England and other European countries, it is believed that peacock feathers, despite their beauty, should never be brought into a house, because they will bring bad luck with them. This belief probably stems from the "eyes" on the birds' tails, which could be construed to be "evil eyes." In eastern cultures, however, peacock feathers were supposed to ward off evil, and umbrellas were made out of them.

● In ancient Greece, the swan was sacred to the god of music, Apollo. It was said to be mute until the moment of its death, when it broke out into song: hence the term "swan song," meaning the final appearance or performance of a well-known personality. The swan's song was not mournful, as we might expect, but joyous, because the beautiful bird knew that it would at last be united with its beloved deity.

● In the rural South, if you manage to sprinkle salt on the tail of a bird, you will have good luck.

● On some sections of the English coast, sea gulls are believed to be the souls of drowned sailors.

● In Italy, if you hear a rooster crow three times, someone in your household will die. But this can be prevented by shutting the bird up. This is accomplished by rubbing its head with olive oil and placing a garland of vines around its neck.

● An old Hebrew superstition says that a bride and groom will have good luck if a live hen and rooster are tossed over the couple.

● Crowing roosters have been thought to influence the weather. An old Ozark rhyme says:

> *If a cock crows when he goes to bed,*
> *He'll get up with a wet head.*

● In an effort to bring rain in medieval Germany, a white rooster was killed and its body filled with myrrh, white pepper, frankincense, milk, and wine. The bird's body was then held up toward the sun, and incantations were recited over it.

● Other Germans believed that every seven years, a rooster could lay one egg. If the egg was thrown over your house, the dwelling would always be safe from thunderstorms.

- Perhaps because they are creatures of the night, owls have often been associated with death and destruction. In the Ozarks, the owl was called the "witch chicken" and was thought to be able to charm chickens off their perches. In some parts of Asia, you could frighten evil spirits away by placing a dead owl above a child's bed (you might also succeed in scaring the heck out of the kid, too!).

- If an owl hoots, screeches, or perches near your house, it means impending disaster. You can counteract the owl's evil influence, however, by shutting him up, which can be done by wearing your clothes backwards, taking off your shoes and turning them upside down, tying a knot in your pillowcase, wrapping a piece of white string around your hair, or throwing salt over your shoulder. But never, *ever*, kill an owl because this will bring even more bad luck.

- In Jewish folklore, Adam's first wife, the she-demon Lilith, flew about as a night owl, making off with children.

- If the first robin you see in the spring flies upward, you will have good luck for the rest of the year. But if it flies down, you *won't*.

- In Elizabethan times, the pelican was thought to feed its offspring with its own blood, a practice alluded to by Shakespeare in *Hamlet*:

  > *To his good friends thus wide I'll ope my arms*
  > *And like the kind life-rend'ring pelican,*
  > *Repast them with my blood.*

- The albatross, a large sea bird with an enormous wingspan, is sometimes called the "Cape sheep" for its habit of frequenting the Cape of Good Hope. It was thought that the bird harbored the souls of dead men, and to kill one was to invite misfortune. This old legend forms the theme of the British poet Samuel Taylor Coleridge's (1772–1834) poem *The Rime of the Ancient Mariner*, in which a sailor is condemned to a lifetime of sorrow for killing one of these birds:

  > *God save thee, ancient Mariner!*
  > *From the fiends, that plague thee thus!—*
  > *Why look'st thou so?—"With my crossbow*
  > *I shot the Albatross."*

- In many cultures, storks are a symbol of good luck and are ascribed human characteristics. They are said to weep human tears when wounded, and young storks care for their parents in old age. A male stork will kill his mate if she is unfaithful. Storks were so highly valued in Thessaly, in eastern Greece, that a man who killed one could be tried for murder.

- A stork's nest on a building will protect it from fire, but if you steal the stork's nest, the building will burn to the ground.

CATS

- Cats have long been associated with magic. In southern France, many people once believed in *matagots*, or magician cats. One of the most famous *matagots* was Puss in Boots.

- Witches were thought to have cats as familiars and were supposed to be able to turn themselves into felines. But a witch could make this transformation only nine times—matching the nine lives of the cat.

- The cat was created by Noah, the builder of the ark. It seems that the rats and the mice in the ark bred so fast that they threatened to eat up all the food. So Noah passed his hand over the head of a lioness, who sneezed forth a cat.

- To many, a black cat means bad luck, but in some parts of New England, it is believed that a *white* cat will bring poverty to its master. If you do not live in New England, however, and a black cat crosses your path, you can counteract the bad luck by doing one of the following:

> Roll up your pants.
> Hike up your skirts.
> Spit in your hat, or on the road.
> Cross your arms, fingers, and toes.
> Take nine steps backwards.
> Or just go home and start your trip all over again.

- An English superstition says that a cat's tail can cure sore eyes.

- Voodoo practitioners believe that charms made from the teeth, claws, and whiskers of a cat bring good luck. Actually, these items are most potent if taken from a lion, but since this might prove to be rather difficult, any old tabby will do.

- In old Russia, a cat was put in a cradle before a newborn baby was placed in it; this was supposed to drive away all evil spirits. Another Russian superstition says that if a bride-to-be hears a cat sneeze before her wedding, she will have a happy marriage.

- True to his title of "kings of the beasts," it was once believed that lions would not attack a prince or any other royal personage, or a woman or child.

- Clothing wrapped in a lion's skin will be safe from moths.

- Because of its fierce nature and the fact that it sometimes attacks and eats human beings, the tiger was regarded with awe and terror in many cultures. According to Malayan legend, there is an entire city that is constructed of human bones, skin, and hair and inhabited by tigers. In Hindu mythology there is even a special hell just for these striped cats.

- In the ancient world it was thought that there were only female tigers. The father of little tiger cubs was the West Wind.

DOGS

- Dogs are associated with luck, both good and bad. An old Hebrew superstition maintains that if a dog passes between two men, they will have bad luck. And if a dog howls incessantly, it means that the angel of death has come to visit your town.

- Parts of the dog were sometimes thought to have magical powers, as this old Hebrew recipe for curing a fever attests:

> *Take seven prickles from seven palm trees,*
> *seven chips from seven beams,*
> *seven nails from seven bridges,*
> *seven ashes from seven ovens,*
> *seven scoops of earth from seven door sockets,*
> *seven pieces of pitch from seven ships,*
> *seven handfuls of cumin,*
> *and seven hairs from the beard of an old dog.*
> *Now tie them to the neck hole of the shirt with a white twisted cord.*

(It is obviously easier just to take a few aspirins.)

- In eastern Europe, if you want to be able to talk to the birds, all you have to do is cook the heart of a dog and fox together and eat them.

- If you sleep on the same pillow your dog does, you will have the same dreams it does (you also might get a healthy dose of fleas).

- There are many superstitions about wolves. In ancient Rome, if a wolf came into a Roman army camp, it was immediately killed, for if it escaped, it was believed that the army would surely be defeated. In other countries, a wolf's head was nailed to the door for protection against witches and other evil beings.

- In ancient Rome, people who had been robbed were advised to put a wolf's tooth under their pillows. The thief's identity would be revealed through dreams.

DOLPHINS AND PORPOISES

- The Indians of the Amazon region believe that dolphins can transform themselves into human beings. They can even sprout legs and walk. Sometimes dolphins will turn themselves into handsome young men and seduce human women. The female "dolphin people" are sometimes malevolent, turning themselves into beautiful women and luring men to the river, where they drag them to their deaths.

- In the Middle Ages, dolphins were believed to ferry the souls of the holy to Avalon, the Blessed Isle of the Dead.

- Few of us can tell porpoises from dolphins, but many sailors could. The sight of dolphins playing around a ship meant good luck, while the presence of porpoises meant that a storm was brewing.

ELEPHANTS

- Until the seventeenth century it was said that a tired elephant cannot lie down but must lean against a strong tree. If the tree breaks, the elephant will never be able to get up again. It was also thought that at the time of the waxing of the moon, elephants would gather long branches from forest trees and raise them rhythmically in their trunks as homage to the Queen of the Night.

● In India, white elephants are supposed to have the power to produce clouds.

FISH

● If you eat the heart of an eel while it is still warm you will be able to tell the future.

● In the Ozarks, if you dream of a fish, you will get rich.

● If you want to dream of your future spouse, eat a raw herring.

● British fishermen of yesteryear would never throw away the bones of a herring. Instead, they would bundle them in paper and throw them in the water, believing that the fish would reassemble itself and call its fellow fish from the deep and into the fisherman's nets.

HORSES

● Horses have long been associated with magic. The ancient Celts kept a sacred grove full of white horses. By watching the animals' movements, they believed they could predict the future.

● In Rouen, France, a traveling English performing horse was once burned as a witch because it was so clever that it was thought to be a bewitched human being.

● If you hold the hair of a horse in your hand, you will be safe from all harm. For those with strong stomachs, the same effect can be achieved by eating a chopped horsehair sandwich.

● In many parts of the world, including the United States, it is believed that a horseshoe brings good luck. A horseshoe will also protect you from evil, especially one that the horse has lost and you found. When you find it, the prongs should be pointing toward you. To activate the power of the horseshoe, spit through the prongs and toss the shoe over your shoulder, then walk away without looking. Or you can nail the horseshoe above your front door so that the luck will not run out. Where does the belief in the power of the horseshoe come from? One legend says that a blacksmith named Dunstan one day had a strange visitor—the Devil himself! It seems that Old Scratch had come to Dunstan just to have a hoof reshod, but the blacksmith, grabbing him by his tail, tortured him until he agreed that neither he nor his demonic helpers would ever enter a building protected by a horseshoe.

- In some parts of Europe and America, to see a white horse means good luck, while in other regions, just the opposite is true. In England, the following advice was given when buying a horse:

> One foot white, buy him,
> Two foot white, try him,
> Three feet white, look about him,
> Four feet white, go without him.

HYENAS

- I In ancient times, the hyena was thought to be able to change into a male or a female. If you were able to catch this animal while in its male form and castrate it, you could use its testicles to make a fine powder that would cure cramps. Hyena sinew mixed with frankincense was also said to be a cure for sterility.

INSECTS

- If you see a swarm of bees, make a wish and it will come true. Make sure, however, not to tell anyone what you wished for.

- The ancients believed that bees came from the carcasses of dead oxen.

- Another belief about bees is that they had to be informed of the death of their keeper, or they would leave the hive or die. In rural New England, when the bees were informed of the sad event, their hives were dressed in mourning. The quaint custom of "telling the bees" is described in the

Quaker poet John Greenleaf Whittier's (1807–1892) verse of the same name:

> *And the song she was singing ever since*
> *In my ear sounds on:—*
> *"Stay at home, pretty bees, fly not hence!*
> *Mistress Mary is dead and gone!"*

- If a fly lands on your nose, somebody has something to tell you.

- But if it's a dragonfly or a darning needle, as these insects are sometimes called, cover your mouth and your nose, or it will sew them up. It is also advised to cover your ears, or they will fly into one and out the other.

- If a cricket moves into your home, you will have good luck. But if it moves out, bad luck is on the way. The ancient Chinese thought so highly of crickets that they often built cages for them and kept them as pets. Never kill a cricket, or its relatives will move into your house and eat your curtains and slipcovers.

- Although ants were looked upon as industrious and wise in Aesop's fables, other cultures had quite a different view of them. In West Africa, an ant's nest is looked upon as the home of demons, and the Pueblo Indians considered them to be a source of disease.

- In England, to find a black beetle anywhere in your house means bad luck. If a black beetle scuttles across your shoe or crawls over a person lying down, that person will die.

PIGS

- A pig in the house on May 1 brings bad luck. On every other day of the year, though, it brings good fortune.

- In many African-American homes in the South as well as the North, hog jowls along with "hoppin' john" (a dish made of black-eyed peas and rice) is eaten on January 1 to ensure good luck for the rest of the year.

RABBITS AND HARES

- Everyone knows that a rabbit's foot is good luck, but it can not come from just any old bunny. The rabbit must be shot with a silver bullet on a night when the moon is full. Then cut off one of its hind feet (in some places the right foot is better, in others, it is the left). Dip the foot in rainwater that has been collected in a hollow stump. For the charm to work properly wear it in your left pocket. The older and drier it gets, the more powerful it is. A rabbit's foot is said to cure both colic and rheumatism.

● If a rabbit crosses a pregnant woman's path, she should immediately tear a piece of cloth from her dress and burn it. Otherwise, her child may be born with a harelip.

RODENTS

● In ancient Rome, rats were a symbol of good luck.

SALAMANDERS, SCORPIONS, AND SPIDERS

● Salamanders were once thought to breed in fire and could therefore survive the hottest flames.

● Although the scorpion was greatly feared for its poisonous sting, it was once believed that a wound could be cured by placing one of these animals on it.

● Spiders are looked on with fear and revulsion by many, but in some cultures they are considered good luck. An old rhyme advises:

> *If you want to grow and thrive,*
> *Let the spider run alive.*

Here are some other spider superstitions:

> If a spider swings down in front of you, you will hear good news or have good luck.
> If you find a spider in your pocket, you will soon come into some money.
> If you find one of your initials in the threads of a web, you will be lucky forever.
> But if a spider crawls toward you, you will have a quarrel.

● Spiders were also thought to have curative powers. Live spiders were once
   worn in little bags around the neck as a cure for various ailments, and in
   1760, one Dr. Watson advised that a fever could be cured by "swallowing
   a spider gently bruised and wrapped up in a raisin or spread upon bread
   and butter."

Chapter Twenty-Two

ANIMAL-ESE

Did you ever wonder where the phrase "not enough room to swing a cat" comes from? This expression had its origin in the maritime world, when sailors were often punished with a "cat-o'-nine-tails," a whip with a number of long, braided leather cords that were sometimes embedded with glass, bits of metal, or wire. In the close quarters of the sailing vessels of yesteryear, there was often not enough room to wield this cruel instrument, hence the term.

Here are more origins of some popular words, slang terms, and expressions involving animals.

To Badger Someone. This expression, meaning to annoy or bother someone, comes from the vicious pastime of "badger baiting," in which this feisty relative of the weasel was placed in a box or tub and then set upon by specially trained dogs. The dogs would drag the fighting, snarling badger from its prison, at which point the animals would try to tear one another to pieces.

Birdie. Golfers use this term when a hole is completed in one stroke under par (the average score listed for a hole). It comes from the old belief that birds are superior creatures because of their ability to fly. In early nineteenth-century slang, "bird" meant "very good" or "excellent." This slang word later fell out of usage, but remained in golf.

Build a Better Mousetrap. This term can be credited to the American poet and philosopher Ralph Waldo Emerson (1803–1882), who wrote:

> *If a man write a better letter, preach a better sermon, or make a better mousetrap than his neighbor, though he builds his house in the woods the world will still make a beaten path to his door.*

To Eat Crow. Meaning to be forced to eat one's words or do something unpleasant, "to eat crow" allegedly comes from an incident that occurred during the War of 1812. It seems that during a period of truce in this conflict, an American hunter accidentally crossed over into British-held territory and shot and killed a crow. Upon hearing the shot, a British officer approached the American. The unarmed Englishman complimented the American on his good marksmanship and fine gun and asked that he hand it over in order for the Englishman to take a better look at it. Upon being handed the gun, the Englishman accused the American of trespassing and, at gunpoint, commanded him to take a bite out of the dead crow, which the American apparently did. When the officer returned the musket, however, the American ordered him to eat the *rest* of the bird—feathers and all.

Jim Crow. This derogatory term for African Americans, obviously referring to the bird's color, came from a minstrel show song of the early 1800s. After the Civil War, "Jim Crow" laws were discriminatory regulations enacted throughout the South and much of the North.

Crocodile Tears. Crocodiles' eyes produce tears just as those of humans do, and these reptiles are sometimes seen with dark streaks of water dripping down their faces. The crocodiles are not "sad," though; this is probably just a way of ridding their bodies of excess salt. It was once thought that the crocodile moaned and pretended to weep in order to attract the sympathy of unwary animals—which, of course, the animal would then eat. This legend, completely untrue, is the source of the term crocodile tears, meaning tears that are do not reflect a genuine emotion.

Dog Days. This refers to the very hot days that often occur in July and August. It comes to us from the ancient Romans, who thought that the July rising of Sirius, the dog star, joined with the sun in adding to summer warmth.

Every Dog Has His Day. According to the Dutch scholar Erasmus (1466–1536), this saying came about as a result of the gruesome death of the Greek playwright Euripides (484–406 B.C.) who was mauled and killed by a vicious pack of dogs that had been set on him by a jealous rival. This saying usually means that even the lowliest person will someday get his or her revenge on their oppressor, no matter how powerful that person may be.

Gossamer. During warm days, when air currents rise from the ground, spiders climb up blades of grass or twigs and emit long strands of wispy silk from their abdomens. When the lines are long enough to catch this movement of air, the little creatures are borne aloft; this aerial travel is called "ballooning." Sometimes millions of tiny spiders are "ballooned" through the air each day, and when dusk comes and water particles condense on their lines, they drift slowly down to the earth. As they land to the ground, still on their lines, they build little webs, and the next morning vast expanses of ground are covered in glistening spider silk.

To people long ago, this spider silk looked like the goose down commonly seen in late summer when geese were killed and plucked. This time of the year—and the spider silk—became known as "goose-summer" or gossamer. Today, the word is used to describe something light and airy, such as "a gossamer cloud of cotton candy."

Halcyon Days. According to the folklore of the sea, the two weeks before and after the shortest day of the year, December 21, was a time of balmy weather and calm seas. This peaceful period was due to the presence of the halcyon, or kingfisher, who supposedly built her nest on the surface of the ocean and had the ability to quiet the waters. Today, the term refers to a time of peace and prosperity. (It is also the trade name of a controversial sleeping pill.)

Horse Latitudes. This region is located at about 30° to 35° north and 30° to 35° south latitude and is characterized by high pressure, light winds, and sparse rainfall. For centuries, sailing vessels dreaded this zone, because the lack of wind meant that a ship could be stranded there for days, even weeks. The horse latitudes encompass a broad area, including most of North Africa (north) and much of Australia and southern South America (south). Most of the world's deserts, including the Australian desert and the Sahara, are located in this area.

In the days of the conquistadors, horses were transported from Spain in slow, clumsy ships to the New World. Kept in slings on deck for three or four months at a stretch, exposed to drenching storms and boiling sun, and unable to exercise, many of them died. When the ships became becalmed and drinking water began to give out, scores more were killed. So many carcasses of the unfortunate beasts were tossed overboard in the aforementioned region that it became known as the horse latitudes.

One Horse Town. This term can be traced to the mid-1800s and refers to a town so small that it needed just a single horse to carry out all its transportation needs. Today it not only means a hick town, but also is sometimes used to describe a small and amateurish enterprise, such as "a one-horse show."

Mad As a March Hare. In the spring, the male European hare often engages in strange behavior as a prelude to mating, jumping several feet into the air and hopping about wildly; hence the expression.

Raining Cats and Dogs. During a heavy downpour, the French say it is raining like a waterfall, or a *catedupe*. The English mistranslated this expression and got the term raining cats and dogs.

Snake in the Grass. Describing a hidden enemy, this term comes to us from the poet Virgil, who in his *Ecologues* warned of being wary of anyone who is like a snake lurking in the grass.

White Elephant. In the days of imperial Siam, kings who wished to punish a courtier who had displeased them would send him an albino elephant. As we have seen, an albino elephant was considered sacred, and since such a royal gift could obviously not be returned, the unfortunate individual was forced to pay the massive bills for the animal's upkeep, which often led him to financial ruin. The term white elephant has come to mean a possession that despite its uselessness is too costly to discard.

Chapter Twenty-Three

QUIZ ANSWERS

ANIMALS IN CLASSICAL MYTHOLOGY: A MAGICAL BESTIARY QUIZ, PAGES 197-198.

1. n. Harpy. The harpies were sometimes called "the hounds of Zeus," because they tracked and punished individuals who had offended the gods.

2. d. Fenrir. He could be bound only with a magical chain called Gleipnir, which was forged from "the sound of a cat's footsteps, the roots of a mountain, the breath of a fish, the beard of a woman and the spittle of a bird"—not exactly the sort of thing you would find at your local hardware store.

3. i. Epona. Some scholars think that the word *pony* comes from the name of this goddess.

4. g. Satyr. The best known of these lusty creatures was Pan, the horned, goat-legged deity of pasture, field, and woods. All satyrs were male.

5. o. The Erymanthian Boar.

6. a. Python. The pet of the goddess Hera, the Python was slain by Apollo. Pythons were believed to be able to tell the future, and these snakes were kept in a temple at Claros, where they were attended by priestesses known as Pythonesses. These priestesses would become possessed by the spirit of

the Python, and their moans and cries would be interpreted and used to tell the future.

7. t. Sphinx. She was sent to Thebes by Hera to punish the people of that city for their drunkenness. This cranky creature enjoyed asking this riddle:

> *What creature walks in the morning on four feet,*
> *at noon upon two, and at evening upon three?*

The answer is man, who goes on four feet as an infant, two feet in adulthood, and three feet (aided by a cane) in old age. Anyone who could not guess the answer was immediately killed, the preferred method being suffocation in the Sphinx's enormous wings. Oedipus answered the riddle correctly and the Sphinx was so upset by this she killed herself (talk about sore losers)! He went on to become king of Thebes and then married Jocasta, who turned out to be . . . well, that's another story.

8. r. Hippogriff. These creatures were the product of a male griffin and a filly. Curiously, even though they were half equine, hippogriffs and horses were thought to be deadly enemies.

9. c. Sleipnir. Odin was also attended by his twin oracular ravens, Hugin (Thought) and Munin (Memory), who flew around the world daily and told their master of the goings-on of mortals.

10. s. Siren. In Greek, this word means "entangler," referring to the beautiful faces and voices of these creatures, which no man could resist. In Greek mythology, there were three, Leucosia, Ligeia, and Parthenope, who sat on the rocks, one playing the lyre, one the flute, and one singing, respectively, as ships approached. Hearing the unearthly music, sailors would jump overboard and be devoured by the terrible trio. The Greek hero Jason, captain of the *Argo*, thwarted the sirens by asking Orpheus to play a tune upon his flute. Furious at being outwitted, the sirens threw themselves into the ocean, where they became the black rocks off the Isle of Capri—the Sirenusae.

11. h. Minotaur. This monster was supposedly born of a union between the Queen of Crete, Pasiphae, and a white sea-bull. The Minotaur was kept prisoner in a labyrinth beneath the Palace of Knossus. Each year, seven handsome youths and seven beautiful maidens were sent into the monster's maze to serve as dinner. On the walls of the Minoan Palace in Crete, built around 2,000 B.C., there are frescoes depicting bull-riding acrobat-

ics popular during this era, which scholars think may have inspired the myth of the Minotaur.

12. q. Pegasus.

13. f. Chimera. This monster was born of the half-serpent, half-human monster Echidna and the giant Typhon.

14. b. Centaur. The most famous centaur was Cheiron.

15. e. Basilisk. This monster was also called a cockatrice, because it was born from an egg laid by a rooster and hatched by a snake. It could be killed by the sight of its own ugly reflection and would also perish at the sound of a cock's crow.

16. l. Hydra.

17. k. Jomungandar.

18. j. Griffin (also gryfin or gryphon). A creature of Arabian and Indian legend, griffins had a lust for treasure, which they hoarded in mountain caves.

19. p. Cerberus. Another one of Echidna's nasty brood, this mean mutt had a mane of snakes, a serpent's tail, and ever-watchful eyes. His three heads represented the past, the present, and the future. The ancient Greeks would attempt to placate this rude dog by placing offerings of honey and cake in the coffins of the newly dead.

20. m. Catoplebas.

GODS AND GODDESSES OF ANCIENT EGYPT QUIZ, PAGES 198-199.

1. b. Maat. One of her duties was to weigh the souls of the dead for Osiris. She would then use the ostrich feather to test and rectify any imbalance on the Scales of Truth.

2. b. Basht, or Bast. In 1500 B.C., a temple was dedicated to this goddess at Beni-Hassan, a Nile city located about 160 miles from Cairo. Mummified cats were sent from all over Egypt to be buried in the pit behind this great building. In the nineteenth century, this burial ground was excavated, yielding 300,000 cat mummies. Incredibly many of them were shipped to

England and used as fertilizer; fortunately, some did make their way into museums.

3. d. Ra. The sun was thought to be the eye of Ra, who traveled the sky in a magnificent golden barge.

4. c. Anubis. He was also the patron of embalming.

5. b. Sekhmet, or Sekhnet. She was also the goddess of sickness.

6. b. Nut. Her epithet referred to her customs of "eating" the sky every night and then "giving birth" to it from her womb the following morning.

7. c. Seth.

8. d. Horus. One of his eyes is the sun, the other the moon. Horus was always at odds with Seth.

9. a. Ptah, or Ptath. Ptah was believed to have created the earth by kneading mud with the aid of water from Nun, the Egyptian father of the gods.

10. c. Osiris. A sacred bull named Apis was regarded as Osiris incarnate. Apis was recognized by its black hide, white triangular mark on its forehead, the figure of a half-moon on its left side, and a knot in the shape of a scarab beetle under its tongue. He was said to be able to foretell the future and lived in a magnificent dwelling with his own attendants. When the bull reached the age of twenty-five, however, it was ceremonially drowned in the Nile and mummified, and the search began for a replacement.

Osiris sometimes took the form of a creature called the Ba-bird. The Ba-bird had beautiful turquoise feathers tipped with crimson and although his body never left the Underworld, his soul often wandered among human habitations, observing the affairs of man. Near sunset each day, the Ba-bird's beaked profile became that of Osiris, looking toward the great Nile.

WHO SLEW WHO? QUIZ, PAGE 199.

1. Siegfried. This legend is the subject of Richard Wagner's opera *The Ring of the Nibelung*.

2. Bellerophon. When this handsome, vain young man arrogantly tried to ride Pegasus, he was thrown to his death. Other stories say that

Bellerophon did not die, but because his face was shattered by the fall, he was condemned to wander the world as a beggar.

3. Theseus. Theseus was able to kill the beast with the help of King Minos's beautiful daughter, Ariadne, who presented him with a ball of magic twine to help him find his way out of the labyrinth.

4. Perseus, one of the many offspring of Zeus. Perseus was able to accomplish his mighty feats with the aid of a magic sword, winged sandals, and a helmet that made him invisible.

5. Hercules.

Part III

A
Z

THE
PEACEABLE
KINGDOM:
ANIMALS
IN RELIGION

Chapter Twenty-Four

ANIMALS IN THE JUDEO-CHRISTIAN HERITAGE

The righteous man regardeth the life of his beast:
but the tender mercies of the wicked are cruel.
—Proverbs 12:10

The Gemara tells the story of the famous Rabbi Judah the Prince, who was known for his piety and wisdom. It seems that one day, as a calf was being taken to slaughter, it hung its head under Rabbi Judah's cloak and cried. Rabbi Judah turned the beast away, crying "go, for this was thou created!" The Gemara states: "[In heaven] they said, 'since he has no mercy, let suffering come upon him. . . .'" Because of his insensitivity Rabbi Judah suffered excruciating pain for many years, until one day he came upon his maidservant sweeping the house. Some young weasels were lying near her, and as she prepared to sweep them away, Rabbi Judah said to her, "Let them be, it is written 'and His tender mercies are over all His works' [Psalms 145.9]. [In heaven] they said, 'since he is compassionate, let us be compassionate to him.'" Because of his concern for the helpless animals, Rabbi Judah the Prince was suddenly delivered of the pain that had tormented him for decades.

This account shows the reverence traditional Judaism shows for all living things. Verses such as Job 38:41 illustrate how God, or Yahweh, cares for all of His creation.

However, Genesis 1:28 ("Be fruitful and multiply, and fill the earth and subdue it, and have dominion over the fish of the sea and over the birds of the air and over every living thing that moves upon the earth") has led many, including Christian theologians such as St. Augustine, to take the view that man should dominate the earth and that animals were placed on this planet to serve him. This attitude has wreaked havoc on the earth for centuries, resulting in the extinction of hundreds of species and the devastation of the natural world.

Fortunately, many people of faith have come to see the inherent weakness in this philosophy, taking seriously the commandment in Genesis 2:15 to "keep" and "till" the garden (the Hebrew word *till* also means to "serve"). Pope John Paul II has spoken about man's responsibility to the environment, and The World Council of Churches, composed mainly of liberal mainline denominations, held an international conference in March 1990 entitled "Justice, Peace, and the Integrity of Creation." *Christianity Today*, a leading journal of evangelical thought, recently published an article on animal rights in which the British theologian Andrew Linzey states, "to affirm God is to affirm that every creature is a loved creature."

A BEVY OF BIBLICAL BEASTS

The Bible is considered by Christians and Jews to be the inspired word of God. It consists of the Old and New Testaments.

The word *apocrypha* comes from a Greek word meaning "hidden." It consists of fifteen books or part of books and was written in the period between the Old and New Testaments, from about 200 B.C. to A.D. 100.

Both the Apocrypha and the Old and New Testaments contain hundreds of references to animals. In some instances, the meanings of the words have changed over the centuries. For example, the "dragon" mentioned in the Bible is probably a crocodile, a creature that was a greatly feared creature in biblical times.

Although ancient peoples, except among the very wealthy, rarely had pets, they were much more dependent on animals than we are, using them as a source of food, transportation, and clothing, and often as sacrifices.

Sheep, cattle, goats, and swine are mentioned throughout the Bible. Cats, on the other hand, are the only domestic animals not referred to in its pages. The ancient Hebrews hated cats, perhaps because they reminded them of their captivity among the feline-loving Egyptians. The word *chatu*, which does

"Peasant Life"—*Although Marc Chagall lived in Paris for many years, he drew heavily upon his Russian-Jewish background for inspiration. Animals figure prominently in his work, as in this 1925 painting. Courtesy of the Albright Knox Art Gallery, Buffalo, New York, Room of Contemporary Art Fund, 1941.*

appear in the Torah, probably refers to a polecat rather than a domestic cat. In the Old Testament Apocrypha, the Letter of Jeremiah tells of bats, birds, and cats that light on the images of idols, proving these false idols to be useless and helpless.

There are forty-one references to dogs in the Bible, almost all of them uncomplimentary. Among ancient peoples, dogs were loathsome creatures, often running in yapping, growling, barking packs through cities, scavenging and generally causing a nuisance. The Book of Tobit, in the Old Testament Apocrypha, however, tells of a dog who accompanies his master Tobias (Tobit's son) on a long and difficult journey.

In addition to the more familiar animals, more exotic creatures are mentioned frequently in the Bible, including leopards, tigers, and peacocks.

QUIZ: ANIMALS OF THE BIBLE

Test your knowledge of biblical animals with the following multiple-choice questions. Answers can be found on pages 255-256.

1. Which four creatures were sent as plagues upon the Egyptians?

   a. Rats, fleas, snakes, and spiders   b. Frogs, lice, flies and locusts

   c. Vultures, gnats, mice, and ticks   d. Mosquitoes, frogs, snakes, and ticks

2. Which tribe of Israel was compared to a serpent?

   a. Reuben   b. Dan   c. Asher   d. Levi

3. According to Mosaic law, which of these creatures were the ancient Israelites *forbidden* to eat?

   a. locusts   b. rabbits   c. lambs   d. antelopes

4. Job, "beloved servant of the Lord," had 14,000 of these animals.

   a. swine   b. goats   c. sheep   d. oxen

5. Which animals devoured the broken body of the wicked queen Jezebel?

   a. vultures   b. lions   c. locusts   d. dogs

6. This pious young Hebrew was thrown into a lion's den by the Persian king Darius.

   a. Job   b. Joshua   c. Daniel   d. Moses

7. This half-fish, half-man deity was worshipped by the Philistines, bitter enemies of the Israelites.

   a. Dagon   b. Baal   c. Asher   d. Ishtar

8. Called the "mercenary prophet" because he was paid to place a curse on the Israelites, he was reproached by a talking donkey, or ass.

   a. Isaiah   b. Nehemiah   c. Balaam   d. Joshua

9. In the Song of Solomon, the "Shulamite maiden" compares her lover to a:

   a. gazelle   b. bull   c. lion   d. peacock

10. The only woman judge in the Bible, her name means "bee."

    a. Esther   b. Deborah   c. Mary   d. Rachel

11. In Ezekiel's strange vision of the creatures with four faces, which bird's face appeared?

    a. dove   b. eagle   c. swan   d. raven

12. When John the Baptist dwelt in the wilderness, he lived on a diet of wild honey and:

    a. locusts   b. manna   c. fish   d. wine

13. When Jesus cast the unclean spirits from the Gerasene demonic, they entered the bodies of a herd of these animals, who then rushed into the ocean and were drowned.

    a. oxen   b. swine   c. sheep   d. goats

14. During his baptism, the Holy Spirit descends on Jesus like a:

    a. dove   b. raven   c. swan   d. eagle

15. In the mysterious Book of Revelations, death is portrayed as riding:

    a. a dragon   b. a pale horse   c. a black horse   d. a winged lion

QUIZ: SAINTS AND THEIR SYMBOLS

Match the name of the saint with the animal he or she is often associated with. Answers can be found on pages 256-257.

a. St. Ambrose   b. St. Blaise   c. St. Fina   d. St. Benedict   e. St. Eustace
f. St. Jerome   g. St. Sylvester   h. St. Roch   i. St. Peter   j. St. Vincent

God's Fool

Saint Francis of Assisi, born Giovanni Bernardone in Assisi in 1182, was the founder of the Franciscan order and is one of the Catholic church's most beloved saints. St. Francis, who proudly proclaimed that he was God's Fool was known for his uncanny rapport with animals. One story concerns the wolf of Gubbio, a huge and ferocious creature who terrorized the Italian countryside. St. Francis, unafraid, confronted the beast, and addressing him as "Brother Wolf," exhorted him to change his beastly ways, whereupon the wolf became so gentle that little children could ride safely on his back. St. Francis is also famous for his beautiful sermon to the birds. In Christian art, St. Francis is often painted with a lily, a crucifix, a wolf, and a lamb.

1. The patron saint of sufferers of the Black Plague, this fourteenth-century French saint was always accompanied by his faithful dog.

2. This medieval French saint is often shown with a rat.

3. One of the Four Latin Fathers of the Church, he is often portrayed holding a beehive.

4. This third-century hermit is the patron saint of wild animals.

5. Another one of the Latin Fathers of the Church, he is often depicted with a lion.

6. Considered by Catholics to be the first pope, he is portrayed with a fish, showing that he is the fisherman of souls.

7. Because he is said to have brought a dead bull to life as proof that Christ was the God of life, he is often depicted with this animal lying at his feet.

8. This saint of the fourth-century is often painted with two crows.

9. This second-century saint, the captain of the guards of the Emperor Trajan, converted to Christianity. Along with his family, he was martyred by being roasted alive in a brass bull.

10. This founder of one of the great religious orders is portrayed with a blackbird, referring to his temptations by the devil.

Chapter Twenty-Five

ANIMALS IN ISLAM

Islam is the "youngest" of the world's major religions, having been started by Muhammad, who Muslims regard as their prophet, 600 years after the birth of Christ. Islam is the world's second largest religion after Christianity, counting some 860 million followers throughout the world, including three to four million in the United States.

The sacred book of Islam is the Quran (also Koran). The Quran is divided into 114 Suras, arranged in descending order from longest to shortest. Muslims believe that the Quran was written by Allah and handed to Muhammad on a stone tablet by the angel Gabriel. A copy of the Quran, bound in gold, is said to be kept in heaven. Islam acknowledges Allah as the creator of all living things (Surah 41:45).

Tradition says that Muhammad was very fond of cats and is said to have preached holding one. He is said to have stated "Cats are not impure, they keep watch around us." One charming story tells of the Prophet's cat, Muezza. One day, while the white cat was asleep on the sleeve of the robe, he was called away on business. Rather than disturb the rest of this beloved companion, Muhammad cut off the sleeve of his garment. On his return, Muezza awoke and bowed to him in thanks. Muhammad then stroked the cat three times down the length of her back. Muslim folklore says that the touch of the Prophet gave cats the ability to always land on their feet. In many Muslim countries, cats are permitted in mosques because they were Muhammad's favorite animal.

Hunting dogs have been bred in Arab-speaking countries for centuries. The saluki, a sleek greyhoundlike dog used for hunting gazelles, first appeared in the Arabian peninsula 1,000 years ago and is thought to be the first canine to emerge as a distinct breed. Nevertheless, dogs do not fare as well as cats in Islam. In many Muslim countries, they are considered to be unclean and eaters of garbage. Muhammad said that angels will not even enter a house with so much as a single dog hair in it.

There are some exceptions to this rule. Most notable is Kashmir, or Katmir, the dog of the Seven Sleepers, an ancient version of the "Rip Van Winkle" story. According to the legend, seven pious young Muslim men hid in a cave to escape religious persecution. They slept there for 309 years. When they awoke, one of the youths went into the nearby city to get provisions. When their companion returned, all the young men fell asleep again until they were eventually admitted into heaven. During the entire time, Kasmir waited outside the cave, going without food, drink, or even sleep (Sura 18:9-16). For his faithfulness, Muslim tradition says that Kasmir is one of the ten animals admitted to heaven, along with Al-Borak, the white horse of the Prophet, and Balaam's ass.

The Arabian Nights is full of tales of fantastic animals, such as the roc, a fabulous bird so enormous that she could carry off an elephant to feed her voracious young. Sinbad the Sailor is said to have mistaken one of her eggs for the dome of a mosque. This tale is probably based on actual sightings of a bird of the same name which became extinct in the Middle Ages.

The jinn, or jinnee, are spirits that can take the form of humans, snakes, cats, dogs, or other animals. Other stories maintain that they are invisible and can be identified only by a whiff of cinnamon in the air. In Arabian folklore, jinn are supposed to have been born from fire, although some sources maintain that they arose from man's shadow.

Unlike angels, these spirits can be good or bad. A good jinn can appear as a beautiful woman, while a bad one can take the shape of a terrifying monster with the head of a hyena and the hindquarters of a wolf. Jinn have magical powers, including the ability to turn onion skins into gold leaf. According to legend, the jinn were trapped in brass bottles or finger ring compartments by the wise King Sulaiman (Solomon) and can be summoned from their prisons to do the bidding of their captors. The jinn are mentioned frequently throughout the Quran, including Sura 72, in which a group of these creatures listen to the words of the Muslim holy book and say, "Surely we have heard a wonderful Quran."

These beings also appear throughout *The Arabian Nights*. One of the stories, "The Porter and the Ladies of Baghdad," tells the story of a young man bewitched by an evil jinn and turned into an ape. But a beautiful princess who was in love with the young man had greater powers than the jinn. In the process of freeing her lover from his enchantment, she and the jinn go through a series of animal transformations. At one stage, the jinn becomes a black cat.

QUIZ: SOME ISLAMIC ANIMALS

Here is a quiz designed to test your knowledge of animals and Islam. Answers can be found on page 257.

1. He is said to have known the language of birds.

    a. Sulaiman   b. Imam   c. Dawood   d. Zakariya

2. The inhabitants of an entire village were turned into these animals for fishing on the sabbath.

    a. swine   b. dogs   c. apes   d. peafowl

3. Which of these is *not* the title of a Sura?

    a. The Bee   b. The Ant   c. The Fly   d. The Cat

4. Muslim legend says that this animal was originally the guardian of the Gates of Paradise.

    a. lion   b. peacock   c. crocodile   d. cow

5. One of Allah's miracles was to bring the dismembered pieces of four of these animals back to life.

    a. goat   b. gazelle   c. sheep   d. bird

6. Muslim tradition says that on his flight from Mecca, the Prophet was saved by the aid of this humble creature.

    a. rat   b. spider   c. ant   d. fish

7. In Muslim tradition, this beast is one of the ten animals admitted to heaven because of its connection with Ibrahim (Abraham).

   a. ram   b. calf   c. she goat   d. ox

8. Among his many miracles, he made clay birds come to life, with Allah's permission.

   a. Muhammad   b. Isa   c. Jalut   d. Mustafa

9. According to Islamic tradition, there are one hundred names of God, ninety-nine of which are known to man. This animal has such a haughty air because only he alone knows the hundredth.

   a. camel   b. horse   c. peacock   d. swan

Chapter Twenty-Six

ANIMALS IN EASTERN RELIGIONS

To see the universal and all-pervading Spirit of Truth face to face one must love the meanest of creation as oneself.

—Mahatma Gandhi

HINDUISM

Between 1700 and 700 B.C., fair-skinned Aryan invaders, possibly from the southern steppes of Russia, arrived into northwest Pakistan. They brought with them their religious beliefs, as well as their sacred texts written in Sanskrit, called the Vedas. The Vedic gods, fused with the beliefs of indigenous peoples such as the Dravidians, became the basis for Hinduism.

Hinduism is notable for its concern for animals. Most Hindus are vegetarians. The Jains, a sect that developed from Hinduism between 500 and 600 B.C., teach the concept of *ahimsa*, (pronounced *ahingsa*), nonviolence to all living things. Some Jains even wear face masks to avoid accidentally breathing in small insects. This concern extends even to inert matter; Jains cannot be farmers, for to plow the earth might cause death or injury not only to small animals and insects, but to the earth as well. Goldsmithing, woodworking, and other crafts are also forbidden. Most Jains are tradesmen and form a prosperous merchant class in India.

Hinduism includes a vast pantheon of gods, many of whom are associated with animals. For example, Yama, the Hindu god of death, has two dogs that he sends out to gather wandering souls.

The three major Hindu gods are Brahma, the Creator of the World; Vishnu, the Preserver; and Shiva, the Destroyer. These deities form the Vedic Triad. Brahma is said to have sprung from a giant golden egg floating in the primeval waters. Some sources say that he became a boar who raised the earth from these waters; others claim that he assumed the appearance of a fish or tortoise at the beginning of the world. He is often depicted as riding on a goose or swan.

One of Vishnu's titles is He Who Pervades, which refers to the way his divine light has infiltrated every part of the universe. The four-armed, blue-skinned god is married to the beautiful goddess Lakshmi. Like most of the important Hindu deities, he is provided with an animal or bird mount, called a *vahana*. Vishnu's *vahana* is the golden-winged bird god Garuda. Garuda's head, talon, beak, and wings are those of an eagle or vulture, but his limbs and torso are human.

Shiva has many contradictory titles, including the Howler, the Terrible One, and the Gracious One. In one of his gentler forms, he is Pasupati, the Herdsmen and Lord of All Beasts. All animals belong to him, and cows are especially sacred to this god. His *vahana* is Nadi, a gentle, peaceful white bull.

Another popular god in Hindu mythology is Hanuman, who has the head and soul of a god, but the face and body of a monkey. His many exploits are related in the epic poem *The Ramayana*. Born of a nymph and the Hindu wind-god Vayu, Hanuman led an army composed of men and monkeys against the evil Ravana, Lord of the Underworld, and his tribe of deformed, evil spirits. Ravana had the beautiful goddess Sita captive on the enchanted island of Sri Lanka. Hanuman and his army attacked Ravana's citadel, but the wind-god set fire to Hanuman's tail. Hanuman then grew to the size of a giant and in turn set fire to the city. By flying to a magic mountain and gathering healing herbs for his war-weary troops, he was able to ensure their success in battle. This is why men and monkeys remain allies, and why simians are held in such high regard in India.

Ganesa, Lord of the Host, has a human body but the head of an elephant. According to legend, his mother, Parvati, assigned her son to stand guard outside her rooms while she was bathing to ensure her privacy. So zealous was he in his duty that he refused entry to her chambers to everyone, even his own father, Shiva. Shiva was so angered by this that he sliced off his son's head. In a fit of remorse, however, he took the head of the first animal that came along, which happened to be an elephant, and placed it on his son's bleeding neck.

Ganesa is depicted riding a rat. He is also the patron saint of literature and knowledge. Hindu students often invoke a prayer to Ganesa before taking exams or starting a new term at school.

Hindus believe in the concept of reincarnation, which states that human beings do not die, but pass from one type of existence to another. According to the Hindu belief in karma, a virtuous life will be rewarded at the next level of existence, while an evil person will be justly repaid for his misdeeds. Hindu folktales relate the story of a foolish man who was reincarnated as a monkey, a cunning, dishonest merchant who came back as a jackal, and an individual who was sentenced to the body of a crow for his greed. Conversely, an animal that has lived a good life may be reincarnated as a human being, even one of high caste.

BUDDHISM

Buddhism was founded in the sixth century B.C. in a North Indian state by Prince Siddhartha Gautama. According to tradition, on the night of his conception, his mother, the beautiful Queen Maya, dreamt that a silver-white elephant with six tusks had entered the side of her body. She told her husband about the strange dream, and he consulted the Brahmins (Hindu priests). The holy men told her not to worry, for a male child had planted itself in the queen's womb. The baby boy, they said, would became a great ruler if he remained within his father's kingdom, but if he forsook the throne, he would become a Buddha, an Enlightened One. Prince Siddhartha chose the later path, forsaking the world's pleasures and becoming an ascetic.

Like Hinduism, Buddhism teaches respect for all living things. Buddhists do not eat animal products of any kind, and many Buddhist monks even strain their drinking and bathing water lest they harm some small insect caught in it. The *ki-lin*, the Chinese unicorn, appears in Buddhist literature (Buddhism spread from India to China in the first century A.D.). Reflecting Buddhist virtues, the *ki-lin* refused to eat any living thing, be it animal or vegetable.

As is the case in Hinduism, monkeys and apes are highly thought of in Buddhist lore. A whole cycle of monkey legends, recorded in the sixteenth century, sprang from the exploits of a seventh-century Buddhist monk who traveled from China to India and back. One tale relates how a monkey traveled to the land of the dead, destroying all the forecasts of when his ape relatives were supposed to die. This is why monkeys live so long.

Curiously, though many beautiful breeds of cats come from Asian countries where Buddhism is dominant, this animal is said to have brought about the Buddha's death. As the Buddha lay dying, after eating some tainted meat, he sent a rat for some medicine to cure him, but a cat captured the rat and ate him. The cat was not invited to the funeral for the holy man, and Buddhists often cast the cat in a diabolical role in their stories.

Chapter Twenty-Seven

QUIZ ANSWERS

ANIMALS OF THE BIBLE QUIZ, PAGES 244-245.

1. b. Frogs, lice, flies, and locusts (Exodus 8, 10).

2. b. Dan (Genesis 49:17).

3. b. Rabbits (Deuteronomy 3:20).

4. c. sheep (Job 42:12). He also had 6,000 camels, a 1,000 yoke of oxen, and a 1,000 she-asses.

5. d. dogs (2 Kings 9:36).

6. c. Daniel (Dan. 6:16).

7. a. Dagon. In 1 Samuel 5:1, the Philistines place the Ark of the Covenant beside the statue of Dagon, only to find Dagon face-down in the morning before the Ark.

8. c. Balaam. (Numbers 22–28). The king of Moab wanted Balaam, a Midinaite magician, to curse the Israelites as they crossed his land. On his way to Moab, however, Balaam's path was blocked by an angel of Yahweh holding a sword, who was invisible to Balaam, but could be seen by the donkey. Balaam, furious at the animal's refusal to budge, cursed him and finally beat him, upon which the ass said, "What have I done to you, that you have struck me these three times?"

9. a. gazelle (Song of Solomon: 2:9)

10. b. Deborah.

11. b. eagle (Ezekiel 1:10).

12. a. locusts (Mark 1:6).

13. b. swine (Mark 5:13).

14. a. dove (Mark 1:10).

15. b. a pale horse (Rev. 6:8). The rider on the pale horse is one of the Four Horsemen of the Apocalypse.

SAINTS AND SYMBOLS QUIZ, PAGES 245-246.

1. h. St. Roch. After many years of nursing those who had the dreaded disease, St. Roch was stricken by the plague himself in the town of Piacenza. He withdrew to the woods to die, but his faithful dog refused to abandon him, bringing him a loaf of bread each day and nursing him back to health.

2. c. St. Fina. After a lifetime of service to the poor, St. Fina was stricken by paralysis. As she lay unable to move, rats came to attack her. After her death, however, when her body was lifted from the hard wooden board on which she had died, it was found to be covered with sweet-smelling white violets.

3. a. St. Ambrose. Legend has it that as an infant, a swarm of bees landed on his mouth, foretelling his future as an eloquent orator.

4. b. St. Blaise. A physician by profession, St. Blaise moved to a cave in the mountains to live the life of a hermit in an area full of ferocious wild animals. Instead of attacking him, however, the beasts welcomed him and became his companions. According to legend, like many saints, he died a grisly death—after being tortured by the Romans with iron combs (the type used to comb wool), he was beheaded.

5. f. St. Jerome. Legend has it that a limping and whimpering lion once appeared at the door of the monastery in Bethlehem where the saint lived. The other monks fled in terror, but St. Jerome, upon closer inspection, found that the animal had a thorn deeply embedded in its paw. Unafraid, St. Jerome removed it, and the lion became his constant companion.

6. i. St. Peter was a fishermen in Galilee. He also is often shown with a set of keys: ("Thou art Peter, and upon this rock I will build my church, and the gates of hell shall not prevail against it. And I will give unto thee the keys of the kingdom of heaven" - Matthew 16:18–19).

7. g. St. Sylvester.

8. j. St. Vincent. According to legend, two crows accompanied the vessel that brought the relics of the saint from Cape St. Vincent to Lisbon, where they now lie.

9. e. St. Eustace

10. d. St. Benedict

SOME ISLAMIC ANIMALS QUIZ, PAGES 249-250

1. a. Sulaiman (Solomon), son of Dawood (David) (Sura 27:16).

2. c. apes (Suras 2:65; 7:163-166). Sura 7:166 states: "Therefore when they revoltingly persisted in what they had been forbidden, we said to them: Be (as) apes, depised and hated."

3. d. The Cat.

4. b. The peacock had this job (nice work if you can get it) until it swallowed the devil. Inside the bird, the devil entered paradise, where he brought about the fall of Adam and Eve.

5. d. bird (Sura 2:260).

6. b. spider. When the Prophet was hiding in a cave, Allah caused a large tree to grow miraculously in front of it. A wood pigeon nested in its branches, and a spider finally wove her web between the tree and the cave. When Muhammad's enemies saw the web, they concluded that no one had been to the cave in some time, and Muhammad was able to leave his hiding place safely.

7. a. ram.

8. b. Isa (Jesus) (Sura 3:10). Although Muslims revere Jesus as a great prophet, they do not consider him to be the son of God, as Christians do.

9. a. camel.

Part IV

A–Z

ANIMALS IN POPULAR CULTURE

Chapter Twenty-Eight

WHAT A CHARACTER: ANIMAL ENTERTAINERS

Both television and the movies have had a major impact on American life. Numerous animal actors have shared the spotlight with, and in some cases have even stolen it from their human costars.

Probably the most popular and enduring animal actor of all time is Lassie. The original Lassie was selected from 300 other collies who auditioned for the part and was bought from his owner for five dollars in 1941 (like subsequent Lassies, the dog chosen was actually a "laddie," because male collies have better markings and more even temperaments than females). This bargain-basement pooch starred in *Lassie Come Home* in 1941. The film was a big success, and Lassie became a celebrity, with his own apartment, a generous salary, and a contract that stipulated he was allowed to work only seven hours per day, and then, only a few days per week. A doggie double was even used to prevent the star from getting hurt.

Before there was Lassie, however, there was Rin Tin Tin. This German shepherd had served as a messenger dog for the Germans during World War I. Wounded in battle, he was found by an American sergeant named Lee Duncan, who took the dog back home to California. In the twenties and early thirties, Rin Tin Tin starred in twenty-two very popular films. When he died in 1932, United Press International (UPI) released the following message: "The most celebrated dog in the world has left to go to the hunting grounds in the Elysian fields."

QUIZ: POOCHES, PONIES, PARROTS, AND PIGS

Here's a menagerie of animals from the stage, screen, and written page. Match the description on the left with the name on the right. Answers are on page 266.

a. Bull's eye b. Fred c. Tribbles d. Darwin e. *National Velvet* f. Bubbles g. Sounder h. Spuds MacKenzie i. Cheetah j. Polynesia k. Boxer l. Arnold m. *The Hound of the Baskervilles* n. Sandy o. Pig p. Chanticleer q. *Mighty Joe Young* r. Gummitch s. Precious t. Orangutan u. J. Fred Muggs v. Beethoven w. Benji x. *Old Yeller*

1. This television dog's real name was "Honey Tree Evil Eye."

2. This bottlenose dolphin starred in the 1993 series "seaQuest."

3. This "he" is really a "she," a daughter of the original star.

4. Dr. Doolittle's tart-tongued parrot.

5. Tarzan's jungle buddy.

6. A faithful hound dog supplied the title for Martin Ritt's 1972 film about a sharecropper's family, which starred Cicely Tyson.

7. This classic 1957 film about a troubled boy and his dog has a two-hanky ending.

8. This was the name of the clever pig on "Green Acres" and also the dog on the television series "Life Goes On."

9. This gentle horse in George Orwell's *Animal Farm* comes to a tragic end.

10. Charles Grodin's furry nemesis in the 1992 film of the same name.

11. Lady killer "Buffalo Bill's" pampered pooch in Thomas Allen's thriller *The Silence of the Lambs*.

12. In Edgar Allen Poe's short story *Murders In The Rue Morgue*, ghastly killings are committed by this animal.

13. Robert Blake's feathered friend in the 1970s television series "Baretta."

14. The name of the hateful Bill Sikes's dog in Charles Dickens's *Oliver Twist*.

15. Feline with an I.Q of 160 in Fritz Leiber's classic fantasy tale *Space-time for Springers*.

16. "Little Orphan Annie's" lovable mutt.

17. Megastar Michael Jackson's chimpanzee, who likes to feast on Oreos and McDonald's hamburgers.

18. Glen Campbell provided the voice for this character in the Don Bluth film *Rock-a-Doodle*.

19. This Sherlock Holmes tale is based on an old English legend about a ghostly hell-hound.

20. This 1944 girl-meets-horse film made a beautiful violet-eyed twelve-year-old named Elizabeth Taylor a star.

21. In Jay Anson's bestseller *The Amityville Horror*, the red-eyed demon named "Jody" takes the form of this animal.

22. This 1949 film starred a ten-foot ape almost as scary as King Kong.

23. On an episode of the original "Star Trek" series, these prolific little critters caused a lot of trouble.

24. Dave Garroway's chimpanzee cohost on "The Today Show."

QUIZ: DISNEY'S ENTERTAINING ANIMALS

Ever since *Snow White* hit the silver screen more than fifty years ago, Walt Disney Studios have been providing pure enchantment. *Pinnochio*, *Sleeping Beauty* and dozens of other films remain enduring classics, enjoyed by generation after generation.

Animals have proven to be some of the most appealing characters in Walt Disney films. Who can forget the childlike innocence of Bambi, the perky Jiminy Cricket, or the simple but good-natured Baloo the Bear in *The Jungle Book*? Here is a word puzzle containing some of Disney's most unforgettable characters.

Find the answers to the twenty-three questions below. Answers are horizontal, vertical, diagonal and backwards. The answers can be found on pages 268–269.

```
P  T  X  T  R  P  S  T  I  G  G  E  R  Y  S
E  C  N  A  H  C  O  F  R  A  J  A  H  I  E
G  F  R  N  K  I  N  G  L  O  U  I  E  S  D
M  O  P  P  O  N  G  O  J  S  P  O  P  H  E
I  X  U  U  S  E  O  X  R  X  B  M  R  E  M
C  S  X  R  I  E  F  L  N  M  P  I  O  R  I
K  S  T  D  M  Y  T  M  U  S  H  C  L  K  H
E  R  H  Y  B  O  H  D  M  M  I  E  I  H  C
Y  N  P  O  A  R  E  A  R  N  L  P  F  A  R
M  N  O  D  X  E  S  Q  F  R  L  N  E  N  A
O  Y  R  C  C  R  O  C  O  D  I  L  E  O  R
U  S  A  S  S  Y  U  U  X  P  P  I  A  G  O
S  O  M  O  N  S  T  R  O  U  E  A  Y  S  U
E  X  F  N  O  O  H  S  H  A  D  O  W  Y  U
S  E  B  A  S  T  I  A  N  Q  U  P  L  B  T
A  N  I  S  A  M  O  H  T  L  X  N  A  D  X
```

1. This cheerful murid is one of the world's most beloved cartoon characters.

2. Aladdin's simian sidekick in the 1992 film of the same name.

3. The "Uncle Remus" tales provided the inspiration for this movie.

4. The names of the three animal heroes in the 1992 flick *Homeward Bound: The Incredible Journey.*

5. In *Peter Pan* (1953) the treacherous Captain Hook lived in deadly fear of this reptile.

6. The nervous crab in the 1991 movie *The Little Mermaid.*

7. This courageous pair rescues their pups from the wicked Cruella De Vil in *101 Dalmatians* (1961).

8. The "king of the swingers" in the 1967 flick *The Jungle Book.*

9. In *Cinderella* (1950), these animals became a team of handsome horses.

10. In *Pinocchio* (1940), Jiminy Cricket describes him as "a whale of a whale."

11. The treacherous tiger in *The Jungle Book.*

12. The blockheaded Pinocchio is betrayed not once, but twice by this slick-talking canid.

13. Merlin's winged pal in *The Sword and the Stone* (1963).

14. In *Robin Hood* (1973) The Prince of Thieves is portrayed as one of these animals.

15. Peggy Lee provided the voice for this blowzy pup in *Lady and the Tramp* (1941).

16. Belle's horse in the 1991 hit *Beauty and the Beast*.

17. Movie about a large-eared flying probiscidean.

18. Princess Jasmine's kittenish tiger in *Aladdin*.

19. This Scottish kitty had three lives, not nine.

20. Goofy feline friend of Winnie The Pooh and Christopher Robin.

21. Another inhabitant of the 100 Acre Woods, a sad-sack patchwork donkey.

22. Comedian Gilbert Gottfried supplied the voice of this obnoxious parrot in *Aladdin*.

23. The hero of Disney's latest release, *The Lion King* (1994).

Chapter Twenty-Nine

QUIZ ANSWERS

POOCHES, PONIES, PARROTS, AND PIGS QUIZ, PAGES 262-263.

1. h. The late Spuds MacKenzie, spokesdog for Budweiser Light Beer. Spuds died in spring of 1993 of kidney failure.

2. d. Darwin

3. w. Benji

4. j. Polynesia

5. i. Cheetah

6. g. Sounder

7. u. *Old Yeller*. Old Yeller contracts rabies and must be "put to sleep."

8. l. Arnold

9. k. Boxer

10. v. Beethoven

11. s. Precious

12. t. Orangutans are animals who almost never attacks humans, but in 1846, when the story was written, the great apes were thought to be vicious monsters.

13. b. Fred, a Moluccan cockatoo.

14. a. Bull's-eye

15. r. Gummitch. Despite his high intelligence, Gummitch is fated to live the life of an "ordinary" cat, "for as Gummitch knew very well, bitterly well indeed, his fate was to be the only kitten in the world who did not grow up to be a man."

16. n. Sandy.

17. f. Bubbles

18. p. Chanticleer

19. m. *The Hound of the Baskervilles*

20. e. *National Velvet*

21. o. Pig

22. a. *Mighty Joe Young*

23. c. Tribbles

24. u. J. Fred Muggs

DISNEY'S ENTERTAINING ANIMALS QUIZ, PAGES 263-265

```
P  T  X  T  R  P  S  T  I  G  G  E  R  Y  S
E  C  N  A  H  C  O  F  R  A  J  A  H  I  E
G  F  R  N  K  I  N  G  L  O  U  I  E  S  D
M  O  P  P  O  N  G  O  J  S  P  O  P  H  E
I  X  U  U  S  E  O  X  R  X  B  M  R  E  M
C  S  X  R  I  E  F  L  N  M  P  I  O  R  I
K  S  T  D  M  Y  T  M  U  S  H  C  L  K  H
E  R  H  Y  B  O  H  D  M  M  I  E  I  H  C
Y  N  P  O  A  R  E  A  R  N  L  P  F  H  R
M  N  O  D  X  E  S  Q  F  R  L  N  E  N  A
O  Y  R  C  C  R  O  C  O  D  I  L  E  O  R
U  S  A  S  S  Y  U  U  X  P  P  I  A  G  O
S  O  M  O  N  S  T  R  O  U  E  A  Y  S  U
E  X  F  N  O  O  H  S  H  A  D  O  W  Y  U
S  E  B  A  S  T  I  A  N  Q  U  P  L  B  T
A  N  I  S  A  M  O  H  T  L  X  N  A  D  X
```

1. Mickey Mouse

2. Abu

3. *Song of the South* (1946)

4. Chance (a street-wise mixed breed), Sassy (a saucy Himalayan), and Shadow (a long-suffering golden retriever)

5. Crocodile

6. Sebastian

7. Pongo and Purdy

8. King Louie

9. Mice

10. Monstro

11. Sher Khan

12. Mr. Fox

13. Archimedes

14. Fox

15. Peg

16. Phillipe

17. *Dumbo* (1941)

18. Rajah

19. Thomasina (*The Three Lives of Thomasina*, 1963).

20. Tigger ("The wonderful thing about tiggers/is that tiggers are wonderful things/their tops are made out of rubber/their bottoms are made out of springs!")

21. Eeyore

22. Iago

23. Simba

GLOSSARY

Aestivation: A sleep similar to hibernation that occurs in hot or dry weather, in which animals hide in mud or other cool places.

Albino: An animal lacking pigment in its skin, hair, and eyes. The opposite of albinism is melanism. A leucistic animal lacks pigment in its hair and skin, but not its eyes.

Amphibian: A vertebrate that lives part of its life on water and part on land.

Anthropoids: A group of primates that includes monkeys, apes, and man.

Anurans: Amphibians that belong to the order Anura. Frogs and toads are members of this group.

Arboreal: Describes an animal that spends most of its time in trees.

Browser: An animal that feeds on the leaves of trees and bushes.

Carnassial: A type of tooth, found in flesh-eating animals, that is designed to cut up meat in guillotine fashion.

Carnivore: An animal that feeds on flesh.

Cebids: New World monkeys belonging to the family Cebidae. The cebids, which live in Central and South America, include marmosets, howler monkeys, and squirrel monkeys.

Cercopithecids: The Old World monkeys, which belong to the family Cercopithecidae. Cercopithecids are found in Africa, Asia, the Philippines, and Japan, and includes such animals as the baboons, mandrills, and languars.

Cervids: A group of ungulates which includes deer and antelopes.

Cetaceans: Whales, dolphins, and porpoises, which belong to the order Cetacea.

CITES: The Convention on International Trade in Endangered Species (CITES) was implemented in 1975. The CITES treaty was designed to protect wildlife against overexploitation by trade and to prevent international trade from contributing to the extinction of a species.

Crepuscular: Referring to an animal that is active between the hours of twilight and dawn.

Crustacean: A member of the class Crustacea, a group of animals characterized by having hard exosekeltons. Shrimp, lobsters, crabs, and barnacles are crustaceans.

Dimorphism (sexual): The presence of different features or characteristics in the males

271

and females of the same species. The great difference in size between male and female hawks is an example of sexual dimorphism.

Ectotherm: An animal whose body temperature depends on the temperature of the environment around it. Ectothermic animals are also called *heterothermic*.

Endangered species: According to the Endangered Species Act, any plant or animal species "which is in danger of extinction throughout all or a significant portion of its range."

Endangered Species Act: An act passed by Congress in 1973 protecting species in danger of extinction.

Endemic: Referring to an animal that is typical and exclusive to a given place. Lemurs, for example, are endemic to Madagascar.

Fissipeds: A group of land-dwelling and semiaquatic carnivores. Dogs and cats are fissipeds.

Folivore: An animal whose diet consists largely of leaves.

Frugivore: An animal that feeds on fruit.

Grazer: An animal that feeds on grasses.

Gymnophions: Amphibians that belong to the order Gymnophiona.

Herbivore: An animal that eats only vegetable matter.

Invertebrate: An animal without a backbone.

Linnaean System: A system developed by the Swedish biologist Carolus Linnaeus, which classifies all life on earth into five kingdoms: Animalia, Plantae, Fungi, Protista, and Monera.

Mollusks: Members of the phylum Mollusca, invertebrate animals with a soft, unsegmented body that is usually protected by a shell. Snails and clams are mollusks.

Mustelids: Musk-bearing animals. Mustelids include such animals as weasels, skunks, badgers, ferrets, and otters.

Passerines: Birds that perch, including robins, starlings, blue jays, and other common species.

Pinnipeds: A group of aquatic carnivores. Seals and walruses are pinnipeds.

Plantigrade: This term refers to an animal that walks with the entire soles of its feet on the ground. Human beings and bears are plantigrade animals.

Primates: A group of highly advanced mammals, of which man is a member.

Sericulture: The cultivation of silk, a fiber made from the cocoons of the moth *Bombyx mori*.

Threatened species: According to the Endangered Species Act, a plant or animal species is one that is likely to become endangered within the foreseeable future throughout all or a significant portion of its range.

TRAFFIC International: The Trade Records Analysis of Flora and Fauna in Commerce, which helps determine whether or not a species is endangered by trade. TRAFFIC is under the auspices of the World Wildlife Fund.

Ungulates: Animals with hooves. They can be divided into two orders: the Artiodactyla, or even-toed ungulates, which includes goats, cows, deer, hippos, and pigs; and Perissodactyla, or odd-toed ungulates, which includes horses, tapirs, and rhinoceroses.

Urodeles: Amphibians that belong to the order Urodela. Newts and salamanders are urodeles.

Vertebrates: Animals with backbones.

SELECT BIBLIOGRAPHY

Part I. The Animal Kingdom

Articles

Barrett, Wayne M. "Stinging Sensation on the Texas Border." *USA Today* (Special Newsletter Edition), June 1991, Vol. 119, No. 2553.

"Bears In Trouble." *International Wildlife*, May/June 1992.

Begley, Sharon. "Killed by Kindness." *Time*, April 12, 1993.

Braaf, Ellen. "Man's Best Friend?" *Woman's Day*, April 27, 1993.

"Can Animals Think?" *Time*, March 22, 1993.

Capuzzo, Mike. "The Raven of Poe's Famous Poem Is a Feather in Free Library's Cap." *The Philadelphia Inquirer*, June 13, 1993.

Chua-Eoan, Howard G. "Reigning Cats and Dogs." *Time*, August 16, 1993.

Fellman, Bruce. "Guess Who's Coming to Dinner." *International Wildlife*, February/March 1993.

Gugliotta, Guy. "How to Stop Dreaded Killer Bees? U.S. Hasn't a Clue." *The Philadelphia Inquirer*, Sunday, August 1, 1993.

Harrison, George. "Wolves of North America." *Sports Afield*, December 1991.

Kelley, Tina. "Forget the Birds; Learn About Bees." *The Philadelphia Inquirer*, June 7, 1991.

Lemonick, Michael D. "The Hunt, the Furor." *Time*, August 2, 1993.

Mee, Charles L. Jr. "How a Mysterious Disease Laid Low Europe's Masses." *The Smithsonian Magazine*, February 1990.

Mills, Judy. "Milking The Bear Trade." *International Wildlife*, May/June 1992, Vol. 22, No. 3.

Mills, Judy. "I Want to Eat Sun Bear." *International Wildlife*, January/February 1991, Volume 21, No. 1

Pollack, Andrew. "They Eat Whales, Don't They? The Fight Resumes." *The New York Times*, Monday, May 3, 1993.

Sitwell, Nigel. "Monkey See, Monkey Pick." *International Wildlife*, May/June 1988, Vol. 18, No. 3.

"The Birds and the Trees." *Newsweek*, April 5, 1993.

Turbak, Gary. "A Reason To Whoop." *International Wildlife*, January/February 1990, Vol. 20, No. 1.

Books

Carrington, Richard, and the Eds. of Time Life Books. *The Mammals*. New York: Time Life Books, 1963.

Boitani, Luigi, and Stefania Bartoli. *Simon & Schuster's Guide to Mammals*. New York: Simon & Schuster, 1983.

Hanson, Jeanne K. *The Beastly Book: 100 of the World's Most Dangerous Creatures*. New York: Prentice Hall, 1993.

Pugnetti, Gino, and Elizabeth Meriwether Schuler, Eds. *Simon & Schuster's Guide to Dogs*. New York: Simon & Schuster, 1980.

Salvadori, Francesco B. *Rare Animals of the World*. New York: BDD Promotional Book Co., Inc., 1990.

Tuchman, Barbara. *A Distant Mirror: The Calamitous 14th Century*. New York: Ballantine, 1978.

Part II Tales of the Dreamtime: Animals in Myths, Folklore, and Superstition

Article

Reid, T.R. "Earth Spiders and Careful Tigers." *International Wildlife*, March/April 1992, Volume 22, No. 2.

Books

Allardice, Pamela. *Myths, Gods, & Fantasy*. Santa Barbara, CA: ABC-Clio, 1991.

Bierhorst, John. *The Mythology of Mexico and Central America*. New York: William Morrow & Co., 1990.

Courlander, Harold. *A Treasury of African Folklore*. New York: Crown Publishers, Inc. 1979.

Erdoes, Richard, and Alfonso Ortiz, Eds. *American Indian Myths and Legends*. New York: Pantheon Books, 1984.

Kirk, Mildred. *The Everlasting Cat.* Woodstock, NY: The Overlook Press, 1977.
Mercatante, Anthony S. *Zoo of the Gods: Animals in Myth, Legend, and Fable.* New York: Harper & Row, 1972.
Spence, Lewis. *North American Indians: Myths and Legends.* New York: Avenel Books, 1986.

Part III The Peaceable Kingdom: Animals in Religion

Articles

Stafford, Tim. "Animal Lib." *Christianity Today,* June 18, 1990.
"The Cow Mooeth, the Lion Roareth." *Christianity Today,* July 19, 1993.

Books

Bancroft, Anne. *Religions of the East.* New York: St. Martin's Press, 1974.
Ferguson, George. *Signs and Symbols in Christian Art.* London: Oxford University Press, 1961.
Hindu Gods and Goddesses. London: Victoria and Albert Museum, 1982.
Holy Qur'an. Translated by M.H. Shakir. Elmhurst, NY: Tahrike Tarsile Qur'an, Inc., 1986.
May, Herbert G., and Bruce M. Metzger, Eds. *The New Oxford Annotated Bible.* New York: Oxford University Press, 1973.

INDEX

A

Aardvark, 56
Adventure World Zoo (Japan), 69
African folklore, 210–15
Agua (cane toad), 9–10
Ahimsa, 251
Albatross, 220
Albinism, 3–4
Aleuts, 91
Algonquin tribe, 207
Allen, Thomas, 262
Alligator River National Wildlife
    Refuge (North Carolina), 76
Alligators, 4, 160–62, 173
Alpacas, 144
American Association of Poison
    Control Centers, 32
American Bison Society, 156
American Fur Company, 154
American Indian Myths and Legends
    (Erdoes and Ortiz), 206
American Kennel Club (AKC), 71
American Sign Language (ASL), 5
Amphibians, 6, 7–11, 216–17
Amphisbaena, 196
Anacondas, 167
Anansi, 211–12
Anchovies, 16
Anderson House Hotel
    (Minnesota), 88

Angelfish, 27
Angler fish, 26
Animal entertainers, 261–69
Animal superstitions, 216–28
"Animal-ese," 229–32
Anson, Jay, 263
Anteaters, 51, 157–58
Antelopes, 145, 151
"Anting," 19
Antivenoms, 166–67
Ants, 36, 38–39, 56, 226
Apes, 5, 6, 116, 119–24, 185, 217
Aphids, 39
Apocrypha, 242, 244
Arapaho tribe, 207
Aristotle, 183
Ashanti tribe, 211
Asian folklore, 203–6
Astor, John Jacob, 154
Aughisky, 203
"Aunt Nancy," 211
Aurochs, 173
Aztecs, 209–10

B

Baboons, 116, 118
Badgers, 94, 95, 229
Barbary lions, 177
Barnacles, 34
Barnum, P.T., 185